Victory for Hire

Victory for Hire

PRIVATE SECURITY COMPANIES' IMPACT ON MILITARY EFFECTIVENESS

Molly Dunigan

Stanford Security Studies,
An Imprint of Stanford University Press
Stanford, California

Stanford University Press
Stanford, California

Special discounts for bulk quantities of Stanford Security Studies are available to corporations,
professional associations, and other organizations. For details and discount information,
contact the special sales department of Stanford University Press. Tel: (650) 736-1782,
Fax: (650) 736-1784

Printed in the United States of America on acid-free, archival-quality paper

Library of Congress Cataloging-in-Publication Data

Dunigan, Molly.
  Victory for hire: private security companies' impact on military effectiveness / Molly Dunigan.
    p. cm.
  Includes bibliographical references and index.
  ISBN 978-0-8047-7458-1 (cloth : alk. paper) — ISBN 978-0-8047-7459-8 (pbk. : alk. paper)

  1. Private military companies. 2. Private security services. 3. Military policy. I. Title.

  UA13.5.D86 2011
  355.3'5—dc22

                                                              2010035617

Typeset by Thompson Type in 10/14 Minion

For Mom & Dad
Thanks for all you do

CONTENTS

LIST OF FIGURES AND TABLES

Figures

Tables

ABBREVIATIONS

ABC	American Broadcasting Corporation
1AD	First Armored Division
AOR	Area of Responsibility
APC	All People's Congress
BAPSC	British Association of Private Security Companies
BW GPSOI	Blackwater Global Peacekeeping & Stability Operations Institute
CATT	Command, Administration, and Training Team
CBS	Columbia Broadcasting System (now CBS Corporation, a major U.S. television network)
CF	Coalition Forces
CIA	Central Intelligence Agency
CIDG	Civilian Irregular Defense Group
COIN	Counterinsurgency
CONOC	Contractor Operations Cell
CONUS	Continental United States
CRC	CONUS Replacement Center
CRG	Control Risks Group
DoD	(U.S.) Department of Defense
DoS	(U.S.) Department of State

DIA	Defense Intelligence Agency
DS	Defense Science Board
DSL	Defence Systems Limited
DTAP	Democracy Transition Assistance Program
ECOMOG	Economic Community of West African States Monitoring Group
EO	Executive Outcomes
EODT	Explosive Ordnance Disposal Technology
FCO	(British) Foreign and Commonwealth Office
FDFA	(Swiss) Federal Department of Foreign Affairs
FSLN	Sandinista National Liberation Front
GAO	Government Accountability Office (Formerly the General Accounting Office)
HV	Hrvatska Vojska (Croatian Armed Forces)
ICDC	Iraqi Civil Defense Corps
ICRC	International Committee of the Red Cross
IDF	Israeli Defense Forces
IHL	International Humanitarian Law
IPOA	International Peace Operations Association
IR	International Relations
ISF	Iraqi Security Forces
ISOA	International Stability Operations Association
ITAR	International Transfer of Arms Regulations
JNA	Jugoslovenska Narodna Armija (Yugoslav People's Army)
KBR	Kellogg, Brown, & Root
KMS	Keenie Meenie Services
LAF	Lebanese Armed Forces
LN	Local National
MCM	Manual for Courts Martial
MEJA	Military Extraterritorial Jurisdiction Act
MNF	Multi-National Forces

MNF-I	Multi-National Force-Iraq
MoD	Ministry of Defense
MPRI	Military Professional Resources Incorporated
MRE	Military Readiness Exercise
NATO	North Atlantic Treaty Organization
NBC	National Broadcasting Corporation
NPR	National Public Radio
OAU	Organization of African Unity
OEF	Operation Enduring Freedom
OIF	Operation Iraqi Freedom
OOTW	Operations Other Than War
PCO	Project Contracting Office
PKSOI	Peacekeeping & Stability Operations Institute
PLO	Palestinian Liberation Organization
PMC	Private Military Company
PMF	Private Military Firm
PMSC	Private Military & Security Company
POW	Prisoner of War
PRT	Provincial Reconstruction Team
PSC	Private Security Company
PSD	Personal Security Detail
QRF	Quick-Reaction Force
RMA	Revolution in Military Affairs
ROC	Reconstruction Operations Center
RSO	Regional Security Office
RUF	Revolutionary United Front
SAS	Special Air Services
SIGIR	Special Inspector General for Iraq Reconstruction
SIRs	Serious Incident Reports
SLPP	Sierra Leone People's Party

SMTJ	Special Maritime & Territorial Jurisdiction
SOFs	Special Operations Forces
SR	Sponsored Reserve
S&R	Stability & Reconstruction
SSTR	Stability, Security, Transition, & Reconstruction
TCN	Third-Country National
TOW	Tube-launched, Optically tracked, Wire-guided (antitank missiles
TRADOC	Training & Doctrine Command
UAV	Unmanned Aerial Vehicle
UCMJ	Uniform Code of Military Justice
UK	United Kingdom
UN	United Nations
UNAMSIL	United Nations Mission in Sierra Leone
US	United States
USCENTCOM	United States Central Command

ACKNOWLEDGMENTS

I AM INDEBTED TO MANY who have supported me throughout the process of writing and publishing this work. Professors Matthew Evangelista, Judith Reppy, Peter Katzenstein, and Colonel Isaiah Wilson III all deserve special thanks for their roles in advising me as this project first came together. I feel extremely blessed to have had the chance to work with each of you. My editors at Stanford University Press, Dr. Geoffrey Burn and Jessica Walsh, also deserve my heartfelt thanks for their guidance and support throughout the review process, and my copyeditor, Margaret Pinette, deserves gratitude for her patience with me throughout the editorial process. Both the Jennings Randolph Peace Scholars Program of the United States Institute of Peace and the Peace Studies Program of Cornell University deserve special thanks for funding this research.

The openness of numerous military and private security company officials and operators made this study possible—words cannot express my appreciation for your willingness to participate in this project. I would particularly like to thank Colonel Timothy Cornett, Colonel Tom Johnson, Alan Brosnan, Todd Taylor, Doug Brooks, and J. J. Messner, all of whom went above and beyond the call of duty to help me as I conducted this research. I am also grateful to my colleagues at the RAND Corporation for allowing me time to revise the manuscript.

Numerous colleagues read through various versions of the draft and, while all errors and omissions are my own, I am indebted to all of you for your assistance. Jessica Watkins in particular deserves special recognition and enormous thanks for her research and editing assistance. Deborah Avant, Ulrich Petersohn, and three anonymous reviewers for Stanford University Press also provided extremely useful insights on various portions of the book. Jennifer Erickson was a very helpful critic in the early stages of the project's design, and my brother Seth was kind enough to proofread early versions of the draft.

Finally, my deepest thanks are due to Ben, who has been by my side throughout this endeavor, and to Seneca and Tahoe, who are the best "writing buddies" I could ever ask for.

Victory for Hire

1 INTRODUCTION

AS OF DECEMBER 31, 2007, at least 1,123 private contractors working for the U.S. government or U.S. companies in Iraq had been killed, according to the U.S. Department of Labor. Private contractors constituted the largest occupying force in Iraq during this time period, outnumbering even U.S. forces, with roughly 155,000 contractors employed there as of February 2008.[1] Contractors operating in Iraq have come from around the globe, ranging from citizens of English-speaking countries such as the United States, United Kingdom, Australia, and New Zealand, to contractors from countries such as Chile or Fiji that were not directly involved in the conflict (third-country nationals, or TCNs), to local Iraqis (local nationals, or LNs). Of the DoD contractors, approximately 10,422 were security contractors as of March 2009, although estimates of the numbers of security contractors employed by all entities in Iraq had ranged as high as 30,000 at earlier points in the conflict.[2] This study is primarily concerned with this subgroup of contractors, the armed security contractors, at least insofar as the Iraq case is concerned.

In Afghanistan, meanwhile, the number of DoD contractors was substantially higher than the number of U.S. troops as of March 2009, with 68,197 contractors compared to 52,300 uniformed military personnel. Again, this does not take into account the number of non-DoD contractors employed in Afghanistan during this period, so the ratio was likely quite a bit higher than these numbers reflect. Nonetheless, these figures reportedly represented the highest recorded percentage of contractors used by the Department of Defense in any conflict in the history of the United States, with contractors comprising 57 percent of the DoD workforce in Afghanistan during this period.[3]

Such a story would have been unimaginable thirty years earlier, when superpower competition fueled national militaries. Not until the fall of the Soviet Union and the corresponding "Peace Dividend" were national militaries—particularly the U.S. military—downsized to the extent that outsourcing of non-core military tasks would be deemed acceptable and necessary. Indeed, it was during the Reagan and Thatcher eras that the economic logic and culture of outsourcing government functions gained prominence. Neoliberal economic thinking and government reports throughout the 1980s and 1990s on the cost-saving benefits of privatization and outsourcing led to the development and expansion of private companies that could provide all non-core military services for the troops, leaving the skilled war fighters free to perform the actual combat tasks. These companies provided services such as weapons system maintenance and upkeep, supply transport, cooking, cleaning, and base construction, among many others.

The industry expanded when former U.S. and U.K. military officers, particularly from the Special Forces, built on the legacy of 1960s British and 1980s South African officers in developing the notion of the "private security company" (PSC)—a company that would provide armed bodyguards and convoy security services for various actors in high-risk areas of operation. Former British Special Air Services (SAS) Colonel David Stirling formed the first of the modern private military companies, WatchGuard International, in Britain in 1967. The firm employed former SAS personnel to train the militaries of the sultanates of the Persian Gulf, to provide support for their operations against rebel movements and internal dissidents, and eventually to provide military advisory training teams to clients in the Middle East, Africa, Latin America, and East Asia.

WatchGuard became the model for all future private military companies, and several other British private military companies grew out of this model in the next few decades, including Kulinda Security Ltd., KAS Enterprises, KMS ("Keenie Meenie Services"), Saladin Security, and Defence Systems Ltd. (DSL). Then, in 1989, a member of the South African Defence Force—Luther Eeben Barlow—formed Executive Outcomes (EO). Executive Outcomes operated in conflicts throughout the African continent during the 1990s, most notably in Angola, Sierra Leone, Congo, and Burundi. Executive Outcomes was disbanded in 1999, but many former EO officers went on to form their own private military firms, including Alpha 5, Stabilco, Omega Support Ltd., Panasec Corporate Dynamics, and Southern Cross Security.[4]

To distinguish themselves from the less reputable private military companies that operated mainly in African states in the 1980s and early 1990s, modern private security companies are adamant that they provide only defensive services and will not fight offensively or for non-democratic causes. The United States and its allies used private military firms in both the 1990–1991 Iraq War and the Balkans conflicts in the mid-1990s, but the majority of the companies involved in these conflicts were employed to perform logistical functions, not security services. Notably, the United States and its allies employed many fewer contractors in these conflicts than they do in the current wars in Iraq and Afghanistan. The rapid expansion of the private security industry over the past several years is unprecedented in modern times, as is the current practice in Iraq and Afghanistan of deploying private security personnel in large numbers on the ground alongside coalition forces. This is particularly true because today's private security personnel are not formally integrated into the military structure, as is the case with, for instance, French Foreign Legion troops and the French military. Security contractors' position in the military chain of command is therefore constantly in question, which, among other things, leads to a host of potential PSC–military coordination problems.

The privatizing reforms of the 1980s and 1990s that preceded this rapid expansion of the private security industry were designed to make government operations more efficient. Yet some media and governmental reports portray such privatization, when applied to the military sphere, as having actually decreased military effectiveness. This book therefore addresses the puzzle of why reforms that were intended to increase performance may be serving instead to decrease it. The book expands its theoretical inquiry beyond the issue of military effectiveness, however, to examine the ramifications of security privatization for the likelihood that democracies will be victorious in their conflicts.[5] I examine the impact of private security forces on military effectiveness in three different types of situations: instances of PSC–military co-deployment, such as the current Iraq War; instances of PSC deployment in place of military deployment; and historical cases in which mercenary forces other than PSCs are structurally integrated in a manner similar to, or are actually integrated into, regular military forces. In using these cases to probe this puzzle, the book has two interrelated goals. The first is to compare different situations of privatized force employment, to illustrate PSCs' potential effects on military effectiveness and on the likelihood that democracies will be victorious in their conflicts. The second is to understand the different effects of structure and identity on the effectiveness of military forces composed of national armies combined with PSCs, with an eye to providing policy prescriptions for current U.S. policy.

Of primary importance to PSCs' impact on military effectiveness, I argue, are the following: (1) the structural integration of private security contractors into the military forces with which they are deployed; (2) the cohesiveness of the collective identities of private and national military forces deployed together; and (3) the extent to which private security companies and their personnel operate in an ethical manner, complying with the rules and norms of international humanitarian law. In exploring the three different types of cases mentioned above, I conclude that private forces tend to decrease military effectiveness and prospects for the democratic advantage in modern cases of PSC–military co-deployment due to a combination of these structural, identity, and ethical issues. Meanwhile, PSCs often increase the military effectiveness of host nation forces in situations in which they are deployed in place of intervening military forces, yet decrease the chances that the methods of operational behavior are performed with due respect for established legal norms and decrease the prospects for the democratic advantage due to their impact on states' conflict selectivity. Interestingly, however, PSCs do not appear in such instances to have a *better* impact on the host nation forces' military effectiveness than would the regular militaries of democratic intervening states, as indicated by several counterfactual comparison cases in which no PSC was deployed. Furthermore, it appears that if covert PSC activities are revealed to the democratic electorate, a public outcry can result on a scale similar to the outcry that occurs when direct government or state-sponsored military involvement in covert activities is revealed to the public. Finally, PSCs both increase and decrease military effectiveness in historical situations of mercenary forces deployed with national militaries and consistently put ethical force employment at risk, due to a combination of structural and identity-based factors.

While it is hoped that professional, policy, and academic audiences will find these conclusions and this research to be compelling, these different audiences will likely find different aspects of this work to be useful. Policymakers and military professionals who may take for granted that PSCs are here to stay will likely be most interested in the study's recommendations for how to use PSCs most effectively. Those who are more skeptical of the value of PSCs, however, will likely be most interested in two notable implications of the findings elaborated in the following chapters. First, this latter audience will find in the evidence outlined throughout the study a strong critique of the democratic peace hypothesis, as the forthcoming chapters indicate that PSCs can be and are indeed used by democratic policymakers—often in a covert fashion—to avoid accountability to the citizenry for decisions to go to war. Even though covert PSC activities can sometimes be unintentionally revealed to the public, such an implication bodes poorly for PSCs' impact on global efforts to create and sustain a peaceful international system.[6] Second, an audience skeptical of the value of PSCs will note that Chapter 6's prescription for greater regulatory oversight is a potentially costly recommendation that could ultimately render PSCs relatively uneconomical.

CONTEXT OF OUTSOURCING

The turn to private military and security forces would be impossible if much of the world—driven by a desire for cost savings and improved outcomes— had not already embraced a larger ideological shift toward privatization and the outsourcing of a range of government functions, including the exercise of coercive power and violence. Governments and leaders across the globe have relied on mercenaries and other private forces to supplement or replace their own militaries throughout history. Yet the outsourcing of violence in modern times expands beyond traditional mercenarism and occurs according to both a logic of capacity (that is, the need to fill the demand for forces) and a normative logic.

In many cases, governments have insufficient numbers of soldiers and/or are reluctant to institute a policy of conscription, causing leaders to look elsewhere for the forces necessary to defend the state and carry out the military elements of state policy. As Gil Merom notes with regard to the limitations imposed on democratic leaders by having to institute a policy of conscription, "Those most likely and best able to check the president's war powers would not do so unless they had a personal stake . . . there is 'no representation without taxation.'"[7] Hence—despite the fact that democracies may have the political legitimacy to assemble mass armies with reduced resort to coercion—the potential to outsource violence and military functions offers a way for democratic leaders to handle problems of military capacity without having to impose policies of conscription, thus increasing their electoral prospects. In other words, outsourcing occurs in such instances to bolster the capacity of existing forces. This happens, for instance, with U.N. peacekeeping missions, which are outsourced to small, decrepit state militaries such as the Fijian Army. As the *Fiji Times* notes:

> Since the 1970s, this impoverished and remote remnant of the British empire has positioned itself as a discount-soldier surplus store. Its best customer has

been the UN peacekeeping operations. Today, on the post-September 11 battlefield, Fiji is marketing for hire its 3,500 active soldiers, 15,000 reservists and more than 20,000 unemployed former troops.[8]

Such outsourcing practices have a long historical trajectory. Egypt began outsourcing its war-making activities to mercenaries in 1479 BCE, substituting mercenaries for citizen armies for the next 700 years. The Egyptians actively recruited mercenaries from North Africa (the Nubians) and from tribes in the Aegean Islands and along the Anatolian Coast. Both supply and demand dictated this increase in the use of hired soldiers, as Egyptian citizens preferred to avoid the battlefield and enjoy their riches, and large numbers of poor and/or displaced tribes were simultaneously available to fight for money.[9] The Israelites, meanwhile, hired soldiers from foreign lands so that local citizens would be free to maintain the economic output necessary to support both the kingdom and the army. The Hebrews began this practice around 1250 BCE. Although David steadily decreased Israel's reliance on foreign soldiers after he assumed power around 925 BCE, Israel never completely stopped hiring mercenaries.[10]

The Roman Empire also relied on mercenaries to bolster the capacity of its existing forces.[11] When the effects of the Second Punic War on the Italian countryside forced small farmers to sell their land to wealthy landowners and migrate to the cities for menial jobs, poor citizens began to feel distanced from the empire and thus reluctant to risk their lives in the military. Meanwhile, their wealthy counterparts were similarly reluctant to join the military, preferring instead to stay at home and enjoy their wealth.[12] Rome's expansion therefore outgrew its capacity to staff its military with professional soldiers in the fourth century, and the empire was forced to hire mercenaries to keep up with this demand for soldiers.[13]

More recently, both mercenaries and privateers played a critical role in supplementing existing forces in the American Revolution. The British government signed treaties with six German princes in 1776 for the provision of a total of almost 30,000 German soldiers to help fight the colonial uprising in America. Landgrave Frederick II of Hesse-Cassel provided the vast majority of these soldiers, and thus the entire deployed German force was commonly referred to as a Hessian force.[14] The Hessian mercenaries served as British auxiliary forces, fully integrated into the British military system.

On the American side of the conflict, American colonists commissioned approximately 700 ships to fight against the British. These privateers—ships licensed by the Americans to harass British vessels and confiscate their cargoes—bolstered the American sea presence considerably, fighting alongside the American Navy's 100 ships. Both Thomas Paine and General George Washington owned stock in privateers.[15] These private ships also played a large role on both the American and British sides in the War of 1812. Congress even granted legal sanction to privateers during this period. With a few extra cannon and men, therefore, any merchant vessel was easily converted into a privateer.[16]

Outsourcing under the logic of capacity has similarly occurred in Operation Iraqi Freedom and Operation Enduring Freedom in Afghanistan, primarily due to the expanding definition of what constitutes "warfare" in U.S. military and policy circles. The growing tendency to consider stability, security, transition, and reconstruction (SSTR) missions as an integral component of warfare stretches the U.S. military and coalition forces thin, causing U.S. policymakers to rely on private security companies as an ad hoc supplement to regular military forces. The practice of outsourcing violence has become so commonplace in U.S. policy that the DoD now publicly recognizes the private security industry's primacy in developing current notions of warfare. Stability, security, transition, and reconstruction missions are now defined as a core U.S. military activity, one in which the DoD explicitly acknowledges that the private sector must play a defining role. Department of Defense Directive 3000.05 now formally includes the private sector in the emerging Pentagon policies pertaining to SSTR missions:

> It is DoD policy that stability operations are a core U.S. military mission that the Department of Defense shall be prepared to conduct and support. They shall be given priority comparable to combat operations and be explicitly addressed and integrated across all DoD activities including doctrine, organizations, training, education, exercises, materiel, leadership, personnel, facilities, and planning.[17]

This document further indicates that:

> Many stability operations tasks are best performed by indigenous, foreign, or U.S. civilian professionals . . . Military-civilian teams are a critical U.S. Government stability operations tool. The Department of Defense shall continue to lead and support the development of military-civilian teams . . . Participation in such teams shall be open to . . . members of the Private Sector [including private sector individuals and for-profit companies] with relevant skills and expertise.[18]

The explicit connection drawn between the private sector and this new core mission for the U.S. military is a significant one, illustrating the key role that private contractors now play in conflicts, particularly the stability and reconstruction (S&R) operations that are beginning to be deemed a core military activity—at least in the military doctrine of strong states, and particularly in the relatively pacifist democracies of Europe—in the post–Cold War era. In this scenario, policymakers are pre-disposed to privatize operations that have traditionally been considered as falling under the rubric of operations other than war (OOTW), in order to maintain adequate military capacity for actual war-fighting missions.

The outsourcing of violence occurs for normative reasons as well, however. As Gil Merom defines it, *normative difference* is "the distance between the position of the state and that of the liberal forces (that give meaning to the term 'society') concerning the legitimacy of the demand for sacrifice and for brutal conduct [in conquering insurgencies]."[19] In terms relevant to this study's focus, the leaders of democratic societies have, on occasion, outsourced violence to distance the state from actions in warfare that may be considered illegitimate by their electorate. This occurred, for instance, in the 1990s in Croatia, Sierra Leone, and Colombia, when the United States and Britain hired PSCs to play military assistance roles outside of the public view. Chapter 4 explores the cases of Croatia and Sierra Leone in greater depth.

Violence is similarly outsourced according to a normative logic in the diamond-rich states of Africa, where diamond companies such as Endiama in Angola hire private military companies to push artisanal diamond miners (*garimpeiros*) off their land. In many cases, the private military forces resort to human rights abuses to carry out the company's wishes. Yet Endiama and other such firms are still able to claim that their diamonds are "conflict free" and mined in accordance with the U.N.–mandated Kimberley Process.[20]

OUTSOURCING A BROAD RANGE OF GOVERNMENT FUNCTIONS

While the outsourcing of violence has been pervasive throughout history, a broad range of government functions beyond those related to violence has been subject to privatization in recent years. In the case of the United Kingdom, the United States, and much of the Western world, the ideological shift leading to the privatization of government functions took place beginning in the 1980s with the Thatcher and Reagan "revolutions." As British prime minister throughout the 1980s, Margaret Thatcher was devoted to the principles of free enterprise, competition, and the market economy. She was a firm believer that state-owned enterprises were inefficient and politicized, and so she began selling off Britain's nationalized industries in the early 1980s. Industries privatized under Thatcher included the National Freight Corporation, part of British Aerospace, Cable and Wireless, British Oil, British Rail Hotels, Associated British Ports, the British water supply, and the country's bus systems.[21] What began as a slow privatization push gained popularity by Thatcher's later terms in office, as each privatization helped to fund tax cuts, won political support from business and further weakened the opposition Labour Party. British Airways was privatized in 1987, as were Rolls Royce, the British Airports Authority, and the government's remaining shares of British Petroleum. British Steel was privatized in 1988.[22] After Thatcher left office, privatizations that had been planned under her leadership—including the continued privatization of the electricity industry—were carried out by her successor, John Major.[23]

Meanwhile, in the early 1980s in the United States, Ronald Reagan began espousing what has since become a key tenet of conservative political philosophy: that the nation's basic needs can best be met by private enterprise.[24] Such a philosophy was in line with Reagan's overall economic plan, "Reaganomics" or "trickle-down economics," based on a theory proposed by economist David Stockman. The theory called for a hands-off approach to fiscal management and major tax cuts for the wealthy captains of industry to encourage them to invest and thereby stimulate the economy. The program led to excessive budget deficits and was even denounced by Stockman himself at one point, nearly costing him his job.[25]

In keeping with the privatization pushes of the Thatcher and Reagan administrations, widespread outsourcing and privatization spread to Latin America in the late 1980s and early 1990s. In 1990, economist John Williamson—an expert on international monetary and development issues—coined the phrase "Washington Consensus" to refer to Washington-based economic institutions' political advice to Latin American countries around 1989. These policies included fiscal discipline, tax reform, interest rate liberalization, trade liberalization, liberalization of inflows of foreign direct investment, privatization, deregulation, and secure property rights. Williamson's phrase soon became a synonym for "neoliberal policies" more generally, and the idea of the "Washington Consensus" continues to be pervasive throughout Western economies.[26]

At the same time, privatization began to take hold in Eastern Europe as well, as economies there started transitioning from communism to capitalism. Eastern European privatization by necessity occurred on a much larger scale than did privatization in the West, as each Eastern European country had thousands of state enterprises to privatize (compared with tens of enterprises to privatize in Western countries). Furthermore, Eastern European privatization posed a unique challenge in that it occurred in states that were only beginning to develop market economies, had few markets and very little private property at first, and did not have market-oriented legal systems.[27] Because no comparable privatization has ever taken place, Eastern European countries had no precedent on which to base their privatization policies. Most of the former socialist countries began with small-scale privatization, selling off small shops, bars, restaurants, and workshops at auctions. To privatize the large state enterprises, a number of countries—Czechoslovakia, Lithuania, Mongolia, Poland, Romania, Russia, and Latvia—adopted voucher privatization programs. The principle underlying such programs is that all resident citizens above a certain age receive an equal number of vouchers that can be exchanged, within a particular time period, for shares in thousands of enterprises that are to be privatized.[28] The key lesson derived from the postcommunist privatizations was that the transfer of ownership must happen as quickly and on as large a scale as possible because the state is even less able to manage enterprises during the transition than it was before.[29] There are interesting parallels between this and the current situation of co-deploying private and national military forces in theaters such as Iraq and Afghanistan, where the transition to the large-scale use of PSCs has been rocky at best and has challenged U.S. ability to manage its forces. Chapter 3 elaborates on these cases.

MILITARY OUTSOURCING IN THE UNITED STATES

Privatization of the defense sector in the United States took on new meaning in the post–Cold War era, as military downsizing and smaller defense budgets required the Pentagon to rethink how it did business. During the 1991 Persian Gulf War, one-tenth of the people deployed were private contractors. Then-Secretary of Defense Dick Cheney was determined to increase this ratio, and shortly thereafter he commissioned a study on how to quickly privatize the military bureaucracy. Interestingly, Cheney commissioned this study from the private sector itself, from a division of his own future firm, Halliburton.[30] The Pentagon carefully considered Halliburton's recommendations, but—somewhat ironically, given its later tendencies to outsource a broad range of government functions—found it necessary to commission a follow-up study within the government. This follow-up study by the Defense Science Board (DSB) Task Force examined outsourcing options for the DoD, publishing its findings in August 1996 and citing earlier U.S. government policies that had relied on outsourcing to bolster its claims. For instance, it cited a 1955 statement by the Bureau of the Budget (the predecessor of the Office of Management and Budget): "The Federal Government will not start or carry on any commercial activity . . . for its own use if such product or service can be procured from private enterprise."[31] The Task Force's recommendations were completely in line with this 1955 policy, reporting that "all DoD support services should be contracted out to private vendors except those functions which are inherently governmental or directly impact war-fighting capability, or for which no adequate private sector capability exists or can be expected to be established."[32] The report projected that the Pentagon could realize savings of 30 to 40 percent of function costs through such outsourcing practices, generating a potential total annual savings of $7 to $12 billion by fiscal year 2002.[33]

A subsequent report by the Government Accountability Office (GAO) in December 1997 concluded that the Defense Science Board Task Force's estimates in this 1996 report were overstated. Agreeing that the Pentagon would be able to achieve cost savings by outsourcing certain activities, the GAO found that there were many legislative barriers to outsourcing—thus, not all logistics activities could be outsourced, as the DSB Task Force had originally argued. The GAO further reported that the DSB's cost savings estimates were overstated by approximately $1 billion for contract administration and inventory reduction and by approximately $1 billion more for reliability improvements. The GAO argued that correcting such overstatements would reduce the DSB's projected savings by 30 percent.[34]

This GAO report notwithstanding, Donald Rumsfeld spurred on defense privatization when he entered his post as President George W. Bush's secretary of defense in 2001. On September 10, 2001, Rumsfeld spoke to the Pentagon officials in charge of overseeing defense contracting, stating:

The topic today is an adversary that poses a threat, a serious threat, to the security of the United States of America. This adversary is one of the world's last bastions of central planning. It governs by dictating five-year plans. From the capital, it attempts to impose its demands across time zones, continents, oceans, and beyond. It disrupts the defense of the United States and places the lives of men and women in uniform at risk. Perhaps this adversary sounds like the former Soviet Union, but that enemy is gone: our foes are more subtle and implacable today . . . The adversary's closer to home. It's the Pentagon bureaucracy.[35]

Rumsfeld then announced a major initiative that would shift how the Pentagon was run, replacing the old bureaucracy with a system that would make ample use of private industry. This new policy—which became known as the Rumsfeld Doctrine—would draw heavily on the private sector, with an emphasis on covert missions, greater use of Special Operations Forces and contractors, and highly technical weapons systems.[36] In defense of his new approach to remaking the Pentagon bureaucracy, Rumsfeld wrote, "We must promote a more entrepreneurial approach: one that encourages people to be more proactive, not reactive, and to behave less like bureaucrats and more like venture capitalists."[37]

The Rumsfeld Doctrine forms the basis of the current context of outsourcing and privatization of defense functions in the United States, a basis codified in Department of Defense Directive 3000.05 and other policies pertaining to contractors' role in warfare. The private security industry represents a relatively small fraction of this privatization, with weapons producers and logistics-support companies (such as Halliburton) comprising a much larger portion of the defense privatization activities in this country. Nonetheless, increasing reliance on the private security industry has important consequences for the U.S. military and for the militaries of other democracies that rely on private security companies, as well as for the international system of states as we know it. This book focuses on the private security industry—at least to the extent that it can be clearly distinguished from other private military firms—leaving examination of these other elements of defense privatization for future research. Several scholars working on issues related to the private security industry have developed classification schemes to categorize the various firms and services comprising the industry. Their typologies are useful in delineating the types of firms and activities that I focus on here.

TYPES OF PRIVATE MILITARY AND SECURITY COMPANIES

Peter Singer developed the first typology to classify the various firms providing private military and security services, the so-called tip-of-the-spear typology, which distinguishes firms based on their range of services, the level of force each uses in performing these services, and their proximity to the front lines of battle.[38] "Military provider firms" focus on the tactical aspects of warfare, engaging in activities at "the forefront of the battlespace."[39] "Military consultant firms," on the other hand, offer "strategic, operational, and/or organizational analysis" through their provision of advisory and training services "integral to the operation and restructuring of a client's forces."[40] Finally, "military support firms" provide non-lethal supplementary military services such as transportation, logistics, intelligence, supply, and technical support.[41] While useful in providing distinct categories of private military services, the tip-of-the-spear terminology is somewhat misleading in the context of modern private security companies. First, in modern warfare the conception of a front line of battle is essentially irrelevant; the prevalence of terrorism and insurgent warfare in modern times means that battles are waged from civilian areas not traditionally thought to be included in the notion of the "battlefield." Second, and more importantly, the majority of private security companies are increasingly diversifying and expanding their range of services to include services spanning across Singer's three categories. The companies do this to remain innovative and competitive within the industry, but it means that they are less easily classified.

For instance, Control Risks Group (CRG) expanded its services from crisis management consulting to include armed security to accommodate its involvement in Operation Iraqi Freedom.[42] Olive Group has expanded over time to include close protection security operations, a crisis consultancy, securities design and integration (using state-of-the-art technology), a satellite tracking system, intelligence analysis and assessment, and training for private firms, military groups, and/or international organizations.[43] Xe, the firm formerly known as Blackwater Worldwide, is constantly innovating, and the range of services it has provided over the years run the gamut from research and development of new and improved military technologies—in 2007, Blackwater tested its own unmanned aerial vehicle (UAV), the Polar 400 Airship—to training domestic and international actors in advanced law enforcement and military techniques, special purpose canine training, intelligence, and aviation, ground, and maritime mobility and logistics work.[44] Back when it was known as Blackwater, the firm even appeared to be branching out into humanitarian work with its Blackwater Foundation, which rescued three stranded missionary workers in Kenya in January 2008 and set up a tent city (and donated 10,000 pounds of supplies) for victims of wildfires in Southern California for three months. Both of these services were performed free of charge.[45] Although I examine private security firms that span the range of Singer's three categories, I focus here mainly on companies resembling Singer's "military provider" and "military consultant" firms.

Deborah Avant's typology better accounts for this tendency for firms to innovate and expand their services. Avant distinguishes between external (foreign) and internal (domestic) security support and suggests three categories of services within each of these two broader geographic categories. External security support encompasses operational support, military advice and training, and logistical support, while internal security support includes armed and unarmed site security, crime prevention, and intelligence.[46] Avant's typology makes its most valuable contribution in its use of contracts rather than firms as the unit of analysis. This allows the analyst to look at a certain firm based on its activities in a certain situation, rather than generalizing about the firm based on outdated notions of the services it provides. I focus in this book on both external and internal security support contracts, looking at cases in which PSCs provide operational support, military advice and training, and site security, as well as personal security details (PSDs).

Meanwhile, Christopher Kinsey has developed a typology of private military and security companies based on the distinction between the "object to be secured" and the "means of securing the object."[47] The object to be secured falls along a range between private and public, while the means of securing the object falls along a range between lethality and non-lethality.[48] Thus, an actor securing a public object in a very lethal manner would most closely represent a national military, while an actor securing a private object in a fairly lethal manner would most closely represent a "military provider firm" in Singer's terminology. An actor securing a public object in a relatively non-lethal manner would be representative of a conventional police force. Finally, Singer's "military consultant" or "military support" firms would exemplify an actor securing a private object in a non-lethal manner. Kinsey's typology is interesting in its inclusion of the public realm; it allows us not only to distinguish between PSCs but also to distinguish PSCs from state-sanctioned methods of violence, as well as to see PSCs in the context of state-sanctioned violence.[49] In Kinsey's terminology, the study at hand focuses on both public and private objects secured in a lethal manner—as seen in the Operation Iraqi Freedom case, for instance—as well as private objects secured in a non-lethal manner (for example, training and consultancy operations).

"MERCENARIES" VERSUS "PRIVATE SECURITY CONTRACTORS"

It is necessary to define the term *mercenary* in this study for at least two reasons. The first is methodological: Because the study seeks to compare cases of modern-day PSC deployment with historical cases of mercenary and auxiliary force employment to derive lessons guiding us to the most efficient and effective uses of modern PSCs in relation to the military, it is necessary to have a clear conception of what constitutes a "mercenary" as opposed to an "auxiliary" and a PSC. The second reason to define the term *mercenary* relates to its legal and normative policy implications for PSCs, who are often referred to pejoratively as "mercenaries" by soldiers, the media, and other critics. Only by probing the use of the term and its relationship to actual PSCs can we determine the legal and normative restraints on future uses of PSCs, which will have a direct impact on the policy recommendations generated by this study.

Unfortunately, widely agreed-upon definitions of the term *mercenary* are elusive, with scholars and analysts arguing over many of the most basic components of mercenarism. For instance, Anthony Mockler argues that "the real mark of a mercenary [is] a devotion to war for its own sake," but Janice Thompson points out that individual motives are impossible to determine and instead defines *mercenarism* as "the practices of enlisting in and recruiting for a foreign army."[50] Peter Singer, meanwhile, highlights seven essential characteristics distinguishing mercenaries from other combatants and military organizations. According to Singer, a mercenary is somebody who is foreign (that is, "not a citizen or resident of the state in which he or she is fighting"), independent (that is, "not integrated for the long term into any national force and bound only by the contractual ties of a limited employee"), motivated by individual short-term economic reward and not by political or religious goals, recruited in oblique and circuitous ways to avoid legal prosecution, organized into only temporary and ad hoc groupings of individual soldiers, and focused just on combat service for single clients.[51]

Focusing on the foreign and financial motivation components of these earlier definitions, Sarah Percy points out that these definitions often encapsulate soldiers not traditionally thought of as mercenaries—U.N. peacekeepers or financially motivated soldiers enlisting in the regular, state-sanctioned military, for instance. Percy therefore develops what she terms a "different" definition of *mercenarism*, highlighting in particular a mercenary's level of attachment to, and motivation as a result of, a cause. According to Percy, mercenaries are not motivated by any cause other than financial gain: "Mercenaries are morally problematic because they cannot provide a plausible justification for killing; they cannot point to a cause in the service of which they fight, aside from financial gain."[52] Associated with this lack of attachment to a cause is Percy's argument that mercenaries make the decision to fight independently; thus, they lie outside of and are not affected by the cause for which they fight.

Finally, mercenaries are not under the control of the entity understood to have the legitimate right to wage war, according to Percy. Hence, she argues that "foreign soldiers in permanent positions in other states' armies are not considered to be mercenary, and nor are fighters sent with the approval of their home state."[53]

While Percy's attempt at a comprehensive and different definition of *mercenarism* is thorough and commendable, on close inspection it appears less different from conventional definitions of the term than she would lead us to believe. The claim that mercenaries are notable in terms of their level of attachment to a cause is, after all, just another way of noting the extent of their proclivity toward purely financial motivation. Furthermore, Percy's claim that mercenaries make the decision to fight independently is reminiscent of the earlier debate between Mockler and Thompson. Nonetheless, Percy's work on this issue is relevant to and quite useful for the study at hand in her recognition of a "spectrum of private violence," measured in terms of both a soldier's degree of attachment to a cause and degree of legitimate control. Based on this spectrum, Percy notes that most medieval soldiers, including the condottieri operating in the Italian city-states, are more mercenary-like than are foreign units hired from one state by another (what Machiavelli terms "auxiliary" forces, such as the Hessians hired by the British to fight in the American Revolution), which are in turn more mercenary-like than are modern PSCs.[54] Yet, all three of these variations of non-state, foreign, and/or profit-motivated hired forces *do resemble mercenaries to a much greater extent than do regular soldiers fighting for their own country*, according to Percy. This relationship is depicted in Figure 1.1. I therefore find it appropriate to assess in Chapter 5 both the case of the condottieri fighting for the Italian city-states and that of the Hessian units fighting for the British, as an assessment of historical cases representing a range of mercenary or hired force situations may give us clues to how best to structure PSC deployments in relation to regular military forces so that they have the most beneficial impact on military effectiveness.

Now to the more specific question of how the various members of the modern private security industry compare with the mercenaries of days past. Many industry critics equate the two types of actors. Most PSC personnel, however, find their association with the lawless, stateless image of a "mercenary" to be ridiculous. They cite the fact that most of them are former military, primarily former Special Operations Forces (SOFs). Hence, they do not perceive themselves as qualitatively different from professional soldiers, and they certainly

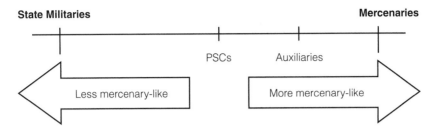

Figure 1.1. Range of hired forces.

associate themselves more closely with the uniformed military than with the traditional image of a mercenary who will fight for any cause, given adequate compensation. They also scorn the "mercenary" label because it is bad for business. Given that the modern PSC industry is predominantly based in democratic states, PSC personnel do not want to be perceived by the voting public as immoral, unpatriotic mercenaries—especially when the price could be the loss of a contract worth multiple billions of dollars, or anywhere from $500 to $1,000 per day, per individual contractor, for the duration of a particular job.

Yet, how unrealistic is the characterization of modern PSC personnel as mercenaries? As noted above, PSCs fit into Sarah Percy's "spectrum of private violence" somewhere halfway between "vagabond" and "medieval" mercenaries and "national soldiers." Nonetheless, according to the legal definition of mercenaries set out in Article 47.2 of Additional Protocol I to the Geneva Conventions, some private security company personnel—namely, third-country nationals—fall much closer to the legal realm of "mercenaries" than they might prefer.[55] Others, such as "local nationals" (LNs) employed to serve in a conflict in their home country, may meet the "profit-motivation" criterion of mercenarism even while falling short of the "foreign" criterion. Despite the fact that some PSC personnel do conform with various aspects of traditional conceptions of mercenarism in certain situations, private security company personnel do have several important traits that distinguish them from the traditional mercenary image. Most importantly, PSC personnel are by definition backed by a corporate infrastructure designed to select, train, and deploy them. This corporate infrastructure similarly bids on contracts and in most cases has a professional portfolio detailing its performance on previous contracts. Furthermore, the modern industry is unique in its scale and transnational nature. Indeed, many PSCs have the capability to hire hundreds of men representing a range of different nationalities at a moment's notice.

Another significant trait distinguishing the modern private security industry from the traditional mercenary is that virtually all of the U.S.– and U.K.–based reputable firms openly competing for government contracts espouse a company ideology in line with the liberal ideals of the United States and its Western allies. One can surmise that this is primarily because a large number of the industry's contracts come from the U.S. and U.K. governments. It is worth considering the counterfactual scenario in which a non-democratic power achieves superpower status and the capacity to buy the industry's services. Where, then, would the company loyalties lie? This is not to say that economic motives would necessarily overpower democratic ideological motives in such a scenario, but that the possibility exists.

Related to this second distinguishing characteristic of the modern private security industry is the fact that—while most do not—some companies do indeed make both explicit and implicit attempts to shape foreign policy. In this sense, the degree of state control over modern PSCs seems to be a rather reciprocal relationship. The former Blackwater Worldwide is a prime example of this phenomenon.[56] While Blackwater/Xe is only one company, and many other private security companies do not engage in the types of policy-related activities outlined above, Blackwater/Xe's size is such that its attempts to affect foreign and military policy are positioned to have an impact. While the condottieri operating in the Italian city-states from the thirteenth through fifteenth centuries did become increasingly involved in politics, as explored in Chapter 5, traditional notions of mercenaries do not generally include such direct involvement in the shaping of state policy.

The third and final trait distinguishing modern private security personnel from traditional mercenaries is the voluntary regulatory system in place in the United States and increasingly in the United Kingdom. The International Stability Operations Association (ISOA—formerly known as the International Peace Operations Association, or IPOA), a trade association for the private military and security industry since 2001, has devised a "Code of Conduct" to which all of its members must adhere. Fifty-five firms were ISOA members as of October 2010, and they must monitor their internal operations to assure that the Code of Conduct is followed. The ISOA has both an open system whereby any person can register a complaint about code violations and a Standards Committee consisting of officials from several member companies who are tasked with investigating such complaints. In the event that a company is found to be in violation of the code and refuses to take actions to remedy the situation, the company's ISOA membership is revoked.[57] The British Association of Private Security Companies (BAPSC) is similar to the ISOA and is developing its own code. Chapter 6 discusses both the ISOA and BAPSC in further detail.

All in all, it appears that traditional conceptions of mercenaries have a profit motivation and/or a foreign component and exist to differing degrees within a historical spectrum of private violence. Auxiliary forces (troops hired out in units by their rulers to serve in foreign conflicts), while not quite mercenaries, are considered to be more mercenary-like than are modern-day PSCs, both because they tend to be less attached to the cause for which they are fighting and because they are less subject to legitimate control by the state actors in question. PSCs, in contrast, are less mercenary-like than are most historical examples of mercenaries and auxiliary forces and have several notable characteristics distinguishing them from traditional conceptions of mercenaries. Yet they resemble mercenaries to a much greater extent than do regular, state-sanctioned forces. Because PSCs differ from regular forces in this manner, the increasing rate of PSC deployment in modern conflicts means that their impact on the operations of regular troops in various deployment scenarios—as explored in this study—is becoming a question of increasing importance. Chapter 5's analysis of the condottieri and Hessian cases draws important parallels between historical mercenary and auxiliary forces and modern PSC forces in this regard. In doing so, it suggests relationships between various types of foreign, profit-motivated, and/or privatized forces and the regular military forces alongside which they often operate and identifies particular outcomes correlated with these various configurations of force employment which may be useful in informing future cases of PSC employment.

PLAN OF THE BOOK

The remainder of the book proceeds as follows: The next chapter frames the problem in terms of theories of the state, military effectiveness, the democratic advantage, and the structure-identity dichotomy in the social sciences. Chapters 3, 4, and 5 examine and compare different cases of modern and historical privatized force deployment, looking at the most recent first and moving backward through time.

Reflecting the book's strong focus on the increasing reliance on PSCs deployed alongside the military in the field, Chapter 3 examines key cases of PSC-military co-deployment—namely, the 2003–2007 portion of Operation Iraqi Freedom, and, to a lesser extent, the concurrent conflict in Afghanistan.

Chapter 4 then examines what were, until 2003, the most common scenarios of modern-day PSC deployment: situations in which PSCs are deployed in place of professional military forces. This chapter looks at the cases of Military Professional Resources Incorporated (MPRI) in Croatia and Sandline in Sierra Leone, comparing them to two counterfactual cases in which regular military and/or government forces were used in similar types of operations, in an effort to determine the effects of using private as opposed to regular forces in such contingencies. To show that the issues apparent in Chapters 3 and 4 are not unique to the modern era and to draw lessons from history to inform more recent cases of privatized force employment, Chapter 5 explores two historical cases in which foreign, profit-motivated groups of mercenaries were either employed in a manner similar to a standing army or were actually integrated into a regular military force. This chapter looks at the cases of the condottieri fighting for the Italian city-states from the thirteenth through fifteenth centuries and the Hessian forces fighting for the British in the American Revolution.

The concluding chapter of the book reflects on the lessons drawn from the case studies in the previous three chapters and develops policy and regulatory recommendations to ensure that PSCs will be used in a manner consistent with democracies' goals of military effectiveness. In developing such recommendations, this chapter examines the current state of the private security industry's regulation, with a specific focus on regulations designed to address abuses in the field.

2 DEMOCRATIC STATES, THEIR MILITARIES, AND SECURITY PRIVATIZATION
Theoretical Considerations

IN CONCEPTUALIZING private security companies' impact on democracies' military effectiveness and propensity to achieve victory in warfare, I draw primarily on several related bodies of international relations theory—those examining the state as an actor in global society, those examining issues of military effectiveness, those arguing that democracies are more likely than other types of regimes to win the wars in which they engage, and the dichotomy between structural and identity-based explanations in the social sciences. The following chapters explore the pressures that the private security industry places on the state and the consequences of such pressures, particularly with reference to democratic states' abilities to successfully and effectively fight wars of counterinsurgency. The book thus uses the proliferation of private military and security companies in modern democracies as a lens to provide a particular insight into the modern state's relation to society and the economy. Yet, the book's theoretical contributions do not fall solely within the realms of state theory, democratic advantage theory, military effectiveness, and the structure–identity debate. In particular, Chapter 3 draws on the profession's literature and civil–military relations theory, as well as various conceptions of structure and identity, to develop a comprehensive analytical framework that helps explain why PSC personnel and the military interact in the manner that they do and to suggest how real and potential frictions between these two groups can best be reduced while maintaining the beneficial impacts of each on military effectiveness. I outline and synthesize these theories in the following discussion, demonstrating their relevance to the topic at hand, and explain the methodology employed throughout the study.

STATE TRANSFORMATION:
THE PRIVATIZATION AND TRANSNATIONALIZATION
OF FORCE PROVISION

Until the recent past, many analysts accepted the Weberian argument that the state enjoyed—and in fact, was defined by—a monopoly on the legitimate use of coercive force, a monopoly that is now increasingly challenged by the private security industry.[1] Max Weber emphasized that "force is certainly not the normal or only means of the state—nobody says that—but force is a means specific to the state . . . the state is a relation of men dominating men, a relation supported by means of legitimate violence."[2] Inherent in Weber's conception of the state is the notion that the state is sovereign, exercising exclusive control over a given territory.[3]

In contrast to Weber, some theorists argue that the Westphalian sovereign state is an ideal form that has never quite been replicated in reality—transnational flows have always existed to some extent. Chief among these arguments is that of Stephen Krasner:

> The term "the Westphalian system" is . . . misleading in suggesting that there has been agreement on the scope of authority that could be exercised by sovereign states. The positive content of sovereignty, the areas over which the state can legitimately command, has always been contested. The claim to exclusive control over a given territory has been challenged both in theory and in practice by transborder flows and interference in the internal affairs of states.[4]

Krasner's argument—particularly the notion of pervasive transborder flows—is certainly supported by the extensive number of kingdoms and states hiring foreign soldiers throughout history, as Chapter 1 outlines. State theorists taking Krasner's view of the persistence of state authority argue that the growth of the private military and security industry does not mark a drastic shift in the history of "the state." Rather, this industry is the result of the evolving material factors—namely, military technology and trade—that enabled sovereign states to become prominent in the first place. Janice Thomson, for instance, explains the rise of the state's monopoly on violence as a trend that is "distinctively modern."[5] Thomson argues that this shift occurred when

> violence was marketized, democratized, and internationalized through the actions of state rulers seeking to escape feudalism's constraints on the exercise

of violence and intent on amassing wealth and military power autonomous from their subjects and other rulers.[6]

Given her argument that the sovereign state's monopoly on violence occurred only when violence was "marketized," Thomson clearly sees the sovereign state and force privatization as having been symbiotically related throughout history.

More recently, British General Rupert Smith makes a compelling case for the decline of the modern state, pointing to the state's diminished role in the future of warfare, a future marked by "war amongst the people." "War amongst the people," according to Smith, means that the industrial army has become effectively obsolete; armies have become smaller, and conscription has largely been abolished; and armies have no clear enemy against whom to fight.[7] Particularly relevant to the issue of force privatization is Smith's observation that "war amongst the people" is characterized by "mostly non-state" actors, "comprising some form of multinational grouping against some non-state party or parties." Interestingly, Smith includes in his definition of non-state parties multinational forces like U.N. peacekeeping troops, coalitions, and alliances in addition to groups traditionally considered to be "non-state" actors.[8]

Krasner and Thomson make convincing arguments regarding the exceptionalism of true sovereignty and the prevalence of transnational flows throughout history, and Smith usefully extends these arguments to the situation of contemporary global conflict. Many scholars, however, while admitting it is an exaggeration, still cite Weber's state monopoly on legitimate violence as a defining feature of the state. As such, many see the private security industry as having the potential to vastly transform the state's control of violence and coercive force. Deborah Avant, for instance, concludes that force privatization should redistribute power over the control of violence both within states and between states and non-state actors.[9]

This book acknowledges that the proliferation of private military and security companies clearly represents a decline in the state's control over the provision of force. The study at hand, however, also acknowledges that states still play a key role in force provision, maintaining state militaries and providing the vast majority of the funding and contracts keeping modern PSCs profitable. The fact that corporations now act as middlemen between the state and individual soldiers-for-hire does not diminish the state's relevance to the force provision equation. This view is in line with that of Avant, who notes,

"Even though states continue to be powerful players, these changes alter expectations about the way international politics works."[10]

Perhaps more significant than the private security industry's impact on the state's role in force provision are the ways in which it interacts with the internal characteristics of states and how it subsequently influences state building activities and the organization of states within the international system. Charles Tilly argues that four interdependent state activities—war making, extraction (that is, taxation), state making, and protection—were crucially significant for the formation and organization of states in Europe before the twentieth century.[11] In the modern era, however, state building activities look very different than they did in pre-twentieth–century Europe, due in part to the global proliferation of PSCs and their impact on these four interdependent state activities.

For one thing, PSCs allow leaders of weak states to protect themselves while simultaneously eliminating the need to create bureaucratic state structures to tax the citizens to pay the military. Avant cites Sierra Leone as an example of this phenomenon:

> Of the four other cases where security was privatized in weak states, in one— Sierra Leone—the government was so weak that it relied on PSCs for control of operations . . . Also, continued and enhanced influence from commercial miners (prominent security consumers) decreased the incentives for politicians to build democratic or capable institutions.[12]

The fact that PSCs eliminate the need to create a bureaucracy to tax the citizenry, coupled with the fact that PSCs often fulfill a greater range of functions in weak states than would the regular military, means that PSCs hinder incentives for state building in weak states when employed directly by the leaders of such states or by their proxies. They similarly hinder the development of the long-term institutional mechanisms necessary for a viable state to develop in the target regions of the world where strong states maintain an interventionist presence, as elaborated in the following discussion.

Strong states such as the United States, meanwhile, are increasingly beginning to focus on stability, security, transition, and reconstruction (SSTR) functions in their military missions and, as Chapter 1 notes, PSCs play an integral role in these missions. In these situations, PSCs free the state's military forces to perform other functions, thus increasing state capacity and the state's power-projection capabilities.[13] In some cases, then, PSCs provide states with a greater range of options for strengthening their own state apparatus and, by extension, their systemic position. Rebecca Ulam Weiner supports this notion, arguing that private military and security companies could step in to fill the widening gap between shrinking state military forces and long-term military commitments because they can be used more discreetly than a state-run military.[14] Yet, the result of such heavy reliance on PSCs for these activities is that the target state in which the SSTR missions take place does not develop its own state-building capacity, and thus it remains a weak state.

Whereas Tilly's view of pre-twentieth-century Europe was that "war became the normal condition of the international system of states and the normal means of defending or enhancing a position within the system," states' abilities to alter their systemic position appear to have changed and to favor strong states to a disproportionate extent in the modern era of such heavy reliance on PSCs as opposed to regular militaries.[15] The extent and corporate organization of the modern private security industry therefore foreshadow significant consequences for the systemic organization and relative power balances of states in today's world. These observations are explored throughout this study with a particular focus on democratic states, as elaborated in the following pages.

THE DEMOCRATIC ADVANTAGE

Many modern PSCs are both based in democracies and predominantly hired by democracies at this point.[16] Because we live in a democracy and security privatization is an issue facing democracies today, this book focuses primarily on democratic states and examines PSCs' impact on theories specific to democracies. A prevalent strand of literature in the international relations field focuses on the democratic peace—the observation that democracies are more selective than are autocracies in choosing their wars and that they rarely fight one another. A subset of this literature focuses on the democratic advantage, or the argument that democracies are more often *victorious* in their wars than are other regime types. This argument originated in David Lake's empirical observation that democracies more often win the wars they fight than do non-democracies.[17]

Two logics exist within the democratic advantage literature, one focusing on military effectiveness and one focusing on selection effects. The military effectiveness argument for the democratic advantage, according to Dan Reiter and Allan Stam, holds that democratic militaries fight more effectively on the battlefield due to better leadership within the ranks and more independent-minded soldiers than those found in autocratic militaries.[18] In other words, democracy's emphasis on the individual is argued to promote more independent-minded soldiers capable of exhibiting strong initiative on the battlefield. Furthermore, Reiter and Stam argue that leadership is stronger in democratic states' militaries than in other militaries, due to the "need for officers in a non-democratic state to be politically unthreatening."[19] Reiter and Stam also look for indicators that morale is stronger in democratic militaries than in others, although their findings do not establish morale as a significant variable. Nonetheless, portions of the interview data examined in Chapter 3 indicate that in some—though by no means all—cases, PSC personnel may have lower levels of patriotic motivation than do professional soldiers.[20] Because Reiter and Stam measure morale partly in terms of patriotic motivation, these data speak directly to their work on morale.

Another argument for the democratic advantage rooted in the notion of military effectiveness emerges from a consideration of democracies' financial advantages. Kenneth Schultz and Barry Weingast argue that liberal democracies are better able than are authoritarian states to establish credible limited government, thereby allowing them to raise massive funds through debt and to finance larger and longer wars.[21] This economic argument directly relates to the use of PSCs, indicating that their use appears to be particularly prevalent among democracies because democracies can afford to hire them. Yet Erik Gartzke's research indicates that, contrary to anecdotal evidence and popular opinion, democracies do not generally substitute capital for labor in preparing for or conducting military foreign policy. In other words, democracies do not spend more money on weaponry or other materiel to minimize casualties. Democracies therefore do not appear to disproportionately protect their citizens, according to Gartzke.[22]

This book examines the military effectiveness side of the democratic advantage literature in depth, looking particularly at how the use of PSCs plays into military effectiveness. PSCs do, however, equally have implications for the selection effects argument. The selection effects argument, as espoused by Dan Reiter and Allan Stam, is based on the idea that democracies selectively involve themselves only in the wars they are likely to win. Reiter and Stam's work is predicated on previous works by Bueno de Mesquita, Lalman, and Siverson, all of which argued that war initiators normally choose conflict adversaries based on which states they believe can be defeated, following the logic that states seek to win wars and thus wage war only if the prospect of victory or the expected benefit is sufficient.[23] Electoral politics play a crucial role here, as the theory holds that democratic leaders will be more beholden to their domestic publics than will autocratic leaders and will consequently be forced to be more selective with regard to the conflicts they enter. As Sven Chojnacki notes, "Democratic elites are thus not per se more averse towards using violence than authoritarian rulers but must consider their decisions more carefully and justify them to the public."[24] Relevant to the issue of PSC use is the fact that democracies—due to these electoral constraints—appear to be particularly casualty sensitive. Indeed, some argue that the more the costs and casualties of violent foreign policy can be restricted (or hidden from the electorate), the easier it is for wars and military interventions to be pushed through democratic decisionmaking processes.[25] Yet, this casualty-sensitivity argument must be considered critically in the context of Gartzke's aforementioned findings regarding the substitution of capital for labor in democracies versus non-democracies. The case studies in the following chapters examine the idea that democratic leaders' sensitivity to casualties may cause them to spend money hiring a PSC to hide conflict casualties from the electorate.

Deborah Avant has examined the possibility that PSCs reduce transparency in democratic decisionmaking and, in the U.S. government in particular, advantage the executive branch relative to the legislative branch, thus making it easier for democracies to become involved in conflicts.[26] She illustrates several cases in which PSCs have weakened democratic structures that cause democracies to be selective in their wars, and in doing so she shows how PSCs very plausibly can weaken the selection effects argument of democratic advantage theory. In particular, the selection effects argument of democratic advantage theory implies the expectation that the democratic advantage would be less likely in cases where PSCs are deployed in place of national military forces because the electorate is less likely to learn of such a deployment—or to consider it to be an actual act of war making—and thus is less likely to pressure policymakers to be selective with regard to conflict involvement. Following this logic, the selection effects argument also implies the expectation that situations of PSC-military co-deployment and private forces' integration into the regular military would hold prospects for the democratic advantage similar to those of a regular military deployment. In such situations, the deployment of national military forces would attract the electorate's attention to the conflict in question, causing the public to put pressure on policymakers to be selective with regard to conflict involvement. The case studies in Chapter 3 in particular explore these implications in greater detail.

The democratic advantage literature has been subject to a fair amount of criticism, particularly in terms of the military effectiveness argument. The selection effects argument, meanwhile, is considered the strongest element of democratic advantage theory.[27] Despite this criticism, I use the democratic advantage literature as a point of departure for this study's analysis because its examination of military effectiveness and conflict selectivity in the specific context of democracies is highly relevant to the topic at hand. Furthermore, if the study at hand finds that PSCs have an impact on military effectiveness, then PSCs are likely to affect the argument and implications of the democratic advantage literature as well. Indeed, with the exceptions of the works of Gartzke and of Schultz and Weingast, democratic advantage theorists largely neglect the economic dimensions of market democracies in their analyses. Some of these economic dimensions—particularly the privatization and outsourcing trends seen increasingly in democratic states over the past few decades—could adversely affect military performance and undermine some of the expectations of democratic advantage theory, or vice versa. This study thus speaks to a broader body of theory and literature than that simply focused on military power and military effectiveness.

One potential challenge to the democratic advantage literature that emerges in this study, however, is that some of the structural constraints noted by democratic advantage theorists as being unique to democracies—in particular, the structural constraints and processes relevant to the military effectiveness and selection effects arguments of democratic advantage theory—appear to play a role in non-democratic regimes as well. This is shown in the cases examined in Chapter 5, for instance, and speaks directly to an emerging research agenda in the international relations field.[28] Future research on this issue might further evaluate some of the cases explored here to examine the prevalence of these structural constraints in non-democracies as opposed to democracies.

Another potential challenge to arguments for the democratic advantage emerges when considering the prevalence of non-conventional forms of warfare today. Gil Merom's research, for instance, shows that democracies have difficulty employing the brutal tactics that, he argues, are essential to waging a successful counterinsurgency. This difficulty stems mainly from the structural constraints of democratic systems combined with the electorate's normative antipathy for brutal tactics.[29] Of course, this challenge to theories of the democratic advantage is rooted in the premise that the "draining the sea" approach requiring the use of brutal tactics is a superior means of waging counterinsurgency (COIN) warfare when compared to the "hearts and minds" approach aimed at co-opting local citizens, an issue that should not be taken for granted and that is explored in greater detail in the case studies of the following chapters.

DEFINING "MILITARY EFFECTIVENESS"

There is a substantial body of literature on military effectiveness itself, of which the democratic advantage arguments mentioned above constitute only a small portion. As Risa Brooks highlights, various different notions of what constitutes "military effectiveness" abound:

> Some studies eschew a formal definition of military effectiveness . . . Some political scientists analyze military effectiveness in terms of a military organization's capacity to prevail over an adversary—in terms of victory or defeat . . . Other scholars place greater weight on the degree to which military organizations and their personnel exhibit particular attributes essential to the planning and preparation for war . . . The term *military effectiveness* is also often used by military professionals and defense officials and analysts. In this context it has a variety of different meanings. Sometimes effectiveness is used to refer to the readiness of forces to deploy to the theater of war. Sometimes it indicates a mission accomplished in a combat zone . . . Sometimes it refers to the attributes of a particular military organization and the quality of its leadership, training, and systems, and the organization's preparation for war.[30]

The neorealist stance on the issue of military effectiveness is the most traditional, emphasizing the relative quantity of material resources in the hands of the military institution in question. Neorealists emphasize factors such as superior technology, superior tactical planning, and numerical supremacy in calculating a military's propensity for effectiveness.[31] A slightly more nuanced view of this perspective is found among offense-defense theorists, who illuminate the benefits of offensive versus defensive military technology.[32] Stephen Rosen expands on traditional neorealist conceptions of military effectiveness, examining the effects of social structures on the amount of offensive and defensive military power that can be generated from a given quantity of material resources.[33] Rosen's work is significant for the project at hand in its recognition of the ways that social divisions can cause unit fissures and decrease military cohesion, or what I will later refer to as *integration*, in line with Risa Brooks's definition.

In *Military Power*, Stephen Biddle also responds to traditional neorealist assumptions in arguing that military capability depends not on technology alone but on how that technology is used—what he terms "force employment." Using this notion, Biddle develops a rather tactically based theory of military capability in terms of three "irreducible capacities": the ability to control territory, the ability to inflict and limit losses, and the ability to prevail quickly.[34]

In an earlier article, Biddle and Stephen Long branch out from neorealist conceptions of military effectiveness and speak directly to the democratic advantage literature, looking at the effects on military effectiveness of various unit-level variables including human capital, civil–military relations, and culture.[35] In this article, however, Biddle and Long similarly conceive of military effectiveness narrowly, in terms of victory in a particular battle or war without any analysis of the means to achieving those results. Biddle and Long do find that the unit-level variables other than regime type are significant for military effectiveness, yet they are unable to definitively prove the direction of the causal arrow linking these unit-level variables and regime type. In its focus on unit-level variables and its suggestion of this causal indeterminacy, Biddle and Long's study encourages this study's focus on the effects of unit-level variables—in this case, PSCs—on military performance.

As is the case with most conceptions of military effectiveness, these definitions pre-suppose a particular type of warfare—Type I warfare, or major conventional war between states. Yet, over the past several decades, asymmetric warfare, counterinsurgency, humanitarian intervention, and nation building have come to the fore as the primary activities of militaries worldwide, overshadowing classic war-fighting activities. As already mentioned, British General Rupert Smith notes that "war amongst the people"—defined by an effectively obsolete industrial army, a reduction in the size of armies and the abolition of conscription, and the lack of a clear enemy against whom armies can fight—is now the dominant form of global warfare.[36] This fact, coupled with the fact that the U.S. military in particular has become increasingly entrenched in these non-conventional war-fighting activities, dictates that this study's definition of military effectiveness take into account the various capabilities necessary for military effectiveness in non-conventional contingencies.

In situations of "war amongst the people," the lessons of COIN doctrine are instructive regarding the capabilities necessary to achieve military effectiveness. Two conflicting schools of thought exist regarding the best approach to counterinsurgency warfare. A strong line of argument insists that compliance with the laws of war better enables militaries to fight effectively, particularly in counterinsurgencies (the so-called hearts-and-minds approach), while another line of argument states that reliance on brutality toward civilians and non-compliance with the laws of war better serves military effectiveness (the so-called draining-the-sea approach).[37] For instance, recent research by Lieutenant Colonel Isaiah Wilson III and Jason Lyall supporting the hearts-and-minds approach indicates that the development of on-the-ground information networks and good relations with local civilians are the keys to waging a successful counterinsurgency.[38] Joseph Felter's research on the correct combination of military capabilities for waging effective COIN supports this, finding that small units possessing superior leadership, training, and access to local information are more likely to conduct effective and discriminative counterinsurgency, and that deploying locally recruited soldiers with specially trained elite forces as cadres is particularly effective at achieving this potent combination of capabilities.[39] Brigadier Nigel Aylwin-Foster of the British Army has reached similar conclusions, arguing that a COIN force must have two traits not required in conventional war fighting: (1) It must be able to see issues and actions from the perspective of the domestic population; and (2) it must understand the relative value of force and how easily excessive force, even when apparently justified, can undermine popular support.[40]

Others argue for the so-called draining-the-sea approach: that brutality against civilian populations can be successfully pursued in counterinsurgency warfare and protracted wars of attrition to weaken the enemy quickly and end the conflict as soon as possible.[41] Due to this indeterminacy in COIN doctrine, it is necessary to consider in a COIN-specific definition of military effectiveness both an adherence to human rights standards and integration with local civilians, and a willingness to undertake the dirty work of acting brutally toward civilians if necessary. As discussed in the following pages, the following chapters assess the relative salience of these two lines of thought with regard to PSC involvement in counterinsurgencies.

Given the plethora of different capabilities and qualities deemed essential to an effective military, it is useful to depict the overlap of these various capabilities across the spectrum of conventional and unconventional contingencies. Table 2.1 does this, using examples taken from the past three decades. Of course, the need for these skills in a particular type of contingency is not given; indeed, controversy abounds over some of them. For instance, some would argue that numerical supremacy has little connection to asymmetric warfare such as counter-terrorism and counterinsurgency.

These disagreements often reflect different research paradigms in the social sciences, with constructivists tending to emphasize the importance of

Table 2.1. Components of effectiveness for contemporary tasks facing the militaries of democracies.

Task	Example	Characteristics commonly argued to be necessary for military effectiveness in achieving tasks						
		Superior technology	Superior tactical planning	Numerical Supremacy	Individual unit morale, expertise	Adherence to human rights standards	Integration with civil/ partner agencies	Willingness to undertake "dirty work"
Conventional (Type I) War fighting	1982: *Falklands War between Britain and Argentina*	●	●	●	●			●
Evacuation mission	1992: U.S. citizens evacuated from *Sierra Leone*	●	●		●		●	
Peacekeeping	1996: U.N. humanitarian operations in *Rwanda and Zaire*	●			●	●	●	
COIN — Military	2001–Present: U.S. military and NATO forces combat Taliban in *Afghanistan*	●	●	●	●	●	●	●
COIN — Civil	2001–Present: NATO runs series of hearts-and-minds campaigns in *Afghanistan*		●		●	●	●	
Counterterrorism	2003: U.S. combat-equipped and support forces deployed to *Georgia and Djibouti* to enhance "counterterrorist capabilities"	●	●	●	●	●	●	●
Security assistance	2004–Present: Coalition forces engaged in training Iraqi army and police forces in southern *Iraq*				●	●	●	
Reconstruction	2003–Present: Coalition forces run civil reconstruction projects throughout *Iraq*				●	●	●	

behavioral norms, political and military strategic culture and morale, and individual and unit-level expertise, and neorealists claiming the primacy of superior material capabilities, as noted above. Even given this disagreement, however, Table 2.1 serves to illustrate how different war-fighting tasks require different military qualities.

Millet, Murray, and Watman support this notion, arguing that the definition and measurement of "military effectiveness" are dependent upon the prevailing conditions in the particular situation being studied:

> . . . it is essential to reach a judgment about the possibilities open to a particular military organization in a given situation. Only then can one compare national armed forces, possessing vastly different characteristics, problems, and enemies in a fashion that can explain their relative effectiveness.[42]

One of the most recent, and arguably most complete, scholarly conceptions of military effectiveness to date that allows for this consideration of situational variation is found in a 2007 chapter by Risa Brooks. Brooks defines military effectiveness as "the capacity to create military power from a state's basic resources in wealth, technology, population size, and human capital" and focuses on four "crucial attributes" that militaries may or may not display: "the *integration* of military activity within and across different levels; *responsiveness* to internal constraints and the external environment; high *skill*, measured in the motivation and basic competencies of personnel; and high *quality*, as indicated by the caliber of a state's weapons and equipment" (emphasis added).[43]

Brooks defines *integration* as "the degree to which different military activities are internally consistent and mutually reinforcing." According to her,

> An integrated military is one whose activities at the tactical level are consistent with those at the operational level and also support broader strategic objectives. Integration also involves maintaining consistency in force development activities, such as procurement, training, and education, with strategy, operations, and tactics. Integration means the achievement of consistency within and across levels and areas of all military activity.[44]

She defines *responsiveness* as "the ability to tailor military activity to a state's own capabilities, its adversaries' capabilities, and external constraints."[45] *Skill* measures "military personnel and their units against some objective standard or benchmark in assessing their ability to achieve particular tasks and to carry out orders" and "also captures a military's capability to motivate soldiers and to ensure that they carry out orders, fight hard, and seize the initiative in combat."[46] Finally, *quality* is the military's "ability to provide itself with highly capable weapons and equipment."[47]

Brooks' categorization of military attributes is a useful and comprehensive method for deconstructing and measuring the effectiveness of particular military actions across a range of different types of contingencies. This study adopts her definitions of *integration, responsiveness, skill,* and *quality,* taking note of the expectations implied by these criteria: that PSCs will have the strongest impact on military effectiveness when integrated into a national military (for they will have the best effect on *integration* and *skill* in such cases), and that PSCs' impact may also be beneficial in situations where they are deployed in place of national forces (when they may have a positive effect on *responsiveness, skill,* and *quality*).

In adopting these criteria, I subsume Reiter and Stam's notions of battlefield leadership and initiative under Brooks' *skill,* for they are essentially one and the same. Indeed, Reiter and Stam note "effective leadership consists of the ability of officers to persuade troops to execute commands, especially under fire, and to competently execute tactics and seize the initiative when opportunities present themselves."[48] This closely matches Brooks' definition of *skill,* although it should be noted that Reiter and Stam explicitly refer to tactical effectiveness. Such a focus is especially appropriate with regard to the issue of *skill.* Thus, this study's references to *skill* focus primarily on activities at the tactical and—to a lesser degree—the operational levels.

However, this study goes beyond Brooks' definition of military effectiveness to focus on tactical, strategic, operational, and political outcomes of warfare. This distinction is highlighted here because a military can clearly be effective in one realm and ineffective in another—comprehensive military effectiveness requires the achievement of the goals of all four realms. Again, Millet, Murray, and Watman's work supports this notion:

> Military activity occurs at four different levels: political, strategic, operational, and tactical. Each category overlaps the others, but each is characterized by different actions, procedures, and goals. Therefore, one must assess military effectiveness separately at each level of activity.[49]

Therefore, in this study an effective military is considered to be one that displays high levels of *integration, responsiveness, skill,* and *quality,* while: (a) accomplishing its tactical goals, or the maneuvers pertaining to the most immediate battlefield goals; (b) accomplishing its operational goals, or the sum of the tactical goals pertaining to a particular theater of operation; (c) accomplishing its strategic goals, or the broader politico-military goals equaling the sum of its tactical goals across various theaters of operation; and (d) accomplishing the political goals of its government. This definition encompasses both the *ends* and *means* of achieving military effectiveness, and its unit-level assessment structure allows for variation in the type of contingency. Yet, this definition maintains the traditional scholarly focus on military power, and the traditional military focus on final outcomes, as indicators of military effectiveness. This focus on outcomes is crucial because, as Stephen Biddle notes, "Military effectiveness matters chiefly because it shapes military outcomes: other things being equal, 'effective' militaries ought to win more often than ineffective ones."[50]

Notably, Brooks' definition of military effectiveness emphasizes the military-technological aspects of warfare—particularly under the rubric of the *quality* component of military effectiveness—even as the volume in which the definition is included focuses on cultural and political elements of military effectiveness. This military-technological focus presupposes a certain type of warfare; namely, Type I warfare or major conventional war. Because the study at hand focuses in large part on Type III warfare or counterinsurgency (COIN), I examine the potential for an additional variable to be considered as a component of military effectiveness—the level of PSC compliance with legal and ethical norms of just war—through four propositions, as elaborated in the following pages.[51]

DETERMINANTS OF PSC–MILITARY COORDINATION: STRUCTURE VERSUS IDENTITY

We now have a solid conception of what constitutes military effectiveness to guide the study, but how do we proceed when we find situations in which PSCs hinder military effectiveness? By more deeply examining the sources of coordination problems within cases of PSC–military co-deployment, we can learn how best to remedy them, and thus how best to improve PSCs' impact on military effectiveness. To examine the underlying sources of such problems, the analysis in Chapter 3 draws on the distinction in the social sciences between structure and identity, as well as the literatures on the professions and civil–military relations. These four distinct theoretical tools, when brought together, create a synthesis from which a policy-relevant framework of analysis can be developed.

In recent years there has been a vibrant debate within the international relations (IR) literature regarding the relative importance of structural and identity factors in shaping international events. However, this IR debate functions mainly at the state or systemic level, giving little attention to analysis of the effects of unit-level structures and individual identities on international relations. While much is written on the effects of domestic political structures on military performance, rarely does this structural analysis come down to the structure of particular military operations. Meanwhile, individual (as opposed to state) identities are rarely seen as relevant to the occurrence of international events, with the exception of political-psychological analyses of particular leaders' identities and perceptions.[52] The introduction of a new tactical and strategic actor—for example, private security contractors—requires deconstruction of the relevant issues down to sub-systemic levels, using different analytical tools than those most commonly used in IR scholarship. Thus, I look at the structure of particular deployments and at military rules, doctrine, and training, and employ measurements of identity at both the collective and individual levels.[53]

The term *structure* has many meanings across numerous disciplines. Wendy Pullan argues that "the desire to define structure in a complete or finite manner is counterproductive . . . structure is an inclusive and open-ended theme that offers itself to interpretation in many disciplines in the sciences, arts, and humanities."[54] The *Random House Unabridged Dictionary* defines structure as: "the organization of a society or other group and the relations between its members, determining its working."[55] Other conceptions of "structure," and particularly "social structure," include "methods of interaction," "the social organization of individuals and groups," "a system organized by a characteristic pattern of relationships," and "the arrangement of components in a complex entity."[56] Of specific relevance to the IR subfield is Kenneth Waltz's definition of political structures: "A domestic political structure is thus defined, first, according to the *principle by which it is ordered*; second, by specification of the *functions* of formally differentiated units; and third, by the distribution of *capabilities* across those units" (emphasis added).[57] Waltz's definition is useful in guiding this study's conception of "structure," as detailed in the following paragraphs.

In the case of PSC–military coordination, one can contrast the *ordering principles* for the military against those for PSCs in terms of their varying levels of hierarchy, as well as analyze the ordering principles for their mutual deployment alongside one another (in terms of the chain of command over contractors). For instance, I conceive of the military as more strictly hierarchical than PSCs, which I conceive of as loosely hierarchical. Differences in pay scales also reflect the divergent ordering principles of the military versus PSCs, reflecting the fact that PSCs place different values on positions similar to military positions and do not necessarily value particular configurations of expertise in the same order—relative to other configurations of expertise— as the military does. Furthermore, the *functions* that each group fulfills are clearly distinct from one another (at least in theory), with private security contractors allowed to fight only defensively and working primarily to guard a person or static site, not to fight offensively to secure a larger strategic goal as the military does. Finally, each group has a distinct level of *capability* associated with it, due to factors such as training and institutional support (the Reconstruction Operations Center in Iraq, for instance), as well as the quality of equipment to which each group is given access. Interestingly, in some cases PSCs have access to better equipment than do military units, which would have a beneficial impact on PSC capability relative to military capability in those cases. References in the interview data to these structural factors as causes of PSC–military coordination problems will provide support for the notion that structural factors have significant ramifications for the success of PSC-military field coordination. Table 2.2 organizes these examples of structural variables alongside identity variables to illustrate the contrast between the military and PSCs in terms of these variables.

The identity variables listed in Table 2.2 are derived from the social science literature on identity, civil–military relations, and the professions. Measurements of identity are just as varied across the social sciences as are measurements of structure. As a recent work by Rawi Abdelal and his colleagues notes, "Despite—or perhaps because of—the sprawl of different treatments of identity in the social sciences, the concept has remained too analytically loose to be as useful a tool as the literature's early promise had suggested."[58] Abdelal and his coauthors develop a framework to operationalize collective identity, dissecting the content of an identity into four non-mutually-exclusive types: (1) constitutive norms; (2) social purposes; (3) relational comparisons with other social categories; and (4) cognitive models.[59] Constitutive norms refer to "the formal and informal rules that define group membership," while social purposes refer to "the goals that are shared by members of a group."[60] Relational comparisons, meanwhile, refer to "defining an identity group by what it

Table 2.2 Structural versus identity variables.

	Structural variables	Identity variables
PSC	**Ordering Principles** • Loosely hierarchical • Order as laid out in doctrine **Functions** • Defensive fighting to guard a person, static site, or convoy **Capability** • Depends on the firm in question • In general, training is not standardized, and institutional support varies • Sometimes better access than military to high-tech equipment	**Constitutive Norms** • Previous military service • Desire to maximize financial earning power • Professional jurisdiction **Social Purposes** • Range from defending country to defending economic enterprise **Relational Comparisons** • PSC self-perceptions relative to their perceptions of military identities **Cognitive Models** • Private sector as innovative and profitable alternative to military service
Military	**Ordering Principles** • Strictly hierarchical • Order as laid out indoctrine **Functions** • Offensive and defensive fighting to secure strategic object **Capability** • More standardized training and better institutional support than PSCs • Equipment sometimes worse than PSCs	**Constitutive Norms** • Personal ethic of civic duty • Professional jurisdiction • Corporateness • Technical love of craft **Social Purposes** • Aim to protect the country, offensively and defensively • Sense of social obligation **Relational Comparisons** • Military self-perceptions in relation to perceived PSC identity **Cognitive Models** • Military as profession • Military as organization

is not, i.e., the way it views other identity groups, especially where those views about the other are a defining part of the identity."

Finally, cognitive models refer to "the worldviews or understanding of political and material conditions and interests that are shaped by a particular identity."[61] In addition to the four types of content, the degree to which a group agrees on its identity (contestation) is an element of collective identity.[62]

As indicated above, both the civil–military relations literature and the literature on professions are key to an understanding of military identities and the potential for friction between military and private security contractors' identities. First, both literatures highlight indicators of "constitutive norms" and "social purposes." Samuel Huntington's work on civil–military relations suggests that a profession is a particular type of functional group with highly specialized characteristics, distinguished by its expertise, responsibility, and corporateness.[63] In the military context, "the modern officer corps is a professional body and the modern military officer is a professional man."[64] Regarding the military officer's professional responsibilities, "The officer is not a mercenary who transfers his services wherever they are best rewarded . . . The motivations of the officer are a *technical love for his craft* and the *sense of social obligation to utilize this craft for the benefit of society*" (emphasis added).[65] This sense of social obligation clearly speaks to the military officer's social purposes, while the love for his craft is a norm constituting his identity. Another norm constituting the military officer's identity is *corporateness*:

> The functional imperatives of security give rise to complex vocational institutions which mold the officer corps into an autonomous social unit . . . The corporate structure of the officer corps includes not just the official bureaucracy but also societies, associations, schools, journals, customs, and traditions.[66]

Huntington thus gives us an idea of the constitutive norms and social purposes comprising a military professional's identity and of its significance in the context of civil–military relations. A leading theorist on professions and the professional workforce, Andrew Abbott, adds to these identity characteristics when he notes that the army is unique in that it is simultaneously a *profession* and an *organization* (cognitive models) and that it is one of the few professions to still develop lifelong *careers* for its workforce (a constitutive norm).[67]

The second contribution of these literatures—particularly the professions literature—is found in its insights on professional jurisdiction and the potential for friction to develop between the identities of different professions. Abbott develops a "turf-war model" to explain competition between professions, writing of a "system of professions" in which "each profession has its activities under various kinds of jurisdiction," and in which "jurisdictional boundaries are perpetually in dispute."[68] Although Abbott later argues that the Army does not fall into this static "turf war" model, Richard Lacquement recognizes the propensity for jurisdictional competition over the core competencies traditionally associated with the professional military:

> Many responsibilities traditionally associated with the Army have been challenged and claimed by others. Moreover, laudable Army service in missions that have little to do with the use of coercive force blur public understanding of the Army's core roles, thus making it easier to challenge those core roles. Strategic leaders must recognize this dynamic context as they define the Army's appropriate roles.[69]

Deborah Avant makes a related point with specific reference to PSCs:

> Its ready use of contractors for tasks that are crucial to both the development of the profession in the future and to the success of new missions . . . has generated competition between the Army and private security companies over who will shape the development of future professionals and has degraded the Army's ability to undertake successful missions on its own.[70]

The extent to which PSC personnel can challenge the military's jurisdiction over its core competencies—which Lacquement suggests include major combat operations (war), stability operations, strategic deterrence, and homeland security—is clearly open for debate.[71] One therefore questions the extent to which competition over professional jurisdiction contributes to any PSC–military resentment and coordination problems that may occur in the field.

I use the framework developed by Abdelal and his coauthors, along with the characteristics of military professionals that Huntington, Abbott, and Lacquement note, to guide the book's conceptualization of military and PSC identities. For instance, in this study I conceive of military identities in terms of a personal ethic of civic duty (a constitutive norm), the aim of defending and protecting the country (a social purpose), relational comparisons in terms of how soldiers perceive their own identities in relation to the identities of PSC personnel, and cognitive models in terms of soldiers' patriotically-motivated worldviews. In contrast, I conceive of norms of previous military service and a desire to maximize financial earning power as constituting the identities of PSC personnel. The social purposes of PSC personnel encompass but are not limited to those of the military, as PSCs may be hired to guard private business installations in addition to governmental sites and targets. Thus, their social purposes range from defending the country to defending an economic enterprise. I conceive of relational comparisons in terms of how PSC person-nel perceive their own identities in relation to military identities. Because most PSC personnel have military backgrounds, which I expect will have been instrumental in shaping their worldviews, I do not anticipate vast differences between PSC and military cognitive models. Again, these identity character-istics are all depicted in Table 2.2.

If any of these identity characteristics are repeatedly cited in the interview data as causes of poor coordination between PSC personnel and soldiers in the field, such statements will support the notion that identity factors play a significant role in controlling PSC–military field coordination. Continuous references to competition over either group's professional jurisdiction will support this notion as well, as professional jurisdiction is a constitutive norm defining each group's collective identity. Analysis of interview and survey data illustrates the relative salience of these identity characteristics versus struc-tural factors as explanations for particular PSC–military field interactions.

PSCS' IMPACT ON MILITARY EFFECTIVENESS
AND THE DEMOCRATIC ADVANTAGE: SIX PROPOSITIONS

As relatively new actors in the field of combat, modern private security com-panies and their personnel are likely to have some effect on military effective-ness and, by extension, on the democratic advantage. The task at hand is to determine what these effects are and how the relevant actors can best deal with them.

Media reports abound about friendly fire incidents between PSC person-nel and the military in Iraq, about the decrease in military retention rates as senior military professionals leave the service for the private sector, and about increasing numbers of security contractors killed in Iraq.[72] These events have ramifications for military effectiveness, as do many other issues related to PSCs. On one side of the debate, scholars and PSC industry representatives argue that PSCs constitute force multipliers who are highly skilled, usually have prior military training, and serve only defensive purposes on the battle-field.[73] Such claims lead to the notion that PSCs will cause a net increase in military effectiveness by augmenting both the quantity and *quality* of exist-ing forces, by increasing the military's *responsiveness*, and by increasing *skill* through the strengthening of commanders' tactical leadership capabilities as they are relieved of non-core military tasks. If this proposition is strongly supported by the data, it will indicate that the growth in PSC hiring will make those actors hiring PSCs more militarily effective. Assuming that the PSC trend continues to operate strongly among democracies, growth in PSC hiring will also increase the prospects for these democracies to experience the military effectiveness side of the democratic advantage. Greater PSC use will translate into more battlefield success for democracies in such cases, *as long as the use of private force does not have a negative impact on the selection effects side of the democratic advantage to an equal or greater degree than its positive impact on military effectiveness.*

However, because PSCs provide democratic policymakers with covert warmaking options that may be used in cases where the electorate would otherwise constrain the decision to become involved in a conflict, they can have a very real impact on the selection effects side of the democratic advantage. Therefore, the benefits of PSCs for military effectiveness do not necessarily translate into battlefield success for democracies, though the potential certainly exists. PSCs' impact on military effectiveness and selection effects must be explored simultaneously to determine whether democracies will experience more or less battlefield success from the employment of PSCs. The logic of PSCs' beneficial impact on military effectiveness is depicted in Figure 2.1.

The findings presented in the following chapters show that a situation such as that depicted in Figure 2.1 is most likely when PSCs are deployed in theaters in place of the military or when they are structurally integrated into the military alongside which they are deployed, as both of these scenarios avoid the problems of PSC–military field coordination that can effectively decrease military effectiveness. History has shown that PSCs are typically deployed instead of the military in relatively small or covert conflicts, particularly in situations where major powers want to shape conflict outcomes without highly visible involvement. However, such situations do not necessarily involve democratic actors, or at least not only democratic actors. Furthermore, the selection effects side of the democratic advantage is more likely to be negatively influenced in situations in which PSCs substitute for national military forces. Thus, the net effect of PSCs on the democratic advantage in these scenarios must be assessed on a case-by-case basis.

In contrast to the notion that PSCs will cause a net increase in military effectiveness, reports from the field in Operation Iraqi Freedom indicate that the presence of PSCs there caused coordination problems between the military and PSCs, and among military units themselves.[74] These reports lead to

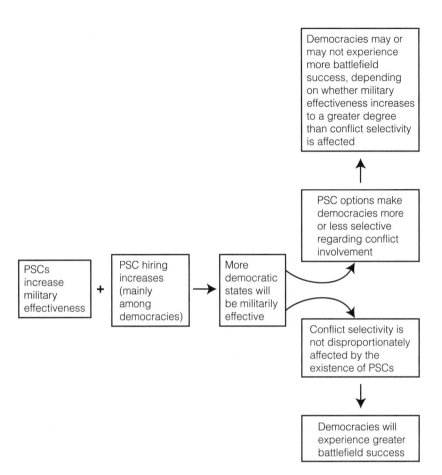

Figure 2.1. The relationship among PSCs, military effectiveness, and the democratic advantage when PSCs increase military effectiveness.

another major proposition to be explored in the following chapters: that PSCs cause a net decrease in military effectiveness by decreasing *integration* and decreasing *skill* through their hindrance of commanders' leadership capabilities and soldiers' motivation levels.[75] If this proposition is strongly supported by the data, such evidence will indicate that the growth of the PSC hiring trend will make actors hiring PSCs less militarily effective. Assuming that PSCs continue to be prominent mainly among democracies, support for this proposition will also indicate a decrease in the propensity for democracies to win the conflicts into which they enter and a corresponding decrease in the strength of arguments touting the benefits of democracy. Again, however, this is assuming that the selection effects side of the democratic advantage is held

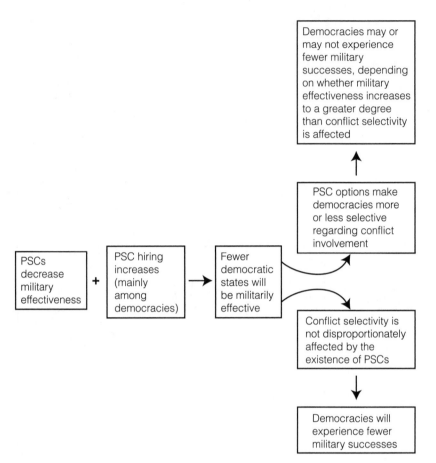

Figure 2.2. The relationship among PSCs, military effectiveness, and the democratic advantage when PSCs decrease military effectiveness.

constant. As the depiction in Figure 2.2 indicates, the relative impacts of PSCs on military effectiveness and conflict selectivity must be assessed on a case-by-case basis to determine PSCs' impact on the democratic advantage.

Of course, we must leave open the possibility that PSCs have no discernible impact on military effectiveness. This could happen either because they do not affect military effectiveness in any manner that would show up in this study or because their positive and negative effects on military effectiveness completely offset one another.

The following chapters assess four additional propositions related to the debate surrounding the legal and ethical basis for warfare and the opaque status of PSCs under the laws of war. Numerous reports have emerged detailing legal and ethical abuses in the field by contractors who, by and large, are not held responsible for their actions by any legal authority.[76] As illustrated by the local outrage caused by the highly publicized September 2007 incident in which Blackwater USA personnel shot and killed seventeen Iraqi civilians and wounded twenty-seven others in Baghdad's Nisour Square while guarding a diplomatic convoy, private security personnel can undermine the military's war for the hearts and minds of local civilians by failing to abide by the laws and norms of just war. Furthermore, as discussed earlier in this chapter, a strong line of argument insists that compliance with the laws of war better enables militaries to fight effectively, particularly in counterinsurgencies (the so-called hearts-and-minds approach). Yet another line of argument states that reliance on brutality toward civilians and non-compliance with the laws of war better serves military effectiveness (the so-called draining-the-sea approach).[77] Because there is a vicious debate at present regarding PSCs' accountability under the laws of war, and due to this study's focus on counterinsurgency warfare, it is appropriate here to explore the impact of private security contractors' compliance with legal and normative rules of ethical warfare on military effectiveness. Hence, the following chapters analyze whether and to what extent private security contractors' compliance with the laws of war increases military effectiveness by supporting the war for the hearts and minds of the citizenry, thus increasing *responsiveness*.

Looking at the issue in another light, from the view that non-compliance with international humanitarian law (IHL) is a means of hindering guerilla warfare (the draining-the-sea approach), I explore a second proposition related to IHL: that private security contractors' compliance with the laws of war decreases military effectiveness by limiting PSCs' ability to take on the dirty jobs necessary to defeat insurgencies, thus decreasing *responsiveness*.

Because PSC compliance with the rules and norms of IHL should not be assumed, I also explore whether private security contractors' non-compliance with the laws of war increases military effectiveness by enabling PSCs to take on the dirty jobs necessary to defeat insurgencies, thus increasing *responsiveness*. Finally, I assess the merits of the view that private security contractors' non-compliance with the laws of war decreases military effectiveness by undermining the war for the hearts and minds of the citizenry, thus decreasing *responsiveness*.

Findings in the following chapters that support the hearts-and-minds school of thought on counterinsurgency will indicate to governments and companies

Table 2.3 Six propositions regarding PSCs' impact on military effectiveness.

Proposition 1 (P1)	PSCs cause a net increase in military effectiveness by increasing the quantity and *quality* of existing forces, increasing *responsiveness*, and increasing *skill.*
Proposition 2 (P2)	PSCs cause a net decrease in military effectiveness by decreasing *integration* and decreasing *skill.*
Proposition 1a (P1a)	PSC compliance with IHL increases military effectiveness by supporting the war for the "hearts and minds" of the citizenry, thus increasing *responsiveness.*
Proposition 1b (P1b)	PSC noncompliance with IHL increases military effectiveness by enabling PSCs to take on the dirty jobs necessary to defeat insurgencies, thus increasing *responsiveness.*
Proposition 2a (P2a)	PSC compliance with IHL decreases military effectiveness by limiting PSCs' ability to take on the dirty jobs necessary to defeat insurgencies, thus decreasing *responsiveness.*
Proposition 2b (P2b)	PSC noncompliance with IHL decreases military effectiveness by undermining the war for the "hearts and minds" of the citizenry, thus decreasing *responsiveness.*

purchasing PSCs' services that they should discriminate against those firms not employing practices and rules of engagement that comply with IHL and other laws of war. Thus, the findings related to these propositions could have grave ramifications for the conduct and future business opportunities of PSCs, putting certain firms at risk of losing business unless they modify their practices. Findings that are strongly supportive of the notion that brutality is necessary to effectively wage COIN warfare, on the other hand, will indicate to purchasers of PSC services that firms' records of compliance with IHL are irrelevant to contracting decisions, or even that poor records of adherence to international laws of war are desirable traits when seeking out a private security firm. Table 2.3 lists each of these propositions.

VARIABLES AND CASE SELECTION

The topic of modern-day military and security privatization carries with it the problem of very few available cases, owing to the relative novelty of the security privatization trend (at least in its current form) and the inherently secretive nature of the industry and its work. This problem is compounded by the fact that the few cases that do exist show little variation in the democracies involved in them, with the United States and Britain accounting for almost all of the democratic state involvement in these cases. Yet both the transnationalization of warfare and the U.S. hegemonic position make it likely that future democratic wars will be fought in multinational coalitions that include the United States.[78] Above all, this study focuses on cases involving the United States because security privatization is a serious issue facing U.S. policymakers at present, and because the United States is a major democracy, a major military power, and a major innovator. Indeed, the fact that U.S. defense expenditures are greater than the next twenty-four countries combined means that the United States will likely continue to be one of the most relevant actors for the private security industry.[79] Therefore, it makes sense to examine PSCs' impact in the context of the United States. Furthermore, because the United States is a major democracy with arguably the strongest military in the world, cases relevant to this topic that involve the United States are hard cases in which we would expect PSCs to have very little incremental effect on military effectiveness and the democratic advantage.

This study categorizes the available historical and modern cases into three different "types" of cases: cases in which the democratic state's military is directly involved in the conflict alongside PSCs in their current corporate form ("co-deployed"), cases in which democratic states hire PSCs to become involved in a conflict instead of the democratic state's professional military (substitution), and cases in which a mercenary or auxiliary force is structured in a manner similar to or is actually assimilated into a regular military force (integration).[80]

In selecting the cases for Chapter 3, I looked first for cases in which modern PSCs were deployed to the same theater but not integrated into the regular military, in a relatively high ratio of PSCs to military personnel. I also aimed to consider the most policy-relevant cases for the United States. Chapter 3 therefore examines the U.S. use of PSCs in the Iraq conflict from 2003–2008, and, to a lesser extent, the use of PSCs in Afghanistan during the same time period.

In selecting cases to include in Chapter 4, I looked first for cases in which modern PSCs were substituted for the regular military. I then narrowed that pool of possible cases by looking only at those cases in which a democratic state was involved. To further slim down the pool of cases, I conducted preliminary research to determine how easily data and evidence could be retrieved for each case. I therefore chose to include in Chapter 4 only those cases on which ample evidence existed in the public domain and for which I could find two counterfactual cases closely resembling the PSC cases but involving regular military and/or government forces as opposed to a PSC. The inclusion of counterfactual cases here is significant because they illustrate the extent to which PSCs substituting for the military influence particular types of operations differently from the effects that the regular military would have on these operations. Chapter 4 therefore looks at MPRI in Croatia, Sandline in Sierra Leone, and the counterfactual cases of U.S. assistance to Lebanon during the Lebanese Civil War and U.S. government involvement in the Iran-Contra affair.

Finally, in selecting cases to include in Chapter 5, I looked first at the pool of historical cases in which profit-motivated mercenary or auxiliary forces were structured in a manner similar to, or were actually integrated into, the regular military, in order to inform modern cases in which PSCs must coordinate smoothly with regular military forces. I then narrowed my pool of possible cases by looking for cases that included a normative element and could speak to the issue of compliance with humanitarian norms of warfare. Chapter 5 therefore examines the condottieri and the "free companies" of mercenaries fighting for the Italian city-states during the Renaissance period and the Hessian forces fighting alongside the British in the American Revolution.

A NOTE ON DATA SOURCES AND METHODS OF ANALYSIS

Owing to the sensitive nature of research focused on private security companies and the military, primary source data on this topic are extremely difficult to come by. Yet the topic of military privatization has been gaining popularity in recent years among the media and academics, and it is thus possible to glean a considerable amount of information from newspaper and magazine articles, as well as from the numerous secondary accounts being published on the subject. In addition, democratic governments (particularly in the United States and Britain) are publishing an increasing number of unclassified reports relating to military and security privatization issues. The private security industry and its trade associations also increasingly publish articles relevant to the study at hand, including some authored by government officials. This project thus relies extensively on such media, industry, government, academic, and secondary-source documents, particularly in Chapters 4 and 5.

Chapter 3 similarly draws on media, industry, academic, and secondary source accounts for background information but also strongly relies on two types of interview data. The first is a set of transcripts of interviews conducted by researchers for the Government Accountability Office (GAO) in connection with its 2005 and 2006 reports on "Actions Needed to Improve the Use of Private Security Providers in Iraq." They comprise twenty-four individual and small group interviews of military personnel of all ranks, U.S. Central

Command (USCENTCOM) officials, U.S. and international private security company personnel and officials, officials from the Project Contracting Office (PCO) in Iraq, and U.S. government officials. Of these, I analyzed only the GAO's interviews of PSC and military personnel who had experience fighting or working in Operation Iraqi Freedom. These included interviews with fourteen military and thirty-three PSC personnel, conducted between 2004 and 2006.

The second type of interview data that Chapter 3 relies on is a comprehensive set of thirty-two original semistructured interviews that I conducted in 2006 and 2007 specifically for this study. These interviews include conversations with academic experts on the issue of military privatization, high-level private security company officials, private security company operators (lower-level personnel), and U.S. Army soldiers of various ranks, ranging from noncommissioned officers to colonels. The private security company personnel and professional soldiers interviewed possessed experience in various theatres, ranging from Iraq to Afghanistan, the Balkans, South America, and several regions in both Africa and Asia. I intentionally sought out several of my interviewees due to their position—for instance, I selected various high-level PSC officials in this manner—and selected the remainder of my interviewees via "snowball" sampling, in which each interviewee referred one to three other potential interviewees. Due to the relatively small number of respondents, the sample cannot be said to be representative of all military or PSC views. The interviews do, however, illustrate distinct trends among the responses. Furthermore, they reinforce many of the things seen in the GAO interview transcripts, indicating the robustness of the findings elaborated in Chapter 3.[81]

I analyzed the content and discourse of both my own and the GAO's interviews, looking specifically at instances where PSC–military coordination successes and failures were mentioned and coding the causes of these coordination successes and failures as either structural or identity-based causes. I employed a similar method in analyzing the documentary evidence relevant to Chapters 3 through 5, looking for structural- and identity-based indicators that PSCs were having a positive or negative impact on military *integration*, *responsiveness*, *skill*, or *quality*. In doing so, I traced the processes through which PSCs and their historical predecessors had an impact on military tactics, operations, and strategy in all of the cases examined in this study. While the data do not lend themselves to a highly quantified analysis, particular answers to the interview questions used in Chapter 3 are broken down into proportions in order to demonstrate the relative frequency of different responses among various groups of respondents.

Due to the difficulty in acquiring extensive, accurate, and quantifiable data on the topic of military privatization at this juncture, primarily qualitative methods of analysis are appropriate to the types of data collected and to the purposes of the project at hand. However, the analysis in Chapter 3 also relies on quantitative survey data collected by researchers at the RAND Corporation in 2008. RAND surveyed 249 military personnel and 892 U.S. State Department personnel who had deployed at least once to Operation Iraqi Freedom, questioning them about their exposure to and experiences with armed contractors while deployed to Iraq. The RAND study examined the costs and benefits that private armed (security) contractors (PSCs) have imposed on U.S. military operations, with specific focus on the case of Operation Iraqi Freedom.[82] In doing so, the researchers touched on a number of issues relevant to the study at hand, and thus these survey data are used to reinforce the interview findings elaborated in Chapter 3.

CONCLUSION

This chapter, using a synthesis of state theory, democratic advantage theory, theories of military effectiveness, and the structure-identity dichotomy, develops a framework of analysis based on six propositions regarding the impact of PSCs on the military. Using these propositions, the analysis in the following chapters seeks to build on several of the dominant works in the IR field examining private security forces and military effectiveness in the context of democracies and counterinsurgency warfare. In particular, I aim to draw from, synthesize, and expand on the works of Deborah Avant, Risa Brooks, and Gil Merom.

I build here on Avant's research on the impact PSCs have on the state, adopting her notion of PSCs' different effects on state building in weak versus strong states to conceptualize how PSCs interact with democracies in counterinsurgency scenarios. As noted in the preceding pages, PSCs allow weak state leaders to outsource their violent activities so that they can remain in power without having to develop a state apparatus. Meanwhile, PSCs allow strong interventionist states such as the United States to outsource the operations traditionally thought of as "operations other than war" to maintain their military capacity for more traditional war-fighting roles. In doing so, PSCs hinder the prospects for the development of long-term viable state apparatuses in the target regions of the world where strong states have an interventionist presence.

PSCs also allow both weak and strong states to outsource violence to distance themselves from the normative implications of potentially unethical actions in warfare and, in a related fashion, to hide their intentions to circumvent electoral constraints. Such rationales for outsourcing violence are particularly relevant in the context of democracies fighting counterinsurgencies, which, as Merom notes, are often difficult wars for democracies to win due to the democratic electorate's unwillingness to use brutal tactics. Yet because there is a strong argument in the international relations and strategic studies fields that focuses on winning the war for the hearts and minds of the public as opposed to the use of these brutal tactics, this study questions whether outsourced brutality in counterinsurgency warfare or PSC compliance with international humanitarian law has a better impact on military effectiveness. This addition of an IHL component to Brooks's otherwise comprehensive definition of military effectiveness is necessary due to her definition's apparent focus on major wars as opposed to counterinsurgencies.

In light of this synthesis, the view espoused in the following pages is that PSCs allow states to circumvent structural constraints on leaders' behavior, often at the cost of the public's normative preferences. Simultaneously, PSCs have varying effects on military effectiveness, depending on the consistency between their own structure and identity and that of the relevant military forces, as well as on whether the public learns of their deployments and the possible moral implications of such deployments.

Seeking to expand on this chapter's insights regarding the impact of PSCs on military effectiveness and the democratic advantage, and the structural and identity-based sources of particular PSC-military interactions, the next chapter uses the framework of analysis developed here to examine recent cases in which the PSCs and the regular military are deployed alongside one another in relatively equal numbers.

3 BROTHERS IN ARMS?

PSCs Deployed Alongside the National Military

AS CHAPTER 1 NOTES, there were approximately 173,300 private contractors employed by the United States in Operation Iraqi Freedom as of December 2008, compared with 146,000 U.S. troops.[1] This ratio of contractors to troops had increased since February 2008, when there were 161,000 private contractors and 155,000 U.S. troops in Iraq.[2] These contractors were hired to perform a variety of functions—including personal security details, convoy security, static site security, weapons maintenance, transportation, logistics, base support, police and military training, reconstruction, and translation, among others—for a number of different contracting organizations.[3] The U.S. Department of Defense (DoD) hired the vast majority of these contractors (163,000), while the State Department (DoS) employed 5,500, and the U.S. Agency for International Development (USAID) employed 4,800. Forty-nine percent of the DoD contractors were local Iraqis (local nationals, or LNs), 34 percent were third-country nationals (TCNs) from neither the United States nor Iraq, and 17 percent were U.S. citizens. All but 1,000 of the State Department's 5,500 contractors were U.S. citizens.[4] Aside from these U.S. government agencies, multinational corporations and NGOs operating in Iraq hired contractors to perform security or other services for them. Of the total number of contractors in Iraq during this period, between 20,000 and 30,000 were private security contractors (PSCs).[5] Significantly for U.S. interests, PSCs provide personal security details (PSDs, or bodyguarding teams) for U.S. government civilians and key parties to the reconstruction and stabilization effort in Iraq and Afghanistan.[6] They also provide limited support to Provincial Reconstruction Teams (PRTs), civil-military teams active in building the capacity of local governments and institutions in both theaters.[7]

As the Iraq example indicates, governments increasingly hire private security companies to operate *alongside* the state-run professional military in
theatres of combat—mainly in close-protection, convoy security, and static
site security roles. As already noted, this practice of placing a large number of
private security contractors in the field alongside the military is also prevalent
in Operation Enduring Freedom in Afghanistan. The two cases together speak
to a strengthening trend in U.S. military policy, one focused on outsourcing
traditional military tasks to an unprecedented degree in modern warfare. The
practice of placing the military and private security contractors in the same
theater of combat has led in some cases to a surprising outcome: multiple reports of hostilities, tensions, and a general lack of coordination between these
forces have emerged from the field. Other reports indicate that PSC personnel act in a hostile or threatening manner toward civilians in their area of
operation. Such actions, if pervasive, can have a grave impact on the overall
military operation and long-term strategic goals in that region. To what extent
do PSC personnel coordinate well with professional soldiers in the field and
vice versa, and how does their co-deployment with the military impact overall
military effectiveness? This chapter attempts to answer these questions, seeking to address also the underlying reasons for PSCs' impact on the military in
co-deployment situations, as well as the policy implications of this impact.

Focusing on the conflict in Iraq and, to a lesser extent, the conflict in Afghanistan in the early period of the twenty-first century, this chapter seeks to
improve our limited understanding of PSCs in several ways. First, it contributes original interview data to a research topic suffering from a dearth of ac-
cessible evidence, using these data to illuminate the difficulties and successes
that private security firms have interacting with the professional military in
conflict zones. Because PSC–military coordination problems can impact the
military's levels of *integration, skill, responsiveness, quality,* and compliance
with the laws and norms of just war, they can have an impact on military
effectiveness and the democratic advantage. Therefore, the chapter's second
contribution is in its analysis of how PSC–military co-deployment impacts
military effectiveness and the democratic advantage.

Analyzing these data and drawing on the theoretical literature on both
civil–military relations and the professions, the chapter then questions the
extent to which PSC-military field interactions are caused by structural factors (such as shortcomings or incompatibilities in deployed military and
PSC units' ordering principles, capabilities, and/or functions) as opposed to

identity factors—the norms, social purposes, relational comparisons, and cognitive models constituting PSC and military identities, respectively. The structure-identity dichotomy leads to an enhanced understanding of the underlying causes of PSC–military coordination issues and therefore helps in the development of appropriate policy recommendations to remedy coordination problems. In performing this undertaking, I find that *both* structure and identity are indeed significant shapers of PSC–military interactions: When confronting weakness in the structures guiding their interactions, PSC and military personnel base their actions on actual and perceived identity-based factors. The chapter then develops a model demonstrating this connection between structure and identity at both the individual and collective levels, therefore contributing to the "structure versus identity" debate within the field of international relations.

The chapter's fourth contribution is in its development of a typology of firms based on their levels of "operational professionalism"—in other words, their pursuit of the practices most likely to have a beneficial impact on military effectiveness. The chapter concludes with an analysis of its findings' implications for policy. In Chapter 6, I recommend a set of policies and regulations based on what can realistically be achieved.

THE PROBLEM:
PSC–MILITARY COORDINATION
IN IRAQ AND AFGHANISTAN

The U.S. Government Accountability Office (GAO) issued a revealing report in July 2005 titled *Actions Needed to Improve the Use of Private Security Providers* in Iraq. In this report, the GAO noted:

> The military and private security providers in Iraq have an evolving relationship based on cooperation and coordination of activities and the desire to work from a common operating picture. However, U.S. forces in Iraq do not have a command and control relationship with private security providers or their employees. Initially, coordination between the military and private security providers was informal. However, since the advent of the Reconstruction Operations Center in October 2004, coordination has evolved into a structured and formalized process. While contractors and the military agree that coordination has improved, some problems remain. First, private security providers continue to report incidents between themselves and the military when approaching military convoys and checkpoints. Second, military units may

not have a clear understanding of the role of contractors, including private security providers, in Iraq or of the implications of having private security providers in the battle space.[8]

This passage clearly indicates that PSC–military coordination in Iraq at this time was problematic.

The GAO authored a follow-up to its 2005 report in June 2006, noting that PSC–military coordination problems still remained in Iraq. In both reports, the GAO recommended structural changes to the system of PSC–military co-deployment in Iraq, pushing specifically for a pre-deployment training program to better train both military and PSC actors to coordinate with each other in the field. The 2006 report noted improvements that had been made, focusing particularly on the development of the five regional Reconstruction Operations Centers (ROCs). The ROCs were established in 2004 to remedy the lack of communication and coordination between private security forces and coalition forces by serving as information coordination hubs for the U.S. military and private security and military companies operating in Iraq.[9] The ROCs were later supplemented with six Contractor Operation Cells (CONOCs), which served to coordinate movements of both Department of Defense and State Department contractors and which—like the ROCs—were managed by the private military firm Aegis. Both DoD and DoS contractors were required to give notice of their movements to a CONOC, which could then alter, deny, or approve the movement request.

A July 2009 report by the Special Inspector General for Iraq Reconstruction (SIGIR) highlights structural changes made since late 2007 with regard to the deployment of private security personnel in Iraq. In addition to noting the establishment of the six CONOCs throughout the country, the SIGIR report points out that the Multi-National Force-Iraq (MNF-I) established the Armed Contractor Oversight Division (which became operational in May 2008) to provide oversight and serve as its overall point of contact on policies that govern incidents involving PSCs employed by the U.S. Department of Defense. The SIGIR report also notes that MNF-I published comprehensive guidance related to the oversight of DoD's PSCs and made military units more responsible for providing oversight of PSC missions, incident reporting, investigations, and contract management.[10]

Furthermore, in December 2007, the Department of Defense and the Department of State signed a Memorandum of Agreement to define the agencies' authority and responsibility for the accountability and operations of PSCs in

Iraq. In addition to establishing common rules for the use of force and for the preparation of serious incident reports and investigations, the agreement also established coordination and control procedures for PSC missions and assigned liaison officers to monitor and coordinate the operations of their separate PSCs.[11]

In early 2008, the State Department also issued its own new directives to improve PSC mission coordination, establishing separate PSC movement reporting requirements for its two types of missions. So-called Tier 1 missions aimed to support the Chief of Mission or provide security to other State Department personnel, diplomats, and senior government officials. Tier 1 missions were to be approved by the Regional Security Office (RSO) in Baghdad and did not require DoD approval to proceed. Instead, the RSO was to forward information on the mission to the MNC-I liaison officer and the field commander where the movement would take place, a minimum of twenty-four hours in advance. The liaison officer then would share this information with the MNC-I Joint Operations Center. Field commanders could recommend that the movement be altered or cancelled based on their own battle area information, despite the fact that DoD approval was not required. "Tier 2" missions, on the other hand, aimed to support all other embassy operations. These missions operated within the MNC-I/CONOC system and followed the same procedures as the DoD-managed PSCs. Tier 2 PSCs were to submit their movement requests to the central CONOC at least seventy-two hours in advance of the movement. The central CONOC would then assess the request and forward it to the responsible regional CONOC and the applicable field commander for their approval.[12]

The SIGIR, relying on interviews conducted with CONOC officials, DoD field commanders, State Department Regional Security Office officials, and PSC officials, reports that these post-2007 structural changes improved mission coordination between PSCs and the military.[13] Evidence of such improvements suggests both that structural changes can be effective at improving PSC-military coordination issues, and—relatedly—that PSC-military coordination is the sum of multiple dynamic processes capable of producing comprehensive change over time, either positively or negatively, as the groups become more accustomed to working alongside one another.

Despite the fact that such improvements were reportedly made to alleviate PSC–military coordination issues in the Iraq theater in the fourth and fifth year of the U.S. military's deployment there, a 2008 GAO report points out that staffing and training challenges remained for the DoD. In particular, the GAO reports that the DoD did not develop plans or a strategy to sustain the increase in contractor oversight personnel that it has assigned to the Iraq theater, nor did it update military unit training on PSCs to reflect the changes made since September 2007 to increase oversight. As a result, the 2008 GAO report expresses concern that military units may be unaware of their expanded oversight and investigative responsibilities.[14]

Furthermore, the 2005, 2006, and 2008 GAO reports, in addition to multiple other media reports, would lead us to believe that there is a high potential for PSC–military coordination problems to occur on a regular basis in co-deployment situations such as Operation Iraqi Freedom, particularly in the absence of structural remedies intended to ameliorate such problems.[15] The 2006 GAO report noted, for instance, that "private security providers continue to enter the battle space without coordinating with the U.S. military, putting both the military and security providers at a greater risk for injury."[16] On the other hand, a number of PSC and military personnel have indicated that ad hoc coordination has occurred regularly between PSC and military personnel in Iraq and Afghanistan. How pervasive were PSC–military coordination problems in these theaters in reality during the 2003–2008 time frame, and to what extent does change over time appear to be possible?[17]

Of the original interviews conducted for this project, six out of eleven military respondents and fourteen out of fourteen PSC respondents agreed that successful coordination between the military and PSC personnel in the field did occur regularly during this timeframe, though many noted that such coordination was often ad hoc and depended on the personalities of those involved. A few examples include security contractors notifying the relevant military commander(s) when traveling into or through a particular area of responsibility (AOR), contractors and military personnel exchanging cell phone numbers when they knew that they would be working in the same AOR, and contractors holding up U.S. or coalition flags when passing through military checkpoints.[18] "Success" in this case is conceptualized in terms of a scale of success ranging from the basics of communicating and not shooting at each other, all the way up through success in achieving the desired tactical, operational, or strategic goal.

A U.S. Air Force pilot with experience commanding a Provincial Reconstruction Team (PRT) in Afghanistan from April 2006 to April 2007 illustrated an instance of this higher level of success. He noted that when training the Afghan National Police, DynCorp contractors' assistance "was invaluable in getting the mission up and running, and in the removal of two highly corrupt police chiefs."[19] Meanwhile, one official from a private security firm who was deployed to Iraq in 2004 highlighted the types of PSC–military coordination practices employed by his firm:

> Always important to coordinate, but stay the hell out of the way. At Camp Taji we had nightly meetings [with the U.S. government] to stay coordinated. At night my job was to ensure that our last Iraqi guard outpost was tied in with the U.S. Army's first position on the perimeter.[20]

PSC–military coordination at all levels in the field enables the entire force to be more responsive to its own needs and capabilities, as well as to external conditions. It also increases the entire force's level of integration. Successful coordination should therefore increase military effectiveness through its impact on *integration* and *responsiveness*, as defined in Chapter 2.[21] The fact that much of this coordination has been ad hoc, however, poses a challenge in terms of how to institutionalize the coordination processes so that they occur more regularly. While the post-2007 structural measures noted in the SIGIR report have undoubtedly remedied PSC–military coordination problems to some extent, the fact that the GAO noted as late as 2008 that coordination problems were still apparent in Iraq indicates that further improvements are needed. Because the concept of "military effectiveness" used throughout this book is broader than the narrow scope of the issues addressed in the SIGIR report, moreover, military effectiveness may still suffer despite the improvements noted by the SIGIR, making further recommendations necessary. Finally, to the extent that these issues have been solved in Iraq, there is nonetheless room for improvement in other theaters—most notably Afghanistan. Through its focus on both structural deficiencies and identity issues underlying the various problems of PSC–military coordination in the field, this chapter aims to develop both structural and identity-based recommendations that will help to institutionalize and standardize coordination processes in Iraq, Afghanistan, and other future threaters to which PSCs and the military will be co-deployed.

When coordination problems have occurred, they have brought with them many interrelated problems that can influence military effectiveness, including friendly fire incidents between PSC and military personnel (so-called blue-on-white incidents), resentment over PSC–military pay differentials, the military's lack of knowledge regarding PSCs' presence in their AOR, and PSCs' often negative impact on local civilians' perceptions of the entire military operation. These issues, which are discussed in detail in the following pages, have occurred both in Operation Iraqi Freedom (OIF) and Operation Enduring Freedom (OEF).[22]

Blue-on-White Incidents

Newspaper accounts detailing events in Iraq indicate that something other than structural improvements might be necessary to remedy PSC–military coordination problems in co-deployment scenarios. At their most extreme, these problems are reflected by friendly fire or blue-on-white incidents, in which the U.S. military fires on PSCs working for various U.S. government agencies or other U.S. contractors (such as PSCs working as security for construction companies in Iraq), or vice versa. Reports of the Baghdad ROC indicate that the most likely blue-on-white victim during the November 2004 through August 2006 period was a private security company employee. Blue-on-white victims during this period were most likely to be fired on by coalition forces (as opposed to Iraqi Security Forces), during the late morning (10:00 to 11:00 a.m.). Victims were most likely to be approaching a checkpoint or overtaking (or being overtaken by) a convoy. The number of reported blue-on-white incidents decreased significantly following the establishment of the ROC in 2004, indicating the potential for improvement over time with the creation of structural coordination mechanisms.[23] Figures 3.1, 3.2, and 3.3 illustrate these data.[24]

While these friendly fire incidents are disturbing, interview data indicate that they were not as pervasive as some media reports made them out to be. Indeed, only six of this project's eighteen PSC interviewees and four of the fourteen military interviewees were ever involved in or had firsthand knowledge of a blue-on-white incident.[25] Of course, one should consider the possibility that the figures detailing blue-on-white incidents are prone to error. An in-depth report published in January 2008 notes that significant incidents are likely to be both underreported and misreported by security contractors. Human Rights First reviewed 610 serious incident reports (SIRs) filed with the ROC between July 2004 and April 2005, finding that the vast majority of SIRs were in regard to threats perceived by contractors and did not touch on contractors' conduct toward others.

The report notes, "Among all of these SIRs just one even suggests unwarranted weapons discharge by a security contractor."[26] Human Rights First points out that such underreporting is likely due to the fact that the self-reporting

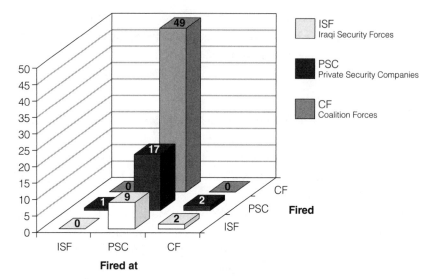

Figure 3.1. Blue-on-white incidents involving coalition forces and PSC personnel in OIF (November 2004 through August 2006).

SOURCE: The ROC Watch Officer originally produced this charts. I would like to thank Colonel Timothy Cornett for providing me with access to these data, which he presented at the Combat Training Center Commander's Conference at the Combined Arms Center at TRADOC on September 26–27, 2006.

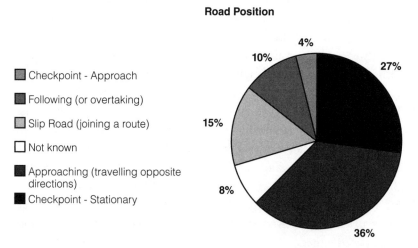

Figure 3.2. The majority of blue-on-white incidents involve approaching checkpoints and following/overtaking convoys (November 2004 through August 2006).

SOURCE: The ROC watch officer originally produced this charts. I would like to thank Colonel Timothy Cornett for providing me with access to these data, which he presented at the Combat Training Center Commander's Conference at the Combined Arms Center at TRADOC on September 26–27, 2006.

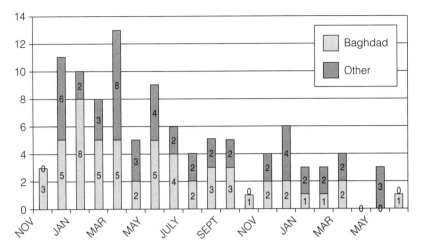

Figure 3.3. Month-by-month breakdown of blue-on-white incidents reported to ROC (November 2004 through August 2006).

SOURCE: The ROC watch officer originally produced this charts. I would like to thank Colonel Timothy Cornett for providing me with access to these data, which he presented at the Combat Training Center Commander's Conference at the Combined Arms Center at TRADOC on September 26–27, 2006.

system is built for coordination and contractor protection, and not for the purpose of monitoring or investigating PSC personnel.[27]

Furthermore, contractors have little incentive to report incidents, given that:

> The individual risks his job, and the private security companies themselves may be concerned that a high number of compromising incidents may be viewed by the military contracting authority as evidence of improper training, supervision or conduct, leading to potential cancellation of current contracts or a decreased chance to secure future contracts.[28]

It is impossible to conclusively know the extent of underreporting. Additionally, the RAND Corporation's large-*n* survey data indicate that, whatever the true number of blue-on-white incidents, fairly large percentages of State Department personnel perceive that neither armed contractors nor the military make an effort to work smoothly with each other. As noted above, RAND surveyed 892 State Department personnel (and 249 U.S. military personnel) who had OIF deployment experience during the 2003–2008 time frame. Of the 842 State Department respondents who answered this question, 16 percent of those who had experience interacting with armed contractors, as well as 16 percent of those who did not have such experience, thought it "typically false" that "armed contractors make an effort to work smoothly with the U.S. military (compared with 57 percent and 24 percent, respectively, who thought this statement was "typically true"). Moreover, 29 percent of the "experienced" DoS personnel thought it "typically false" that U.S. military personnel make an effort to work smoothly with armed contractors (with 5 percent of the less experienced DoS personnel feeling this way).[29] While a larger number of both experienced and unexperienced respondents therefore thought that armed contractors and the U.S. military make an effort to work smoothly with each other than the number of those who thought the opposite, it is troubling that such large minorities of respondents felt that the two types of actors did not make an effort to work together. This is particularly true in light of the fact that armed contractors are deployed to augment U.S. military forces, as the RAND study points out.

Yet a PSC official with extensive U.S. Army Special Forces experience, and experience working as a contractor in OIF in 2004, provides some hope that improvement in PSC–military coordination is possible. He notes that, "fights [between PSC personnel and the military] are less common than you would expect, but there is a structural problem—doctrine supported by training and simulations are lacking . . . much more needs to be done at the Training and Doctrine Command (TRADOC) and within the Marine Corps."[30]

The vast majority of both PSC and military personnel interviewed specifically for this study agreed that most of these incidents occur because of the lack of interoperable communications devices and shortcomings in young soldiers' training regarding PSC personnel and how to deal with them. Many young reservists in particular were not accustomed to working alongside PSCs and were occasionally referred to as "trigger happy" by their PSC counterparts. A PSC operator involved in several blue-on-white incidents while in Iraq from February 2004 to May 2005 noted:

> I personally was shot at four times by the military, but I never shot at a military person. So what's the real problem? Training on the military side. Don't just shoot at something because you don't know what it is. Simple solution we had: We requested and were issued a Marine Corps radio so we could talk to the gate before we rolled up. Problem solved . . .[31]

Whatever their cause, blue-on-white incidents have an unmistakable impact on the force's *integration*, as they decrease the level of trust between military and PSC personnel fighting the same enemy.

PSC–Military Pay Differentials

Both PSC and military interviewees frequently cited the high pay of PSC personnel for jobs similar to their military counterparts as a source of resentment between the two groups. In some cases, security contractors can make nearly a soldier's annual salary in just one month. Two PSC interviewees who served in OEF in 2002 and 2003 (with one returning to Afghanistan for one month in late 2004) noted that they were making approximately $1,000 per day while deployed, working as PSC team leaders.[32]

Zapata Engineering   One colorful example of pay differentials leading to dangerous levels of resentment is seen in the Zapata Engineering incident of May 28, 2005, when sixteen employees of the U.S.-based firm Zapata Engineering were arrested for supposedly firing upon a U.S. military checkpoint watchtower in Iraq. Zapata was under contract with the U.S. Army Corps of Engineers at the time, tasked with managing a storage depot for captured ammunition in Iraq. The sixteen contractors were held in military custody for three days and, as documented in a report on National Public Radio (NPR), were harassed and treated disrespectfully by the Marines during their detention. Referring to Matt Raiche, a former Marine working for Zapata, the NPR report notes:

> While in Marine custody for three days, Raiche and some of the other contractors say they were abused and humiliated. One Marine derided the group as rich contractors, Raiche says, and another Marine slammed a contractor to a cement floor and crushed his testicles. Raiche says a Marine sergeant pushed him to the ground with a knee to his back while other Marines mocked him.[33]

Another report of this incident notes:

> All 16 of the Zapata convoy were imprisoned in small, six-foot by eight-foot cells, dressed in orange prison garb for three days without legal charges or legal counsel . . . Some of the security convoy said the Marines also roughed up the contractors before taking them to jail and that they were slammed down on the concrete one by one, bruising some pretty badly . . . One of the contractors, Rick Blanchard of Shelbyville, Tennessee, said a Marine put a knee to his neck and applied his full body weight as another cut his boots off and stripped him of his wedding ring and religious ornaments. Twenty or thirty other Marines laughed, he added, as a uniformed woman with a military dog snapped photographs. Taunts were made about the large salaries of private security

contractors . . . The gathering crowd of Marines was saying things like "how is that contractor money now," said Blanchard, a Marine veteran.[34]

This treatment allegedly occurred despite the fact that some if not all of the employees were former military personnel themselves and despite the contractors' claims of innocence with regard to firing on the checkpoint.

The Marines dispute this account of the Zapata employees' detention, however. Marine spokesman Lieutenant Colonel David Lapan told reporters, "The contract personnel were treated professionally and appropriately the entire time they were in the custody of military personnel . . . Before they were taken to the detention facility, they were placed on the ground, flex-cuffed and searched per standard practice. They were not thrown to the ground."[35] The Zapata contractors were never charged for the alleged offense, reflecting the problems regarding contractors' legal accountability discussed in Chapter 6.

Such encounters—though not usually this severe in nature—underscore how sentiments of resentment or competition between the military and PSCs, particularly over issues of pay differentials, can become a major problem. Of the military and PSC respondents interviewed specifically for this project, seven of eight military respondents and fourteen of seventeen PSC respondents cited resentment between PSC and military personnel, often based on contractors' higher wages for similar work, as a major cause of field coordination problems. As one U.S. Army Major with experience in Afghanistan from August 2003 to May 2004 noted:

> There was always resentment between my soldiers and the contractors because the contractors were making several times more money than my soldiers and doing basically the same job . . . Everybody rolls their eyes when we start to mention private security contractors. It seems that none of my colleagues have had a positive experience when interacting with them.[36]

A former Army Airborne Ranger and Special Forces officer with fifteen years of military experience who worked for Triple Canopy in Iraq from February 2004 to May 2005 dissected the issue of PSC-military resentment:

> In my two years I learned that most of the problems between military and security contractors were ego/jealousy driven . . . Example: Two guys with the same background. One stays in the military and gets deployed to Iraq. The other gets out of the military and deploys to Iraq during the same time period as a contractor. The guy in the military is making $40,000 a year working twelve-hour shifts seven days a week while the contractor is making $240,000

a year and working four- to six-hour shifts four to six days a week. The guy in the military sleeps in a room with ten other guys while the contractor has his own trailer with air-conditioning, television, a DVD player, and a fridge. The military guy is under the control of the military, so no sex or drinking—the contractor isn't. The military guy wears a uniform while the contractor wears whatever he wants. The military guy stays seven months and is forced to stay longer while the contractor can leave whenever he wants. And so on and so on.[37]

These findings are supported by the RAND survey data, which found that just over half of lower ranking enlisted personnel (E4 to E5) and of those under age thirty-five responded "typically true" to the statement, "the pay disparity during OIF between contractors and U.S. military personnel was detrimental to morale in my unit during my time in theater."[38] Interestingly, 70 percent of lower-ranking officers and 45 percent of higher ranking officers, as well as 58 percent of those under age thirty-five and 50 percent of those over age thirty-five thought it "typically true" that the pay available to armed contractors during OIF negatively impacted recruiting and retention among U.S. military personnel.[39] Such a perceived negative impact on military recruitment and retention could also stimulate military resentment of contractors.

At issue here is the fact that PSCs are increasingly infringing on the military's professional jurisdiction and are paid more for performing the same jobs. Matt Raiche of Zapata Engineering reiterated this point, describing members of the military as "resentful that we made so much money, the fact that we could come home, you know, every ninety days. They didn't like that. But mainly they're mad about the money we made, four or five times the amount they make."[40] Such resentment strongly influences the force's *integration* and reflects issues of professional jurisdictional competition and identity cleavages based upon different social purposes and relatively hostile relational comparisons.[41] Significantly, though, there are structural differences—for instance, in pay levels and vacation time—at the root of these hostile relational comparisons. Therefore, if this resentment is strong enough to cause PSC–military coordination problems, both structural- and identity-based remedies to these coordination problems will be necessary. The connection between identity cleavages and resentment are explored further in the following discussion of identity issues.

Interestingly, however, the opinions of military personnel regarding their PSC counterparts are not entirely negative. The interview data in some instances actually indicate that increased exposure to security contractors is improving the military's perceptions of PSC personnel and their motives for working as war zone contractors. For instance, two British PSC officials noted that the PSC industry received a warmer welcome from the U.S. military than from the U.K. military precisely because the U.S. military has a longer history of working alongside contractors.[42] Furthermore, when asked whether they thought the PSC personnel with whom they had come into contact were as motivated by patriotism as they were by money, six of eleven military interviewees answered in the affirmative, as did twelve of fifteen PSC interviewees. Though this level of PSC affirmation is not surprising, the military's level of agreement with them on this issue is fairly unexpected, given the military's professional incentives to frame PSC personnel as unpatriotic. A former Heavy Brigade Combat Team Commander with OIF experience from November 2005 to November 2006 noted that "contractors were generally well-meaning patriots trying to make a living."[43] Another U.S. military major with OIF experience in 2003–2004 and again from November 2005 to November 2006 said, "Money is obviously a strong incentive for contractors to work in a combat zone and separate from their families when they do not have to. I think most also have a sense of patriotic duty, since many are prior military."[44] Meanwhile, on the PSC side, a retired U.S. military general working as an official at DynCorp noted:

> Honestly, I believe that significant numbers of our employees are motivated by a sense of duty to our Nation. While money is a strong incentive (and most employees earn significantly more deployed than in their regular law enforcement jobs), it takes a sense of commitment and a desire to help those that can't help themselves. I see that in most of our employees.[45]

These findings speak directly to Reiter and Stam's variable of morale, discussed in Chapter 2, which they measure in terms of patriotism.[46] Based on these findings, it would be difficult to argue that PSCs have a negative impact on military effectiveness based on claims that they are less patriotically motivated in the field than are regular soldiers. A similar finding bolsters this conclusion, with nine of the study's fourteen military respondents and twelve of the eighteen PSC respondents saying that they do *not* believe PSC personnel are likely to abruptly abandon their posts. While it is virtually impossible to find actual data to substantiate this finding at this point in time—due to the plethora of firms operating worldwide, the lack of any comprehensive study of this issue up to this point, and the incentives for firms to cover up instances of employees abandoning their posts—it is nonetheless an interesting finding that speaks directly to a common critique of private military and security firms. For instance, Peter Singer has warned potential purchasers of PSC services that:

> while firms may have market incentives not to abandon their posts or jump ship for better paying contracts elsewhere, their employees often do not. Operations will thus depend on soldiers, unaccountable to the code of military justice, who make their own personal risk vs. reward analysis.[47]

All in all, the interview findings on the one hand bode well for PSCs' impact on the military's *skill* in terms of soldiers' motivation, as they indicate that private contractors comprising part of a co-deployed force will likely be relatively easy to motivate for particular tasks because many are in the field for patriotic as well as monetary reasons. In critically assessing these interview responses, however, one must question whether they apply to all categories of private security contractors or just to U.S. or British expatriates and/or local nationals. One could certainly make the case that these two categories of contractors would be much more likely to be patriotically motivated than would third-country nationals hired by a foreign country and serving in yet another foreign country. The positive impact on *skill* indicated by these interview responses is further tempered by the aforementioned RAND survey finding that a substantial number of military respondents found it "typically true" that the pay disparity between contractors and the military was detrimental to unit morale.[48]

While there is therefore some ambiguity with regard to security contractors' patriotism and impact on *skill*, the data do seem to indicate that PSCs have a positive impact on military effectiveness in terms of *quality*. Twelve out of this study's fourteen military respondents and all eighteen PSC respondents said that they believe that PSC employees are necessary force multipliers. This finding is supported by the RAND survey, in which respondents were asked to respond to the statement: "Armed contractors are force multipliers for the U.S. military." Of the 247 military personnel who answered this question, 151 had experience with armed contractors and ninety-six did not. Of the "experienced" military personnel, 67 percent considered armed contractors to be force multipliers, while 40 percent of the military personnel who had less experience with armed contractors felt this way.[49] Of the 122 "experienced" military respondents who answered a question in the survey about surge capacity, 62 percent thought it "typically true" that armed contractors provide needed surge capacity, while 34 percent of the ninety-seven respondents with less experience with armed contractors felt this way. Finally, 69 percent of the "experienced" pool of military personnel ($n = 151$) and 51 percent of the "inexperienced" pool of military personnel ($n = 97$) responding to the statement "Armed contractors provide security critical to the success of reconstruction projects" found this statement to be "typically true."[50] PSCs therefore improve military effectiveness in this sense by increasing the military's capacity, or *quality*. Again, the fact that such a high proportion of military respondents answered these questions in the affirmative is surprising and particularly informative, given the motives for the military to try to defend their professional jurisdiction by arguing that PSCs are unnecessary.

The Military's Lack of Knowledge of PSC Positions

Both military and PSC personnel have frequently cited the military's lack of knowledge regarding PSC personnel traveling through a particular military unit's area of responsibility (AOR) as a result of problematic coordination between PSC and military personnel co-deployed in the field. Both the GAO interviews and those interviews conducted specifically for this project included numerous statements regarding such a lack of knowledge. Of the GAO's military interviewees, eight of the fourteen complained of not being aware of PSCs' location within their area of responsibility, which in some cases led to unnecessary danger for the troops in that AOR when having to provide assistance or a quick-reaction force (QRF) to PSCs. Again, many interviewees cited the dearth of interoperable PSC and military communications devices as an underlying structural cause of this lack of knowledge: Twenty-two of the GAO's thirty-three PSC interviewees and eight of the GAO's fourteen military interviewees mentioned communications difficulties as the main cause of coordination problems. This was mainly due to the lack of interoperable radio and communications systems between the military and PSCs. These coordination and communications shortcomings can have a significant impact on the force's *integration* and *responsiveness*, as they increase the likelihood that PSC movements will catch military units off guard, thus hindering the military's ability to unify its troops' activities and to respond to the enemy. Many interviewees, however, noted that these communications shortcomings regarding PSC teams' field positions have abated significantly since the establishment of the Reconstruction Operations Center in Iraq, and, as previously noted, the SIGIR reports that the post-2007 DoD and DoS structural changes improved PSC–military communication problems. This bodes well for structural remedies to PSC–military coordination problems.

Despite the fact that improvements are being made to facilitate PSC–military coordination, the problems of the early years in Iraq must not be overlooked, as they hold lessons for future PSC–military co-deployment scenarios in other theaters. The devastation that can occur due to failures in coordinating contractor movements was seen in Fallujah in early 2004, when four U.S. contractors working for Blackwater USA were brutally killed by insurgents. Contractor deaths such as these pose a challenge for the military. In the Fallujah case, moreover, they led to a complete overhaul of the original strategic military plan. The Blackwater deaths caused U.S. policymakers to shift the military strategy and launch an offensive in Fallujah, as elaborated below.

Fallujah   In March 2004, four contractors working for Blackwater USA were ambushed while providing security for a convoy attempting to drive through the city of Fallujah in central Iraq. Insurgents killed the four men in a violent volley of small arms fire and lit their vehicles and the corpses on fire. The riotous scene was soon aired on television stations across the globe, with jubilant insurgents dragging the burned and mutilated corpses of the four men to a nearby bridge and hanging them there.

Both Iraq War experts and the media acknowledge that the gruesome murder and mutilation of these four Blackwater contractors served as the rallying cry and inspiration for the Marines who fought in the November 2004 battle in Fallujah.[51] Journalists Bill Sizemore and Joanne Kimberlin write that the Fallujah ambush "irrevocably altered the course of the war" in Iraq. "U.S. military commanders, who had no advance knowledge of the convoy's presence in Fallujah, were ordered by Washington to change tactics and pound the city into submission, inflaming the Iraqi insurgency to new heights."[52] Meanwhile, former Reagan-era Assistant Secretary of Defense Bing West, who authored an account of the Fallujah battle, noted in an interview that launching the offensive in Fallujah was "a decision by our top leadership against the advice of the Marines. They were not going to change their entire strategy because of a tactical error. They were overruled."[53]

Whether or not this is true, the contractors' deaths certainly served as the motivation for the Marines to roll into Fallujah just five days after the Blackwater deaths—months before November's major battle—in an operation resulting in up to 600 Iraqi deaths, many of them reportedly civilian women and children, along with seven Marine deaths, 100 wounded Marines, and only the temporary pacification of the city.[54] This operation, Operation Vigilant Resolve, followed Paul Bremer's statement that "their deaths will not go unpunished," and the statement of the Deputy Director of Coalition Operations that "it will be at a time and place of our choosing. We will hunt down the criminals. We will kill them or we will capture them, and we will pacify Fallujah."[55] Such statements indicate that the wide publication of the Blackwater contractors' deaths in the international media may have prompted stronger conflict involvement by the U.S. military in this area, thus reducing conflict selectivity and the U.S. chances of experiencing the democratic advantage with regard to Fallujah and the larger Iraq conflict. Notably, such an impact does not follow the conventional logic of the selection effects argument of democratic advantage theory because it relies on the notion that electoral concerns in this case may have *prompted* conflict involvement, not stymied it.

Whether the Blackwater contractors involved in this incident coordinated with the Marines surrounding Fallujah before attempting to travel through the city is unclear. Journalist Robert Young Pelton notes:

> According to one theory, the convoy intended to link up with an American-trained Iraqi Civil Defense Corps (ICDC) team on the eastern entrance to town, which would guide them through the city center, providing more firepower if anything happened. However, this would have required coordination the evening before, and there is no evidence that the marines at Camp Fallujah, or the Blackwater contractors themselves, had made this contact.[56]

A September 2007 congressional inquiry into Blackwater's actions in Fallujah reinforces the notion that the Blackwater team did not adequately coordinate with coalition forces prior to the attack, noting that the Blackwater personnel arrived at the wrong military base the day before the attack because they did not have maps and the mission had not been sufficiently planned. The team was forced to spend the night at this base (Camp Fallujah) when, on attempting to depart for the correct base (Camp Ridgeway), they were prevented from traveling farther by a military checkpoint. At Camp Fallujah, a witness employed by contracting firm Kellogg, Brown, and Root (KBR) assessed that "the mission that they were on was hurriedly put together and they were not prepared."[57]

It is clear that PSC–military coordination in this instance needed improvement to at least some extent, since neither the U.S. military nor coalition forces were accompanying the convoy through what was thought at the time to be a dangerous area of the country. Nor was the military involved in helping the convoy to chart out the safest course through the city or blocking off roads for the convoy—things that the military often does for convoys when coordination occurs ahead of time. In reality, the Blackwater convoy had entered the city by bypassing a Marine checkpoint without the Marines' knowledge.

The Marines first learned of the ambush from television reports detailing the contractors' gruesome murders and the desecration of their bodies.[58]

Also clear in this case is that PSC actions had an impact on military planning and, potentially, on the military's ability to wage war in accordance with its operational and strategic aims. One must consider the counterfactual scenario regarding the battle of Fallujah: What would have happened in that region, militarily speaking, if the contractors had not been attacked? Because the Marines were not planning to launch a massive offensive on Fallujah prior to the Blackwater contractors' gory deaths, and because the battle of Fallujah was a major event early on in Operation Iraqi Freedom, one may sensibly conclude that the PSC and its employees changed the military's plans significantly in this situation, thus having an impact on the military's operational and strategic effectiveness. Of course, as Robert Young Pelton notes, "It can be argued that the battle for Fallujah was part of a larger plan to destroy insurgent strongholds in the Sunni Triangle."[59] The extent and direction of this impact is therefore debatable. The important point to recognize here, however, is that PSCs and their employees can and do have an impact on military planning and the military's ability to achieve its tactical, operational, and strategic goals.

PSCs' Impact on Local Civilians' Perceptions of the Entire Military Operation

Security contractors have been shown, on multiple occasions, to negatively influence local civilians' views of the entire military operation. Contractors' impact on locals in co-deployment scenarios is extremely relevant to military effectiveness, primarily because locals do not distinguish between security contractors and the military in Iraq and Afghanistan. Yet contractors have different tactical aims from those of the military, primarily the aim of protecting the "principal," or the object that they are guarding. They therefore operate differently from the military, particularly with regard to their treatment of local civilians. While the U.S. and coalition forces in OIF and OEF recognize the value of cultivating good relationships with locals in a counterinsurgency—focusing largely on the hearts-and-minds approach in these two theatres—PSC personnel in many reported cases have harmed their own and the military's relations with locals.

Nisour Square   A highly visible example of how PSCs can negatively influence local civilians was seen in Baghdad's Nisour Square on September 16, 2007, when Blackwater USA contractors fired upon and killed seventeen Iraqi

civilians and wounded twenty-four others, in a confusing and ultimately un-
justified shooting incident exacerbated by the "fog of war." Some accounts of
the incident cite Iraqi witnesses who say they saw Iraqi Security Forces open-
ing fire from a watchtower, thus prolonging the firefight and possibly leading
the Blackwater contractors to believe they were under attack. Iraqi officials
have denied this. Ultimately, it is virtually impossible to learn exactly what
happened in Nisour Square, given officials' failure to secure the scene directly
after the massacre and the unwillingness of all parties involved to share information with each other.[60] Meanwhile, the fact that the Blackwater contractors
were immune to prosecution under Iraqi law at that time meant that months
passed before they were indicted in the United States under a controversial version of the Military Extraterritorial Jurisdiction Act (MEJA). The case against
them has since been dropped due to prosecutorial misconduct.[61] Interviews
with the family members of the Nisour Square victims indicate that they and
other Iraqis harbor resentment toward the contractors themselves and Blackwater as a whole. The perception among Iraqis that U.S. security contractors
can act with impunity has engendered some resentment of contractors among
locals and has led the Iraqi government to vow that the perpetrators of the
Nisour Square deaths in Baghdad would be tried in Iraqi courts.[62] This incident was therefore a significant precursor to the January 2009 adoption of a
new Status of Forces Agreement (SOFA) between the Iraqi and U.S. governments that placed American contractors working in Iraq under Iraqi legal jurisdiction for the first time.

While Nisour Square is an extreme example, military personnel have cited a
number of other instances in which security contractors have acted disrespectfully at best toward locals in their AOR. For instance, a U.S. Army infantryman
with experience in Iraq from November 2005 to November 2006 noted that:

> Some commanders are thankful because they have well qualified security con-
> tractors operating in their AO [area of operation]. However, it can become the
> bane of a commander's existence if they are causing more problems than they
> are solving . . . Security contractors do not have to worry about the far reaching
> implications of their actions as it pertains to population perception and the
> like. All they have to do is worry about getting their PC (precious cargo) from
> point A to point B safely. However, the end result falls back on the Army soldier
> in that now Iraqis who have been harassed just associate it with Americans . . .
> and they do not differentiate between contractors and the military . . . they just
> know that an American harassed them.[63]

This statement speaks both to issues of command and control and to issues of contractors' compliance with legal and normative rules of international humanitarian law, which dictate how civilians in war zones are to be treated. Such legal issues are addressed in Chapter 6, but it is worth noting here that such statements provide empirical support for the proposition that PSC noncompliance with legal and ethical norms of just war has a detrimental impact on military effectiveness (Proposition 2b).

Another major in the U.S. military with OEF experience from August 2003 to May 2004 noted:

> the contractors could shoot/kill local nationals without having to deal with ROE [rules of engagement]. The contractors often boasted of how many locals they had killed. We always had to do the consequence management after these events. I don't know if these contractor killings were on legitimate Taliban/ AQ [Al Qaeda] insurgents or not. We still had to deal with the aftermath . . . it provided unneeded friction.[64]

Both statements illustrate how contractors can have a negative impact on overall military effectiveness by harming local perceptions of the military's mission and the legality with which it is conducted, particularly when the military has opted primarily to follow the hearts-and-minds approach to counterinsurgency warfare. Furthermore, by increasing the difficulty of the military's mission, such incidents reinforce military resentment of PSC personnel.

The military has little control over such incidents because PSC personnel are largely outside of the military chain of command. Of the original interviews conducted specifically for this study, only four of nine military interviewees and three of ten PSC interviewees thought that military commanders work well with PSCs. Meanwhile, another four of the nine military interviewees thought that military commanders do *not* work well with PSCs, and six of the ten PSC interviewees said that commanders' abilities to work well with PSCs vary based on commander personalities. A contractor from New Zealand working for both Control Risks Group (CRG) and BLP in Iraq from January 2004 to January 2005, and then again from October 2006 up to the time of his interview in April 2007, stated:

> It depends on who the military commander is and their attitude to PSCs. Some military commanders resented us mainly because of the money we earned in relation to them and also some PSCs were "cowboys" and very unprofessional. I personally got on well with most military commanders and providing we

conformed to their rules and regulations generally there were no problems. Problems usually occurred when the military rotated their units and the new unit had different rules and regulations and their attitude to us varied.[65]

When asked specifically about the chain of command, six of this study's eight military interviewees and four of the eleven PSC interviewees thought that the chain of command does *not* operate smoothly with regard to security contractors in the field. The low percentage of PSC interviewees sharing this sentiment probably reflects the industry's incentives to appear as though it is under clear control in the field. The military's views on this issue may therefore more closely approximate reality. A U.S. Army colonel and former heavy brigade combat team commander who served in Iraq from November 2005 to November 2006 noted that security contractors "did *not* fall under my command. Normally they were attached to another command moving through the area or worked for [the U.S. State Department] . . . The main issue is that they did not have to answer to me, so I had very little leverage over them."[66]

Yet it is crucial not to overstate the significance of these findings, as 45 percent of the RAND survey's military respondents who had experience with armed contractors (n = 152) reported that they "never" had firsthand knowledge of armed contractors failing to coordinate with military commanders, while 20 percent "rarely" had such knowledge, and another 20 percent "sometimes" had such knowledge.[67] It should therefore be noted that, while problematic, PSCs' opaque position in the military chain of command is perhaps not as prevalent of a problem as these interviews would otherwise lead one to conclude. Nonetheless, as the RAND study notes, the numbers of respondents having "sometimes" and "rarely" had such knowledge are sufficiently large enough to cause concern, particularly because, as noted earlier, PSCs are deployed to augment the U.S. military. Difficulty integrating contractors into the chain of command can have a negative impact on both the military's *responsiveness* and its *integration*. They also lower the military's *skill* as it is conceived in this study, by making effective leadership more difficult.

OVERALL IMPACT ON MILITARY EFFECTIVENESS AND THE DEMOCRATIC ADVANTAGE

As illustrated in the examples above, PSC–military co-deployment can have a significant and lasting impact on the military's ability to successfully achieve its aims. While PSCs do serve as force multipliers in Iraq and Afghanistan and thus have a beneficial impact on *quality*, they have a negative impact on *integration* through the structural and identity-based hindrances to their effective coordination with the military. These coordination problems pose further challenges for the military in terms of their effects on *responsiveness*. For instance, when a military unit is pulled away from its activities to send a quick-reaction force (QRF) to the aid of a PSC team in its AOR of which it had no previous knowledge, the ability of the soldiers in question to respond to external threats and changes in enemy capabilities is compromised. The soldiers in question are placed in a dangerous situation for which they had not planned nor prepared, to save the lives of "friendly" contractors who had not coordinated with them.

PSC–military co-deployment's impact on the military's relationship with the local population also detrimentally affects military *integration*, as well as military *quality*. Because contractors in Iraq have, in many instances, fired on civilians and driven recklessly through civilian areas while firing shots, the locals harbor resentment toward them. Many Iraqis also reportedly hold the coalition forces accountable for contractor actions because they associate the contractors with the U.S. military-led coalition occupying their country. This is particularly problematic because the U.S. and coalition forces have opted to follow the hearts-and-minds approach to COIN in these theaters. Such contractor actions further spur resentment of security contractors within the military ranks, making the integration of PSC and military personnel into a cohesive occupying force less likely. Furthermore, a strong line of argument exists that says that because the military's capacity to fight an insurgency depends so strongly on local support, locals can be seen as a type of "weapon" contributing to or taking away from the coalition's counterinsurgency activities. If one accepts this logic, then we can consider the military's *quality* to have been compromised by contractors' alienation of the local citizenry as well.

Meanwhile, although their patriotism mitigates the impact of their presence on soldiers' levels of motivation, the fact that resentment over wage differentials still exists between PSC and military personnel means that PSCs' higher pay has at least somewhat of a disheartening effect on military personnel, decreasing their motivation levels and thus their *skill*. This is illustrated by the fact that soldiers do leave the military to join the private sector, though the extent to which this occurs is debatable.[68] Furthermore, many of the PSC and military personnel interviewed for this study thought that military commanders do not exercise effective control over PSC personnel. This level of doubt indicates that the presence of PSC personnel co-deployed alongside the military in the field likely lowers the military's *skill* by making overall effective military leadership more difficult.

Thus, the OIF and OEF cases demonstrate that PSCs can have a significantly detrimental impact on military effectiveness in situations of PSC–military co-deployment, providing support for the proposition that PSCs cause a net decrease in military effectiveness (Proposition 2). By extension, the democratic advantage should be less likely with democracies' use of PSCs co-deployed alongside the regular military. This is because PSCs tend to diminish the very military effectiveness that, in part, defines the democratic advantage. PSCs logically do not have as much of an impact on the selection effects side of the democratic advantage in these cases of co-deployment as they do in Chapter 4's cases of PSC substitution for regular military forces. This is because the deployment of regular forces alongside PSCs in co-deployment situations draws the electorate's attention to the conflict, diminishing the chances that PSCs will allow policymakers to make conflict decisions without public knowledge. Yet, contractor deaths are not included in official casualty counts for either OIF or OEF. This indicates that the use of PSCs may be enabling U.S. policymakers to continue involvement in these conflicts beyond what U.S. voters would stand for if contractor casualties were widely publicized, also to the detriment of the democratic advantage. Furthermore, U.S. policymaker statements made in response to the widely publicized Blackwater contractor deaths in Fallujah provide some indication that these deaths decreased conflict selectivity and hence the prospects for the U.S. to experience the democratic advantage in this case. However, these deaths did so through a reverse process from that theorized in the "selection effects" argument of democratic advantage theory, by prompting rather than hindering conflict involvement due to a concern with domestic public opinion.[69]

UNDERLYING DETERMINANTS
OF PSC–MILITARY COORDINATION

In the preceding analysis, both structural and identity issues are at the core of PSC–military coordination. As Chapter 2 notes, "structure" in this study is conceived in terms of the ordering principles characterizing PSC–military co-deployments, the functions of the PSC and military units in question, and distribution of capabilities across those units. Meanwhile, identity is studied here in terms of the individual and collective identities of both PSCs and the military, based on Abdelal and his coauthors' deconstruction of the content of collective identity into constitutive norms, social purposes, relational comparisons with other social categories, and cognitive models, or worldviews.[70] Table 3.1 reiterates the different interview responses, categorizing them in terms of identity and structure.

Structural Issues

Of the original interviews discussed in the preceding pages, eight out of eight military interviewees and sixteen of seventeen PSC interviewees cited structural causes for coordination problems. These problems, depicted in Table 3.1, included both shortcomings and incompatibilities in PSC and military capabilities (such as lack of training and lack of interoperable communications devices), and shortcomings and incompatibilities in PSC and military ordering principles (for instance, the failure to effectively integrate contractors' into the military's chain of command).

One Army infantryman with OIF experience from November 2005 to November 2006 said, "I think most of the issues between the military and contractors are tied to incompatibility of equipment (communications, etc.)."[71] A lieutenant colonel in the British Army, speaking of emerging thoughts on

Table 3.1. Structural and identity issues mentioned in the interview data.

	Structural Issues	Identity Issues
What PSCs say	• Communication difficulties • Lack of standard doctrine for PSC–military interactions • Lack of pre-deployment training for military on PSCs • Lack of standard procedures for approaching checkpoints/convoys • Problems identifying PSCs	• Perceive military as "conventional," "slow," "inefficient," "dismissive" of PSCs, envious of PSCs' higher wages • Military commander's personality determines PSC–military relationship
What the military says	• Communication difficulties • Lack of standard doctrine for PSC–military interactions • Lack of pre-deployment training for *both* military and PSCs • Lack of knowledge of PSCs location/PSC failure to notify commander when in AOR • Lack of formal command and control relationship between military and PSCs • Resentment of PSC personnel due to pay differentials	• Perceive PSCs as disrespectful, ranging from "professional" to "pseudo-mercenaries" and "cowboys" • Varying PSC identities • Different operating cultures/styles • Different missions (i.e., social purposes) • Perceive most PSC personnel as at least somewhat patriotically motivated

PSC issues, acknowledged that the ROCs in Iraq are "a major step forward, but correlated pre-deployment training is still not happening because [PSCs and the military] are still not planning for joint operations together."[72] He noted that one example of the multitude of problems associated with this lack of correlated pre-deployment training and planning is that the military has no standard operating procedures in place for what the military should do if PSC personnel get attacked by insurgents in a military unit's AOR.[73] In other words, planning for PSC–military field interactions is not included in each group's stated functions, at least not to the degree necessary for effective coordination. While the post-2007 DoD and DoS policy changes may have remedied this situation somewhat, there is still room for improvement in Iraq and Afghanistan and lessons to be learned for application to other theaters in the future.

These results closely replicate those from the interviews conducted for the 2005 and 2006 GAO reports on coordination problems between the military and PSCs in Iraq, as structural issues were the most commonly cited causes of military field coordination problems in the seventeen relevant GAO interview transcripts. Beyond the capability issues already cited, the second most common response from PSC interviewees regarding the causes of PSC–military coordination problems referred to incompatibilities in ordering principles: the lack of standard military rules, instructions, or doctrine regarding how PSCs and the military should deal with each other in the field. These responses included statements regarding PSCs' ambiguous position in the military chain of command, the ambiguity in the military's responsibility to provide assistance to PSC personnel, and ambiguity in the rules of engagement applying to PSC personnel. One-third (eleven out of thirty-three) of PSC interviewees also noted the lack of pre-deployment training *for the military* regarding security contractors and their roles in the field. Notably, none of the PSC employees interviewed by the GAO mentioned that *PSC employees* should receive pre-deployment training on how to interact with the military. One-quarter (eight out of thirty-three) of PSC personnel interviewed by the GAO noted the lack of standard procedures for approaching military checkpoints and passing convoys as a major problem hindering PSC-military coordination, while six of the thirty-three PSC interviewees stated or implied that problems identifying PSCs as friendly forces contributed to poor PSC–military coordination.

The structural problems noted by the military differed slightly from those that PSC interviewees cited, although eight of the GAO's fourteen military interviewees similarly noted the lack of pre-deployment training as a structural weakness hindering effective military–PSC coordination. Yet, military interviewees thought that *both* groups should receive such training. Furthermore, eight of the fourteen interviewed from the military complained of a lack of knowledge regarding PSCs' location within their AOR, which in some cases led to unnecessary danger for the troops in that AOR when having to provide assistance or a quick-reaction-force to PSCs. Another eight of the GAO's fourteen military interviewees noted the lack of a formal command and control relationship between the military and PSCs as a cause of coordination problems. In a related finding, six of the fourteen interviewed from the military said that they had no knowledge of any formal military rules or doctrine regarding how to interact with PSCs.

Clearly, structural shortcomings are paramount in hindering effective PSC–military field coordination. Development of rigorous, standardized training regimens for both PSCs and the military regarding how the two groups should interact in the field, development of doctrine institutionalizing the guidelines for these interactions, and placement and clarification of PSCs' position in the military chain of command are necessary structural remedies that would help prevent many of the coordination issues cited in the preceding discussion.

In considering these data, it should be noted that there is a potential for change over time as structural improvements are instituted to better facilitate PSC–military coordination. As noted above, as the exposure of military personnel to PSC personnel (and vice versa) increases, and as the number of media reports about their interaction increases, policymakers are slowly instituting changes to remedy coordination problems. The 2004 development of the ROC in Iraq is an example of such a structural change, as are the new measures taken by MNF-I, the DoD, and the DoS that are discussed at the beginning of this chapter.

Identity Issues

Convergence and Divergence along the Four Components of Identity   The discussion earlier in this chapter of resentment based on pay differentials highlights how structural problems can cause collective identity cleavages, which then lead to misunderstandings and envy. The majority of PSC–military resentment is based on these actual or perceived identity distinctions. However, identity issues pertaining to PSC–military relations expand beyond the resentment caused by divergent pay scales.

As indicated in the data cited in the preceding section, PSC personnel and the military are defined by quite different constitutive norms and social purposes in a war zone. For instance, two of the GAO's military interviewees noted that differences in operational cultures and missions made it difficult for the two groups to coordinate. Not only do PSCs vary among themselves in terms of operational styles, they also differ from the military in this sense. One military interviewee noted an indicator of these differing operational styles, saying that the military tends to drive slowly when approaching checkpoints, whereas PSCs drive fast through them to avoid roadside attacks.[74] The two groups also differ rather drastically in their missions in the field: Whereas the military mission is to secure the entire AOR, the PSC mission is to protect certain assets (individuals or static sites, depending on the contract in question).

It is these different social purposes (of which the different missions are an example) and constitutive norms (of which operational culture is an example) that can lead to resentment, despite the fact that PSC and military personnel do have some things in common. The existence of common ground shared by the two groups stems from the fact that the majority of security contractors have previous military experience, and thus they share a common professional background and training with the military. Furthermore, the aforementioned finding that PSC personnel are motivated by patriotism in the conflicts in Iraq and Afghanistan speaks to some similarity of motivation between the two groups, assuming that the majority of military personnel are patriotically motivated as well. If this common ground were better emphasized through structural policy initiatives, the prospects for eliminating PSC–military resentment would grow substantially.

Different perceptions that the two groups hold of each other (that is, "relational comparisons"), however, contribute substantially to PSC–military resentment and make it difficult to overcome coordination problems. PSCs see the military as inefficient, bureaucratic, and envious of the PSC lifestyle, while the military views security contractors as varying from "professional" to "cowboys" or "pseudomercenaries."[75] For instance, two different PSC respondents interviewed by the GAO mentioned their perceptions of the military mind-set as being "conventional" and "dismissive of PSCs," unwilling to risk their lives for "these private security guys who are making nearly five times their salary."[76] The GAO's military interviewees, on the other hand, noted that they perceive PSCs as having little respect for applicable military rules, and that some PSCs act like "cowboys."[77] PSCs' apparent disrespect for a particular division's rules while in their AOR had a particularly strong effect on military personnel: "PSCs acted as though they had the right to do whatever they wanted and thought they were exempt from 1AD [First Armored Division] rules. Sometimes there were confrontations between 1AD soldiers and PSCs that came to fist fights and drawing weapons."[78] Although this statement refers to events in 2004, the interviews with military personnel who served in Iraq in 2005 and 2006 indicate that improvement in PSC–military coordination over time has not been as complete or happened as quickly as some might have hoped.

Spectrum of PSC Identities   Related to these incompatible perceptions of each other is the possibility that PSC identities vary along a spectrum, depending on the background, training, and experience of the men and women that each company hires, as well as on the operating style of the company itself. For example, does the company provide uniforms and armored sport-utility vehicles for its personnel, or operate relatively undercover with indigenous cars and clothing? In the GAO interviews of military personnel, one interviewee noted that PSC identities range from "professional" to "pseudomercenaries," and another commented of PSCs that "some were good, but others were cowboys."[79] Although the GAO's PSC interviewees did not explicitly refer to this variance among PSC identities, some interviewees did speak implicitly of key differences among companies—for instance, different company standards regarding uniforms or the use of armored versus civilian vehicles.

Interviews conducted specifically for this project with high-level British PSC officials from ArmorGroup International, Olive Group, and Control Risks Group supplement this implicit recognition of variance among PSC identities. In each of these interviews, the company official(s) in question made remarks to distinguish his company from other private military and security companies. The variance in how each official defined his company among just two of these interviews is, in itself, suggestive. For instance, an official with a large, multinational private military and security company strongly disapproves of the "private military company" or "PMC" terminology, instead preferring to refer to his company's personnel as "project managers" who comprise an integral part of "national capacity." Relaying a joke shared by industry insiders regarding the debate over the "PMC" label, the same interviewee said they might as well be called "JAC" or "Just Another Contractor."[80] Meanwhile, Eric Westropp of Control Risks Group (CRG) rejects the PMC terminology in favor of "crisis management consultancy," explicitly distinguishing CRG from U.S. companies like Blackwater and Triple Canopy who, he says, are "more proactive" in their willingness to fire their weapons than is CRG (among other differences).[81] This variance in how PSCs identify themselves represents at least a moderate level of contestation regarding the definition of PSCs. Organizing various PSCs into a typology based on the identity characteristics mentioned here is one way to clarify the identity differences between various companies, as elaborated below.

The Potential for Shifts in Identity   Clearly, there are a multitude of ways that identity cleavages may hinder effective PSC–military coordination in situations of co-deployment. Yet because identities are dynamic and mutually constitutive, we would expect to see change over time in these collective identity characteristics—either positively or negatively—as PSC and military personnel become more accustomed to operating alongside one another in the field.[82] Indeed, we do see change over time in these characteristics, but such change is inextricably linked to structure. Identity-related problems improve when extended exposure between contractors and the military helps in the development of ad hoc coordination mechanisms to overcome structural shortcomings in PSC–military co-deployments. On the other hand, identity-related problems worsen when extended exposure reinforces negative perceptions of the other group, especially if there are no structural mechanisms to boost coordination. For instance, as noted earlier, a high-level British PSC official mentioned that his company's experiences with resentment were more acute with the British military than with the U.S. military because the U.S. military is more accustomed to working with private security than is its British counterpart. This suggests that states that are new to the security privatization trend are likely to see more friction between PSCs and the regular military than are states with more experience co-deploying the two groups. Statements regarding variation in PSC identities also indicate the potential for identity shifts over time, with the interviewees noting that the "old hands" were less likely to be "trigger happy" than were new recruits.[83]

MODELING PSC-MILITARY INTERACTION:
THE INTERPLAY OF STRUCTURE AND IDENTITY

Clearly, both structural and identity-based factors are at play in determining the nature and extent of PSC–military coordination in the Iraq and Afghanistan conflicts. Structural factors figured much more prominently in interviewees' answers regarding the causes of PSC–military coordination problems. Beyond the frequent mention of structural issues, however, we can see a pattern of how the interplay of structure and identity affect PSC–military co-ordination. Specifically, where structural weaknesses exist, coordination becomes dependent on individual and collective identities. In such a situation, outcomes vary with the variance of these individual and collective identities. For instance, because communications between PSCs and the military were primarily ad hoc during the 2003–2008 period (a structural weakness), coordination in any particular situation became dependent on the personalities of all involved. This was particularly true with regard to the relevant military commanders—hence individual identities were significant. Coordination also became dependent on the relational comparisons and constitutive norms that each group employed in assessing the other, and thus collective identity was relevant as well.

Both the structure–identity interplay and its relationship to the various components of military effectiveness are illustrated in the framework depicted in Figure 3.4. In this figure, the lower right-hand quadrant reflects the goal that policymakers from the United States and other PSC purchasing states should strive for: very few instances of structural or identity-based shortcomings to insure efficient and effective PSC–military coordination, so that PSCs will have a beneficial impact on military effectiveness. Unfortunately, in Iraq—and to a lesser extent in Afghanistan—the situation most closely matches that depicted in the upper left-hand quadrant of Figure 3.4, especially during the conflicts' early years.

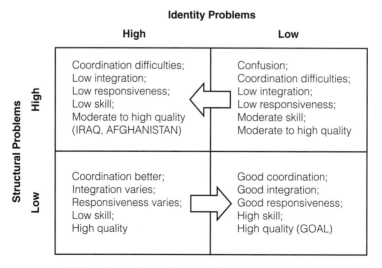

Identity Problems

	High	Low
High	Coordination difficulties; Low integration; Low responsiveness; Low skill; Moderate to high quality (IRAQ, AFGHANISTAN)	Confusion; Coordination difficulties; Low integration; Low responsiveness; Moderate skill; Moderate to high quality
Low	Coordination better; Integration varies; Responsiveness varies; Low skill; High quality	Good coordination; Good integration; Good responsiveness; High skill; High quality (GOAL)

(Structural Problems: High / Low)

Figure 3.4. PSC–military interaction model.

Interestingly, even if the situation reflected that depicted in the upper right-hand quadrant of the figure (high levels of structural problems and low levels of identity problems), the coordination difficulties and confusion spurred by the lack of adequate coordination structures would likely breed resentment between the two groups, thus causing identity-based problems and shifting the situation into that depicted in the upper left-hand quadrant. The arrow in the upper half of the table illustrates this potentiality, which is particularly significant when considering the aforementioned finding that structural weaknesses lead PSC and military personnel to rely more strongly on identity-related factors. If, on the other hand, the situation reflected that in the lower left-hand quadrant (low levels of structural problems and high levels of identity problems), the repeated, structured interactions between PSC and military personnel would likely allow each group to learn more about the other. This could decrease resentment between the two groups and therefore reduce identity problems, shifting the situation into that depicted in the lower right-hand quadrant (as depicted by the arrow in the bottom half of the table).

In other words, structural weaknesses lead to both a greater reliance on identity-based factors and to a greater chance for identity-related problems to emerge. Meanwhile, a rigorous structure of rules guiding PSC-military interactions leads to increased learning and the possibility for improved perceptions of each other. While there is also a risk that increased exposure will lead to negative perceptions of each other, the interview data cited throughout this chapter seem to indicate that increase exposure tends to improve PSC and military perceptions of each other. Therefore, while identity issues will never disappear, military and PSC strategists should: (a) focus on remedying structural shortcomings such as deficiencies in training and doctrine and (b) learn which types of individual and collective identities promote strong PSC–military coordination and provide incentives for the military and PSCs (both as individual companies and collectively) to align their identities with those that promote PSC–military coordination. The practice of aligning these identities will undoubtedly require minor structural changes in order to support the norms constituting these more beneficial identities, but the overall change will be a shift in identity.

For example, let us assume that the PSCs viewed as "professional" in the military's eyes are those providing armored cars and standard uniforms to their employees and that this practice makes it easier for these PSCs to coordinate with the military because it easily identifies the PSCs as friendly forces.

Implementing these suggestions would lead less professional PSCs to make a structural change (in the form of a rule or company standard) to abide by this norm of providing armored cars and uniforms, which, ceteris paribus, will eventually shift these companies' identities to be in line with the more "professional" PSCs.

TYPOLOGY OF PSC "OPERATIONAL PROFESSIONALISM"

As seen in the preceding analysis, certain practices enable PSC and military personnel to engage with each other productively in the field. Taken together, these practices constitute part of the structure of PSC–military co-deployments and, for the purposes of this study, are considered indicative of the private security firm's level of *operational professionalism*. Andrew Abbott defines *professions* as "exclusive occupational groups applying somewhat abstract knowledge to particular cases" and argues that interrelations between professions are determined by how each group controls its knowledge and skill.[84] Part of this control of knowledge and skill, I argue, includes the practices relating to how PSCs and their personnel operate in the field. These practices play a large part in dictating how the military and PSC personnel interact with and view each other. They include, for instance, PSCs' use of armored vehicles and the requirement that PSC personnel wear identifiable uniforms. Other examples of these practices include PSC operational styles that correlate well with the operational style of the military units alongside which they operate—for instance, driving styles—and treating local civilians respectfully. An overarching indicator of dedication to operational professionalism is membership in a major trade association, such as the International Stability Operations Association (ISOA).

Significantly, the scope of this typology is limited to focus only on professional activities at the tactical and operational levels, dictating proper actions while in the field. Limiting the typology's scope in this way is necessary to clearly delineate which firms are best at implementing those structural variables that matter most for PSCs' impact on overall military effectiveness. Some firms may be considered "professional" according to other measurement rubrics—for instance, the dollar amount of contracts they are awarded—but such measurements are irrelevant to the goal of determining a set of practices that will best enable PSCs to have a beneficial impact on military effectiveness.

Some firms adopt the practices most important for operational professionalism relatively easily, while others argue that different operating styles better enable them to act effectively in the field. However, the evidence gathered from the interviews conducted for this study indicates that, in almost all cases, the use of identifiable armored vehicles and uniforms better enables effective PSC–military field coordination than does the use of indigenous vehicles and plain clothes. Furthermore, the facts that many military and PSC interviewees noted the divergent operational styles of the two groups, and that soldiers repeatedly complained of having to manage the consequences of contractors' disrespect of local civilians and of their traditions and customs, indicate that operational styles (as dictated, for instance, by driving procedures) and treatment of local civilians are two additional areas in which a structure of common practices could improve PSCs' impact on military effectiveness.

We can therefore conceive of private security companies along a "spectrum of professionalism," with the firms that employ most of these practices at the "more professional" end of the spectrum and the firms that employ fewer of these practices at the "less professional" end of the spectrum. Figure 3.5 depicts this typology. Notably, no firm is entirely perfect in this regard, and—because the policies of each firm are likely to undergo some fluctuation as contracts and deployments change—firms are likely to move up and down the spectrum over time. Some firms, however, will implement these practices better than others at certain times, and purchasers should recognize this and award contracts accordingly. By doing so, purchasers will create market incentives for firms to employ these "professional" practices, pushing the entire industry closer to the "more professional" end of the spectrum and increasing the prospects that PSCs will have a beneficial impact on military effectiveness. This is particularly true with regard to situations of PSC–military co-deployment, but these professional practices can also have a beneficial impact in situations where PSCs are substituting for an intervening state's military force. In many such cases, the PSC in question will still be responsible for interacting with the military of the state to which the company is deployed, and these practices will assist in that regard. Furthermore, the requirement that PSC personnel act respectfully toward local civilians and local traditions and

Figure 3.5. Typology of PSC operational professionalism.

customs to be considered "professional" will benefit PSC and military actions in all theaters, regardless of the deployment situation.

Of course, the risk that certain individual employees will fail to abide by these practices is ever present, and it is thus necessary that each firm establish rigorous training and vetting standards to minimize this risk among its employees. Furthermore, each firm must establish internal regulations and guidelines for dealing with employees who fail to abide by the company's standards for ethical and professional practices.

IMPLICATIONS FOR POLICY

This chapter shows the interplay among military effectiveness, structure, and identity. As the preceding analysis makes clear, structural factors and identity-based factors are equally relevant in determining the quality of PSC–military interactions and coordination in the context of the Iraq War, though they do operate differently. When structural weaknesses abound, both PSC and military actions rely on identity factors. Simultaneously, the structural weaknesses are likely to cause coordination problems that, in turn, have a negative impact on identity factors by breeding PSC–military resentment and unfavorable relational comparisons. Thus, both structure and identity are important in the context of PSC–military relations, and both must be considered.

Related to this is the preliminary finding that military professionals may not need to worry (at least not as much as some have argued they should) about the takeover of their professional jurisdiction by contractors. In other words, there may be a limit to what you can pay someone to do; necessary actions beyond this limit would thus fall within the purview of the military. Preliminary evidence indicates that this may be the case, at least with regard to some PSCs. For instance, a high-level PSC official who asked to remain anonymous noted that there may be a limit to what PSCs could do in any particular event, with PSC employees not being as fully committed to take and accept risks as are men and women in the military. As a former military officer himself, he noted that he was personally "prepared to stand into harm's way as a serviceman, on active service, when serving [his] nation," whereas his motivation as an employee of a PSC would be "very much more conditional."[85] This limit on the risks PSCs are willing to take has implications for the selection effects argument of democratic advantage theory, indicating that while PSCs may make it easier for democracies to use force covertly, they may also limit the scale and scope of the sorts of operations that can be conducted.[86]

However, this may not be the case with PSCs who have a particular political or ideological leaning. Interviewees from one PSC, for instance, told the GAO that they were not working for a PSC for the money, that they were "doing something that they believed in and as part of their love of the United States and the democratic society for which it stands."[87] Companies sharing this ideological stance may instill a stronger sense of national loyalty into their personnel, essentially providing them with the sense of civic duty found within the professional military. This point has potential as an interesting issue for future research.

CONCLUSION

As this chapter endeavors to make clear, the problems illuminated in the Zapata Engineering, Fallujah, and Nisour Square cases are not anomalous; they are pervasive issues that threaten situations of PSC–military co-deployment. While coordination successes also occur regularly, an examination of the data makes clear that coordination successes and failures are not mutually exclusive. To best harness the beneficial qualities of PSCs and minimize the potential problems associated with using these firms, states must take an active role in dictating how private forces should be structured in relation to the military. In contrast to the co-deployment scenarios explored in this chapter, the next chapter explores the ramifications for military effectiveness and the democratic advantage of situations in which PSCs are deployed in place of a state's military forces.

4 TRADING PLACES
Private Firms Hired in Place of National Militaries

CHAPTER 3 EXAMINED ISSUES facing very recent cases in which PSCs and the military were deployed in largely equal numbers alongside one another (that is, "co-deployed"). While such instances of private forces deployed alongside national militaries are again becoming increasingly common, they are by no means the only deployment scenarios for private military and security companies. Nor is the use of PSCs unique to the Iraq and Afghanistan deployments. Indeed, until recently these private firms were more commonly hired to train and equip struggling state militaries behind the scenes, to fulfill international objectives in place of a state military (as proxy intervening forces) in politically sensitive areas, and/or to supplant state militaries in situations of civil war or open rebellion against a state's government.

What are the consequences of such PSC deployment scenarios for military effectiveness and the democratic advantage, and how do they compare to the other case studies that this project explores? This chapter endeavors to answer this question, focusing on two cases varying both in terms of the actors involved and in the purposes for which the PSC is hired: MPRI in Croatia in the mid-1990s and Sandline in Sierra Leone in the 1997–1998 time frame. Despite this variation, both cases reflect a deployment situation in which a PSC was used in place of a regular military force. In addition, this chapter assesses two counterfactual cases: the U.S. military intervention in the Lebanese Civil War from 1982–1984 and the U.S. government's sale of arms to Iran during the mid-1980s in the so-called Iran-Contra affair. These counterfactual cases are similar to the Croatia and Sierra Leone cases in terms of the types of military assistance provided to the countries in question—that is, training and the provision of weapons, respectively—yet they differ fundamentally from the Croatia and Sierra Leone cases in that the U.S. government and/or military was directly involved in these cases, rather than a PSC. These counterfactual cases are therefore useful in illustrating how outcomes would differ if U.S. or British forces were directly involved in the Croatia and Sierra Leone cases, as opposed to the involvement of PSCs as substitutes for such forces.

Analysis of these cases illustrates that hiring private military and security firms to carry out backdoor assistance roles often results in tactically, strategically, and operationally effective military actions—assuming these operations are based on sound strategies in the first place—due to the beneficial impact of such deployments on *skill, responsiveness,* and *quality.* The potential for resentment between a state's military forces and the PSC in question, and any resulting effects on *integration,* can be tempered by the involvement of a third party in brokering the deal to hire the PSC, as illustrated in the Croatia case. Yet the use of private security firms in such cases does not provide a discernible increase in military effectiveness over what one would expect from U.S. or British (or other potential interventionist) forces employed in a similar manner, as shown in the two counterfactuals in the following pages.

A difference *is* apparent between the use of PSCs and regular military forces in terms of the ability of PSC employment to reduce transparency and accountability to democratic processes, however. PSC deployments in place of regular military forces are therefore predisposed to entail behavior at odds with international legal rules and norms of ethical warfare. Furthermore, precisely because democratic intervening states' militaries are not involved in the conflicts in Croatia and Sierra Leone, PSC deployments in these cases enable these democratic states to become involved in outside conflicts at a reduced risk of political discord from their domestic publics. This increases the likelihood that democracies using PSCs as proxy intervening forces will be less selective about the conflicts in which they become involved and, as such, less likely to experience the democratic advantage. Moreover, because the "selection effects" argument of democratic advantage theory operates according to the same mechanism as the democratic peace hypothesis (that is, the ability of a democratic electorate to constrain its leaders from entering into war), the fact that modern PSCs are used in such a manner poses a strong challenge to the hypothesis that the democratic peace will exist in modern and future warfare.

Interestingly, however, a comparison of the Sierra Leone and Iran-Contra cases highlights the fact that democratically supported covert PSC activities can, if unintentionally revealed to the democratic electorate, engender a political backlash similar to that experienced by democratic leaders when their own governments' covert activities are revealed. This indicates that PSCs' negative impact on democracies' conflict selectivity in cases of PSC substitution for regular government or military forces operates only as long as the PSC activities in question succeed in remaining covert.

The remainder of the chapter proceeds as follows. The next section examines the Croatia case, analyzing MPRI's impact on the Croatian Army's military effectiveness and the prospects for the United States—as the third party intervening to broker the business arrangement between the Croatian government and MPRI—to experience the democratic advantage. This section highlights the ethnic cleansing campaign pursued by the Croatian Army directly following the majority of its training with MPRI, questioning MPRI's impact on the legality with which force was employed in this case. I then examine the counterfactual case of U.S. military assistance to Lebanon from 1982 to 1984, looking in particular at the impact of U.S. forces on Lebanese military effectiveness, and at the U.S. electorate's response to U.S. involvement in this conflict and the resulting effects on policymaker decisions regarding the extent and duration of this involvement. The following section assesses the role of Sandline in Sierra Leone, looking especially at Britain's involvement in this case and its desire for a *covert* force to supply weapons to Sierra Leone during a U.N. arms embargo—a need easily fulfilled by a PSC. Finally, I analyze the counterfactual case of the Iran-Contra affair, again exploring the impact of U.S. government involvement on military effectiveness, the electorate's response to such involvement when it came to light, and the resulting impact on the United States' conflict selectivity. In concluding, I rearticulate the circumstances under which private security companies and their personnel may have a beneficial impact on military effectiveness when used in place of a state military and examine the prospects for the democratic advantage under these circumstances.

DEMOCRATIC USE OF A PSC AS A PROXY
INTERVENING FORCE: MPRI IN CROATIA

Military Professional Resources, Inc. (MPRI), is an Alexandria, Virginia-based firm specializing in private military and government services, primarily security sector reform and development.[1] Founded in 1988 by former Army General Vernon Lewis and several other retired generals, MPRI has a reputation within the private military community for professionalism. Indeed, an official at MPRI's corporate headquarters notes that the company is reputed to be a "military organization in civilian clothing," although the leadership is working to ensure that this is not the company's brand recognition because MPRI has now diversified into many areas other than simply Army support.[2] The firm employs dozens of retired top-ranked generals and over 10,000 former military personnel, many of them elite Special Forces.[3] MPRI has a long history of high-paying government contracts—from both the United States and foreign governments. It is approximately 75 percent dependent on Pentagon contracts and is currently deployed to approximately sixty countries, mostly to build "institutional capacity"—for example, training and restructuring military forces.[4]

In March 1994, the Croatian minister of defense requested military assistance from the U.S. government, stating that Croatia's goal was the transition of the Croatian military "to one which follows the model of the United States."[5] The defense minister therefore requested U.S. permission to negotiate with MPRI over the provision of training in civil–military relations and program and budget services to the Croatian Armed Forces (Hrvatska Vojska, or HV).[6] This action followed Croatia's declaration of independence from Yugoslavia in June 1991 and the ensuing civil war across the region.

The provision of direct U.S. security assistance to aid Croatian defense reform efforts would not have been unusual, as the United States is an active provider of security assistance to reform the defense sectors of many states, particularly former Soviet states seeking admission to NATO and/or the European Union. Furthermore, the use of a private firm to provide such assistance is not completely anomalous; for instance, the firm SAIC was hired to provide guidance to Albanian defense reform efforts from 2002 through 2007.[7] What made MPRI's involvement in Croatia particularly unusual was the private firm's involvement in Croatian defense reform efforts in the midst of an active conflict in the region. As Silverstein notes, "MPRI also offers advice and training to the Croatian military, a relationship that began in April 1995 at one of the most intense periods of fighting in the Balkan war."[8]

Washington's involvement was piecemeal throughout most parts of the conflict, and analysts have cited the lack of a well-coordinated and persistently enforced international strategy to end this conflict as contributing to the long-term destruction and loss of lives in Croatia.[9] This was partially a result of Western jubilation at the recent end of the Cold War and the tendency to see the dissolution of Yugoslavia as a necessary transitional by-product of this geopolitical restructuring.[10] By 1994, however, Washington realized that strong leadership was needed in brokering a cease-fire in the war between the

Croats and Muslims in Bosnia. Through extensive diplomatic contacts among the United States and Croatian and Bosnian Muslim representatives, Washington was able to convince Croatian President Franjo Tudjman to abandon the idea of a Croat statelet in Bosnia. In return, the U.S. negotiators promised U.S. help in hastening Croatia's economic, political, and military integration into the West.[11] The 1994 Washington Agreement thus set the stage for U.S. military aid to be provided to Croatia.

Despite Tudjman's efforts to consolidate the Croat forces into an effective military (the HV), some analysts argue that by 1994 the Croatian armed forces still suffered from poor leadership and an unprofessional organizational structure. Its troops were poorly disciplined and poorly supplied.[12] Others, however, point to the January 1993 Maslenica offensive in which Croatian troops launched a lightning strike across U.N. lines to capture the straits of Maslenica. This offensive was strategically quite significant—it linked central Croatia with the Dalmatian coast, as well as linking the capital city of Zagreb with the country's second city, Split. Some say it was thus an early indicator of growing Croatian military strength and self-confidence.[13]

In August 1994, Assistant U.S. Secretary of State for European and Canadian Affairs Richard Holbrooke persuaded the State Department to license MPRI to provide training to the Croatian army.[14] Regardless of whether Croatian troop strength was increasing on its own, the Croatian defense minister and MPRI President Carl Vuono signed two contracts in September 1994, arguing that MPRI's services were intended to prepare Croatian forces to participate in NATO's Partnership for Peace Program. The first contract, which began in January 1995, provided for long-range management designed to help Croatia restructure its defense department for long-term strategic capabilities. The second contract developed the Democracy Transition Assistance Program (DTAP), providing for the "military education and training of staff officers and uncommissioned officers of the Croatian army."[15] Under the DTAP, MPRI trained Croatian army officers and personnel for fourteen weeks, in eight-hour sessions five days a week. In this endeavor, MPRI used translated textbooks identical to those used at U.S. professional military academies, graduating their first officers in April 1995.[16]

Many analysts take issue with MPRI's work for the Croatian government, citing the Croatian military's "Operation Storm" in early August 1995 as proof that MPRI's military assistance stretched beyond classroom training and resulted in humanitarian atrocities. In Operation Storm, the HV quite easily recaptured the Krajina territory, which constituted 20 percent of all Croatian territory—in other words, a sizable portion of land. As journalist Esther Schrader notes, "The operation played a key role in reversing the tide of war against the Serbs and, consistent with American policy, in bringing both sides to the negotiating table."[17] The Croatian forces' tactics in this operation were reportedly strikingly similar to NATO-style movements, drawing suspicion from observers of the U.S. role in bringing about the results of Operation Storm. As Colonel Leslie of the U.N. garrison in Knin put it, "It was a textbook operation, though not a JNA textbook. Whoever wrote that plan of attack could have gone to any NATO staff college in North America or Western Europe and scored an A-plus."[18] Deborah Avant, meanwhile, speculates on the causes of using MPRI as a conduit for such military assistance, as opposed to the professional military: "Given the awkward nature of sending U.S. military assistance to Croatia during a U.N. arms embargo, a private contract between the Croatian government and MPRI allowed U.S. expertise to flow to Croatia without direct U.S. government involvement."[19] Some argue that MPRI provided doctrinal advice and possibly scenario planning to the Croatians, while others think that MPRI allowed the U.S. government to share satellite information with Croatia.[20] Ken Silverstein, for instance, notes:

> A Croatian liaison officer told the local press that just weeks before the offensive General Vuono held a secret top-level meeting at Brioni Island, off the coast of Croatia, with General Varimar Cervenko, the architect of the Krajina campaign. In the five days preceding the attack, at least ten meetings were held between General Vuono and officers involved in Operation Lightning Storm.[21]

Meanwhile, MPRI denies any claims that it rendered military advice to Croatia, insisting that its classes focused on the sole topics licensed in the contract. Furthermore, the Croatian government claims that its military success resulted from both the government's consolidation of power directly before Operation Storm and the Serbs' simultaneous demoralization due to increasing international pressure. Retired Army Lieutenant General Harry E. Soyster, an executive at MPRI, told a journalist in 2002:

> I can assure you if we had the capability to train an army in a month to turn it around that fast, I wouldn't be talking to you, I'd be flying you over the Riviera on the way to see it for yourself. If we could do that in Croatia, we could straighten out Afghanistan in a couple of months.[22]

MPRI's work in Croatia gradually expanded, including an Army readiness training program and, later, assistance in implementing the Partnership for

Peace Program's requirements after Croatia was admitted to the program in 2001. Even as MPRI's role in Croatia was expanding, the Croatian government began paying less of the bill for its work—Pentagon contributions to MPRI's efforts in Croatia grew from $105,000 in 1995 to $6,000,000 in 2003.[23]

Impact on Military Effectiveness
and The Democratic Advantage

Operation Storm, with its successful "lightning quick" and NATO-like tactics, illustrates that MPRI had a beneficial effect on the tactical abilities of the Croatian military—whether only through classroom training or through other, more covert assistance. In doing so, MPRI increased the Croatian Army's levels of *skill* and *responsiveness*—its ability to achieve particular tasks and to carry out orders and its ability to tailor military activity to Croatia's capabilities, its adversaries' capabilities, and external constraints, respectively. It also likely played a role in increasing the Croatian military's *quality*, or its ability to provide itself with highly capable weapons and equipment (Proposition 1). Indeed, analysts speculate that MPRI may have given advice on procurement and weapons acquisition to the Croatians, as Croatia spent approximately $1 billion on Eastern European weapons during MPRI's initial training mission.[24] *Integration*, moreover, was not hindered in the Croatian case, mainly due to the fact that MPRI was the only PSC involved here, and it is unlikely that the firm provided on-the-ground operators to work side-by-side with the Croatian military during combat. Thus, the issue of PSC-military coordination problems never arose. This is a key distinction between the types of PSC deployment discussed in this chapter and those examined in Chapter 3. In fact, the Croatian military's *integration* most likely improved due to MPRI's training, as suggested by the HV's success in Operation Storm and subsequent operations.

Beyond this improvement in tactical effectiveness, MPRI arguably enhanced the Croatian Army's operational and strategic effectiveness as well. By November 1995, President Tudjman's army had recaptured all but 4 percent of Croatian territory and was occupying 20 percent of Bosnia as well.[25] Clearly, the broader operational and strategic aims of the Croatian military had been realized. Whether this improvement is wholly attributable to MPRI is debatable, but the improvement clearly correlates with the time period in which MPRI began providing its assistance to Croatia. Major General Alain Fourand, who commanded U.N. forces in the area of Operation Storm, said, "I don't think it was the Croats themselves that did that," adding he suspected it was MPRI.[26] Another Canadian Major General reported that he doubted the Croatian army had conducted Operation Storm without outside assistance: "That was done by people who really knew what they were doing," he said, adding he didn't think the Croats had the expertise.[27] Furthermore, a *Washington Times* International Special Report notes that MPRI also helped Croatia to establish a military system that works in harmony with a democratic government, thus easing the military aspects of the democratic transition.[28]

While MPRI's assistance to the Croatian military certainly coincides with the military's improved tactical, strategic, and operational performance, this is not purely a success story for private military assistance to a professional military. This case illustrates the potential for private military and security firms to allow unethical behavior in warfare. According to the Croatian Helsinki Committee for Human Rights, Operation Storm resulted in the massacre of at least 410 civilians in the course of a three-day operation. It has been reported elsewhere that the actual number of civilians killed or missing was much larger.[29] An internal report of The Hague War Crimes Tribunal leaked to the *New York Times* confirmed that the Croatian Army had been responsible for carrying out "summary executions, indiscriminate shelling of civilian populations and 'ethnic cleansing' in the Krajina region of Croatia."[30] In a section titled "The Indictment: Operation Storm, A Prima Facie Case," the internal Hague War Crimes Tribunal report confirms:

> During the course of the military offensive, the Croatian armed forces and special police committed numerous violations of international humanitarian law, including but not limited to, shelling of Knin and other cities . . . During, and in the 100 days following the military offensive, at least 150 Serb civilians were summarily executed, and many hundreds disappeared . . . In a widespread and systematic manner, Croatian troops committed murder and other inhumane acts upon and against Croatian Serbs.[31]

The report concluded that the tribunal had "sufficient material to establish that the three [Croatian] generals who commanded the military operation could be held accountable under international law."[32] The individuals named had been directly involved in the military operation "in theater." Those involved in "the planning of Operation Storm" were not mentioned:

> The identity of the "American general" referred to by Fenrick [a Tribunal staff member] is not known. The tribunal would not allow Williamson or Fenrick to be interviewed . . . Several people who were at the meeting assumed that

Fenrick was referring to one of the retired U.S. generals who worked for Military Professional Resources Inc. . . . Questions remain about the full extent of U.S. involvement. In the course of the three-year investigation into the assault, the United States has failed to provide critical evidence requested by the tribunal, according to tribunal documents and officials, adding to suspicion among some there that Washington is uneasy about the investigation . . . The Pentagon, however, has argued through U.S. lawyers at the tribunal that the shelling was a legitimate military activity, according to tribunal documents and officials.[33]

Furthermore, in the wake of Operation Storm, the Croatian military engaged in an abhorrent ethnic cleansing campaign against the Serbs in the Krajina region. This campaign comprised the largest single forcible displacement of people in Europe since World War II, with the Croatian army attacking the road that the Serbian refugees were using to flee into neighboring Bosnia. Refugees were also forced to run through towns filled with angry Croatians who took to the streets to stone them. "The Croatian authorities had mapped out the route for refugees. An old woman died, her face swollen beyond recognition, of injuries suffered when hit by a rock."[34] Later, the Croatians burned and looted over 20,000 houses in this region owned by Serbs, killing the elderly Serbs who had failed to evacuate. A U.N. report stated, "The lady was tied by fish net and a tire was put around her neck before she was set on fire. The old man was burned to death a few yards away."[35] A Canadian officer operating in the region reported, "We found people in wells. There was an old lady we found head-first in a well. Why did they do that?"[36]

After the assault on Krajina, observers suggested that MPRI's team of instructors had actually trained the Croatians in a set of military tactics, known as "AirLand Battle 2000," which were then used against the Serbs in Krajina.[37] A number of media accounts even reported that MPRI personnel helped plan the Croatian occupation and ethnic cleansing of the Serb-populated region. United Press International reports, "Even the Foreign Military Training Report published by both the State Department and Department of Defense in May refers to these allegations against MPRI not entirely disparagingly."[38] There is also evidence that the United States provided Croatian President Franjo Tudjman with a green light just a few days before the operation.[39]

MPRI, while expressing regret at these incidents, simply claimed that such behavior indicated the Croatian army's need for democratic assistance and thus did not suspend their training efforts.[40] While it is difficult to conclusively determine whether regular military forces would be any less likely to allow or perpetrate violations of IHL in this case, one must consider the possibility that these regular military institutions—the U.S. military, in this case—would be under much greater public scrutiny and would crack down on such behavior, were they to become directly involved. The U.S. military's unwillingness to engage in unethical warfare under similar circumstances was seen in the Lebanese Civil War, as explored later in this chapter. It is therefore plausible that substitution of MPRI for U.S. forces had a negative impact on adherence to IHL in this case. As one military analyst noted, Operation Storm "was followed by massive ethnic cleansing. Now, had American troops been on the ground, we would have been held accountable for that. The fact that it was a private company made the connection a lot less clear."[41]

MPRI's beneficial impact on the Croatian forces' military effectiveness therefore coincides with MPRI's failure to ensure the Croatian forces' adherence to IHL, serving as evidence for draining-the-sea school of thought with regard to treatment of civilians in counterinsurgency warfare, and for the related proposition that PSCs improve military effectiveness because they are less beholden to the electorate and can therefore perform the dirty jobs necessary to win wars (Proposition 1b). It is difficult to argue, however, that ethnic cleansing could ever be a "necessary" tactic of counterinsurgency. Furthermore, it was the Croatian Army that engaged in these IHL abuses, therefore making it difficult to conclusively place the blame for the ethnic cleansing campaign on MPRI. Stepping in during the ethnic cleansing campaign may have been interpreted as undermining the Croatian army's professional jurisdiction, and/or MPRI might have worried that its contract with the Croatian government would have been placed at risk through such intervention. Yet, it is difficult to imagine that U.S. forces would not have reacted in some way to the ethnic cleansing campaign in the Krajina region if they, rather than MPRI, had been providing security assistance to the Croatians. There is therefore something inherently covert in the private nature of the firm in this case that led it to allow such unethical behavior.

While military effectiveness in this case is generally high in terms of tactical, operational, and strategic effectiveness—through MPRI's impact on *responsiveness*, *skill*, and *quality*—the case of MPRI in Croatia bodes ill for the U.S. prospects for experiencing the democratic advantage. When PSCs are deployed in place of the professional military to allow a democratic intervening state some influence in an outside conflict, the electoral checks and balances intended to prevent policymakers from involving the democracy in such an outside conflict do not function as intended. As such, the executive in the democracy in question is able to militarily influence an outside conflict in large part without the knowledge of the domestic public. This leads the democracy to become less selective about the conflicts into which it enters (or to whose parties it provides support) and, subsequently, less likely to experience the "selection effects" aspect of the democratic advantage.

As already noted, the MPRI contract in the Croatian case allowed U.S. government support to flow to the Croatian military without direct U.S. government involvement in the conflict. Indeed, even MPRI acknowledges this role for itself. According to MPRI information officer Joseph Allred, the firm exists so that "the U.S. can have influence as part of its national strategy on other nations without employing its own army."[42] Significantly, domestic public support for a U.S. military deployment to the former Yugoslavia at this time was fairly low: according to a number of polls conducted in the early 1990s by major U.S. news outlets such as ABC, CBS, and NBC, and by major U.S. pollsters such as Harris and Gallup, very few Americans (ranging from 1 percent to 4 percent of respondents) considered the war in Bosnia to be the most important issue—foreign or domestic—the United States faced at the time. Accordingly, the vast majority of Americans viewed military action as largely a European or multilateral responsibility rather than an American one. Indeed, approval for unilateral air strikes ranged from only 20 percent to 25 percent of those respondents polled, and Americans were much more likely to support humanitarian airdrops and U.N. humanitarian or peacekeeping efforts than they were to support the use of U.S. ground troops for combat against the Serbs.[43] The ability to hire MPRI allowed the U.S. government to commit a type of "ground force" to the conflict despite the low public support for such a commitment, without any electoral ramifications.

While the extent of U.S. government support flowing to Croatia via MPRI is debatable, the U.S. government's involvement in the Balkans through the proxy of MPRI could be said to be substantial at the very least, as indicated by the preceding figures showing U.S. government payments to MPRI for the firm's work in Croatia. Meanwhile, Western governments turned a blind eye to the attack on Krajina in Operation Storm, with Western politicians remaining quiet. Prior to the offensive and on his return from a trip to Washington, U.S. Ambassador to Croatia Peter Galbraith told President Tudjman that the United States would tolerate a military offensive to recapture Krajina, provided it was "short and clean."[44] Although then-U.S. Secretary of State Warren Christopher later denied that Washington had played any role in encouraging Operation Storm, he did admit that Croatian success in this operation aided the process of a broader peace settlement in the region. MPRI in this case therefore facilitated the likelihood of the use of force by circumventing the standard electoral consent mechanism that would otherwise constrain democratic leaders. Another official at MPRI has even acknowledged that the idea of the United States or other democratic governments using PSCs in this manner, to bypass electoral risks on politically sensitive foreign policy issues, is a "plausible hypothesis."[45]

COUNTERFACTUAL #1:
U.S. MILITARY ASSISTANCE TO LEBANON
DURING THE LEBANESE CIVIL WAR, 1982–1984

The case of MPRI in Croatia illustrates the effects of a covertly hired PSC for the military effectiveness of a host nation, as well as its effects on an intervening democracy's prospects for experiencing the democratic advantage. The case of U.S. military assistance to Lebanon in the early 1980s, by contrast, illustrates the impact of overt, direct U.S. military assistance on host nation military effectiveness and U.S. prospects for the democratic advantage.

Lebanese Civil War: Background

The Lebanese Civil War lasted from 1975 to 1990, during which time up to 7 percent of the roughly 3.4 million Lebanese people were killed.[46] At least 200,000 are believed to have been injured; some estimates are over twice that figure.[47] Lebanon's major religious sects include Maronites, Greek Orthodox Christians, Sunnis, Shi'a, and Druzes; all of these groups engaged in the fighting and changed their alliances several times over the course of the conflict's fifteen-year duration. Palestinian factions, particularly the Palestinian Liberation Organization (PLO) led by Yasser Arafat, also played a prominent part in the war. Lebanon saw direct intervention from Syria, Israel, Iran and Multi-National Forces—most prominently France (Lebanon's one-time colonial ruler) and the United States.[48]

Until 1918, the land now comprising Lebanon was nominally ruled by the Ottoman Empire. In 1920, the League of Nations granted France a mandate for Lebanon and Syria, and it was the French who drew the borders of "Greater Lebanon" to include the Beq'aa Valley, which historically belonged to Syria.[49]

A Lebanese constitution was adopted in 1926, establishing a democratic republic with a parliamentary system of government. Political independence occurred in 1943.[50] A census carried out by the French mandate in 1932 put the Christian population at just over 50 percent, but the influx of half a million mostly Sunni Palestinian refugees between 1948 and 1968 was later to dramatically change that composition. There was an unwritten national pact in 1943 that the status quo should be a Christian president, a Sunni prime minister, a Shi'a speaker, and a Druze chief of staff. In addition, there would be six Christian parliamentary seats for every five Muslim seats. This was observed but was increasingly resented, particularly by the marginalized Druze and the Shi'a.[51]

Religious frictions were compounded by social upheaval and in particular by the militant campaigns of the Palestinians, which divided public opinion. A combination of leftists of all faiths joined forces in the 1970s under the Lebanese National Movement to push for social reforms and support the Palestinians. The Maronite elite—opposed equally to reform and to the Palestinians—trained Christian militia forces, who later came to be known as the "Phalange."[52] Political tension turned to military conflict when the Phalangist leader Pierre Gemayel was targeted and some of his entourage killed, probably by Palestinian militants, and full-scale civil war broke out in April 1975.[53]

U.S. Interests in the Lebanese Civil War

The U.S. position with regard to the war in Lebanon evolved confusingly, in line with the intricate and rapidly changing alliances within groups in Lebanon and regional and international trends of other players.[54] U.S. policymaking on this issue was influenced to some degree by a concern for Israeli interests, due in part to the strong pro-Israel lobby in the United States. In Lebanon, Israel's objectives were to eject the PLO and to secure a government that was more sympathetic to Israel. In effect, this meant a rightist Christian-dominated government. In the mid-1970s, the Athens station of the U.S. Central Intelligence Agency (CIA) assisted Israel in arming Lebanese Christian militias in preparation for battle against the Palestinians.[55] Many believe that America's diplomatic interventions in Lebanon in 1976 and 1981 were designed to avoid a Syrian/PLO–Israeli confrontation and to encourage a Syrian blow to the PLO:

> Throughout the war, the U.S. looked the other way while Israel fought a war with the Palestinians on Lebanese soil, then cordoned off part of the South to set up a mini-state that blocked retribution against Israeli actions in Lebanon at the U.N.[56]

Nonetheless, the United States did not always act diplomatically in Israel's favor. Despite Israeli hostility to Syria, in the mid-1970s the United States maintained cordial relations with Syria. At that stage, however, the Syrian regime was itself opposed to a strong PLO presence in Lebanon. In 1980, Marius Deeb, discussing U.S. foreign policy with regard to the proposed Syrian intervention in Lebanon, described it as one of "tacit approval" because:

> King Husain on his visit to the United States in late March 1976 had convinced the Ford administration that Syrian intervention would prevent a leftist take-over of Lebanon and would put an end to the conflict and that, after this was achieved, Syrian troops would withdraw from Lebanon.[57]

Indeed, the U.S. envoy, L. Dean Brown, arriving in Lebanon on March 31, 1976, reported to U.S. Secretary of State Henry Kissinger that the role of Syria was constructive and that Lebanon was not in any danger of becoming a Syrian satellite state.[58]

Conversely, and as the Cold War lingered, the United States was intent on undermining Soviet clients wherever they might be. In Lebanon, Syria was such a client, and Syria in turn bolstered the Palestinian presence in the early 1970s, armed the Druze and the Shi'a Amal militia, and promoted the growth of the pro-Iranian Hezbollah. As Daniel Amit writes in his introduction to former Israeli Defense Forces (IDF) Lieutenant Colonel Dov Yermiya's published war diary:

> From the start, the U.S. underwrote Israel's war in Lebanon and, in this sense, Israel in Lebanon became a hostage to U.S. objectives there. The war, beyond a few days, could not have continued without massive economic aid. In the beginning, U.S. aid was forthcoming without much overt Israeli prodding. One has to assume that the U.S. administration perceived potential gains in the war, such as the establishment of a Phalangist regime, humiliation of the Soviet Union through its Syrian proxy, etc. Some of these goals, of course, were shared by Sharon and Begin. But the audible glee with which U.S. leaders greeted the sight of their planes destroying Soviet supplied anti-aircraft underlines that they found this proxy war initially very satisfying indeed.[59]

Any satisfaction felt on the part of the United States quickly evaporated in 1983 when a truck packed with 2,000 pounds of explosives drove into the U.S. Marine base in Beirut and killed 241 Marines, as examined in further detail in the following section.

U.S. Military Intervention in Lebanon

Marines were twice deployed to Beirut in 1982. On June 15, 1982, Israeli units were entrenched outside Beirut. The United States had called for PLO withdrawal from Lebanon, and Israeli Prime Minister Sharon began to order bombing raids of West Beirut, targeting some 16,000 PLO *fedayeen* who had retreated into fortified positions. Meanwhile, Palestinian leader Yasser Arafat attempted through negotiations to salvage politically what was clearly a military disaster for the PLO, an attempt that eventually succeeded once Arafat had gained considerable publicity for his cause and once the multinational force arrived to evacuate the PLO. Fierce artillery duels between the IDF and the PLO and PLO shelling of Christian neighborhoods of East Beirut at the outset gave way to escalating aerial IDF bombardment beginning on July 21, 1982.[60]

By late August 1982, Lebanese sources placed the official death toll in Beirut at 6,776. This figure included victims of the June 4, 1982, bombing, which occurred two days before the actual commencement of the operation. Lebanese police claimed that civilians accounted for 84 percent of the fatalities. This figure squares with the estimate of 80 percent often cited by international doctors who had served in Beirut during the siege. Of the 1,100 combatants among those killed, Palestinians accounted for 45.6 percent, Lebanese for 37.2 percent, Syrians for 10.1 percent, and other nationalities 7.1 percent of the total. Other estimates of the death toll during this entire Israeli campaign, known as "Operation Peace of the Galilee," range as high as 20,000 killed on all sides, including many civilians, and 30,000 wounded.[61]

Direct U.S. military intervention in Lebanon occurred as a result of Israel's invasion of southern Lebanon. U.S. negotiations with Lebanese political protagonists resulted in an agreement for a withdrawal of the PLO together with an Israeli withdrawal, and the deployment of Multi-National Forces (MNF), comprising American Marines, French paratroopers and Foreign Legionnaires, various Italian forces, and 100 men of the Blues and Royals with armored cars from Britain.[62] This first deployment of U.S. Marines to Beirut began in late August 1982 and consisted of the Marines and multinational forces overseeing the evacuation of the PLO from Beirut and acting as a peacekeeping force. They stayed for only a few weeks.

The second deployment of Marines to Lebanon occurred after the assassination of the Christian President-elect Bashir Gemayyel and the consequent vengeful Christian Phalange massacres of Palestinians in the camps of Sabra and Shatilla. The Israeli Defense Forces were seen as being complicit in these massacres, but if there was an element of U.S. self-interest and support for the beleaguered Israeli state in this action, the principle U.S. objective appears nonetheless to have been to restore peace to Lebanon. Indeed, this second deployment was mainly a knee-jerk reaction against perceived humanitarian injustices perpetuated during "Operation Peace of the Galilee," and, as John Laffin notes, the mission statement for the U.S. Marine force was very vague:

> The Americans were simply innocent—if that is not too euphemistic a word. They were committing troops to the most politically complex region in the world without any clear political objective beyond the general aim—laudable in itself—of maintaining peace.[63]

Due to the fact that its main incentive for intervening in the conflict was a response to perceived humanitarian abuses, the U.S. administration wanted the deployment to be fairly high profile: It wanted to be seen as responding to the massacre in the Palestinian camps that had shocked the world.

However, a number of the warring factions in Lebanon—namely the Druze, Shi'a and many of the Sunni militants—did not construe the U.S. intervention as impartial, believing that the MNF had come explicitly to bolster the Christian militias, and attacked them accordingly.[64] Furthermore, the Iranian Islamic Revolutionary leader Ayatollah Khomeini promulgated the idea that Shi'a (both in Lebanon and in Iran) should fight the U.S. presence in Lebanon as part of their religious duty to eject the United States from Muslim lands.

The impression that the U.S. forces were biased in favor of the Christian factions in Lebanon was compounded by their role in training the Lebanese Armed Forces (LAF). Partly in an effort to create a sense of purpose in what was otherwise a poorly defined mission, the Marines and U.S. Special Forces had been tasked with training the Lebanese Armed Forces, equipping them to take control of security in the country.[65] Supposedly a cross-confessional force whose role it was to protect Lebanese sovereignty, the LAF became dominated by Christian groups during the civil war. The United States played an instrumental role in the rebuilding of the Lebanese army after the Israeli invasion. Under President Amin Gemayal, plans were made to create a twelve-brigade 60,000-man army, equipped with French and U.S. arms and trained by French and U.S. advisers. In addition, President Gemayal planned to increase the Internal Security Force to 20,000 and introduced a conscription law to enforce this requirement (and to ensure an intrasectarian mix), but the law was never implemented.[66]

The United States proposed a Lebanese Army Modernization Program composed of four phases. The first three phases entailed organization of seven multi-confessional army brigades, created from existing battalions. The fourth phase focused on rebuilding the navy and air force. The total cost of the first three phases was estimated at $500 million (USD). The United States pledged to pay $235 million of this sum, with the Lebanese government paying the balance. A team of eighty United States military advisers, including fifty-three Green Berets, provided officer training in Lebanon. U.S. Special Operations Command notes, "Despite the chaotic situation in Lebanon, the training programs conducted by the 10th Special Forces Group for the LAF were extremely successful."[67] Furthermore, Lebanese officers were attached to the United States MNF contingent for training in military unit operations. Lieutenant Colonel Matthews, BLT 3/8 Commander, notes:

> Our goal was to allow the Lebanese Army to see how our NCOs function, and they function without officers and they saw that and . . . in many cases absorbed that kind of demonstrated leadership, and they certainly absorbed a lot of our spirit.[68]

Despite considerable progress in training, however, the lack of military leadership within the LAF stymied training efforts, and defection by Druze and Muslim soldiers undermined the concept of a unified army. Increasingly, the Lebanese Army became the target of attacks by Druze and Shi'a forces, hence reifying the image of the United States as the champion of the Christians. On April 18, 1983, a car bomb was detonated next to the U.S. Embassy in Beirut, killing sixty-six people.[69] By the autumn of 1983, after the Israeli withdrawal from Beirut, the Phalange who had occupied the Chouf area during the Israeli occupation were left exposed to attacks by Druze militia. The Lebanese Army lacked the strength to assume the Israeli positions, and the Druze attacked the Phalange and the Lebanese Army. The United States adopted a protective role toward the Lebanese army by providing heavy gunfire from USS *New Jersey* against the Druze, apparently on the direct orders of President Reagan. This resulted in multiple civilian casualties.[70]

Then, as noted above, in October 1983 terrorists drove a truck full of explosives into the U.S. Marine barracks in Beirut, killing 241 Marines in the deadliest terrorist attack on Americans prior to September 11, 2001.[71] Shi'a revolutionaries linked to the incipient Hezbollah are thought to have been responsible. This caused a huge outcry domestically, with the U.S. public demanding to know why the Marines were in Lebanon in the first place:

> U.S. public opinion polls had turned against Reagan's handling of the situation, and even Lebanese President Gemayel had found it necessary to express concern that U.S. support for his government was waning.[72]

Yet, President Ronald Reagan called the attack a "despicable act" and pledged to keep a military force in Lebanon. Secretary of Defense Caspar Weinberger said there would be no change in the U.S. Lebanon policy. U.S. Vice President George H. W. Bush toured the Marine bombing site on October 26, 1983 and said the United States "would not be cowed by terrorists." President Reagan assembled his national security team and planned to target the Sheik Abdullah barracks in Baalbek, Lebanon, which housed Iranian Revolutionary Guards believed to be training Hezbollah fighters. But Defense Secretary Weinberger aborted the mission, reportedly because of his concerns that it would harm U.S. relations with other Arab nations. The Marines were moved offshore where they could not be targeted.[73] When pro-Syrian militias subsequently took over West Beirut in February 1984, domestic public pressure forced President Reagan to order a Marine evacuation. This was completed in late February 1984; the rest of the MNF was withdrawn by April.[74]

The Impact of the U.S. Military Intervention on the Lebanese Military's Effectiveness and on the "Selection Effects" Dynamics of the Democratic Advantage

As the preceding analysis indicates, the U.S. military intervention had a beneficial impact on the Lebanese army's *skill* through its impact on training but was ultimately rendered relatively useless due to its inability to resolve other *skill* and *integration* problems within the Lebanese Armed Forces. Furthermore, much of the successful training was done by Special Forces, not by the general interventionist forces led by the U.S. Marines. The fact that the United States withdrew its support and ultimately had little beneficial impact on the LAF points to the conclusion that the U.S. military in this instance had a less beneficial impact on the indigenous force's military effectiveness than did MPRI in Croatia.

Yet analysis of four reasons commonly cited for the failure of the U.S. military intervention in Lebanon indicates that—while PSCs might have been better suited in some ways than the military for improving the LAF's effectiveness—for the most part, PSCs would not have had a discernibly improved impact on the LAF's military effectiveness when compared to the U.S. military force. For one thing, military historians generally agree that the performance of the Marines in Beirut was hindered by the fact that their mission was ill defined.[75] PSCs would likely perform similarly to the Marines with relation to the issue of the mission's level of definition, as the mission statement would be determined by the administration commissioning the PSC, just as it is with the regular military. Of course, one should nonetheless consider that PSCs might feel less hesitance toward deployment than would the Department of Defense and/or the regular military given a poorly defined mission, mainly due to the fact that larger sums of money would likely be promised to the PSC than to the military. Such financial incentives might motivate PSCs to deploy more willingly and with less hesitation than would lesser-paid U.S. troops, which could have an impact on the ability of the forces in question to work effectively once deployed.

The second reason commonly cited for the failure of the U.S. forces in Lebanon was that the Marines were not the most appropriate force for the deployment. The deployed force in this instance was essentially tasked with playing a peacekeeping and training role, but the Marines are an assault force. It has been argued that they were sent simply because they were in the vicinity and thus were easiest to deploy and required the least support.[76] With regard to whether the peacekeeping ethic would be present in a PSC, this would likely depend on the identity of the PSC in question, for PSC identities vary rather widely (as elaborated in Chapter 3). PSCs are generally considered to be convenient to deploy, however, so a PSC might have been used to replace the Marines in this instance—but with questionable results given the unproven nature of peacekeeping by PSCs and the unpredictable nature of military and police training via PSCs.[77]

The third reason commonly cited for the failure of the U.S. intervention in Lebanon is that the chain of command between the deployed U.S. force and Washington was poor.[78] This was mainly a result of bureaucratic inefficiency and likely would not have been improved by substitution of a PSC for U.S. troops in this case. Indeed, PSCs seem repeatedly to struggle with their own chain of command issues and with questions of how their contractors fit into the military chain of command when deployed alongside a friendly military. Yet one should not rule out the possibility that using PSCs in a relatively covert fashion might bypass bureaucratic obstacles, streamlining the chain of command by involving fewer bureaucratic agencies.

Finally, the fourth commonly cited reason for the failure of the U.S. intervention in Lebanon was the short length of individual deployments, which meant, "The critical civil–military relationships essential to success in fourth generation warfare (i.e., counterinsurgency) could never form."[79] Yet private contractors entirely determine the length of their own tours. They have more leave rotations than the military, but some may stay for several years, while others may depart after a few months. In this sense, PSCs are much more sporadic than the regular military, which would likely have an even more detrimental effect on the training of the LAF in this case.

For the most part, therefore, it appears that PSCs would not likely have had a different impact on the LAF's military effectiveness than the regular military did. However, in one sense, this case provides evidence to support the notion that PSCs may be more effective than the military in "substitution" cases in which they are deployed in place of the military, simply because they can operate outside the public eye and therefore are under less pressure to conform to the rules and norms of IHL. As Laffin notes, "Some of the best-trained troops in the world, with some of the best equipment, had been forced out by a relative handful of primitives whose principal weapons were fanaticism and a relative desire for martyrdom."[80] He argues that the helplessness of the MNF in the face of the guerrilla warfare that confronted it "vindicated the Israeli tactics of a hard-hitting all-out combined forces assault against a strong guerrilla force which was a threat to peace."[81] Such statements provide evidence to support the draining-the-sea approach to counterinsurgency warfare (Propositions 1b and 2a). The fact that the U.S. military failed to enact such an approach in Lebanon, when compared with the lawless Croatian army tactics effectively condoned by MPRI, indicates that PSCs may be better positioned to take such an approach than are the militaries of democratic states.

The dynamics relevant to the "selection effects" side of the democratic advantage, meanwhile, are clearly influenced by the overt employment of a legitimate military force in this case. When compared to the MPRI case, this illustrates that PSCs used as proxy intervening forces can protect democratic leaders from the wrath of the electorate, thus decreasing their conflict selectivity and increasing the likelihood that such leaders will involve their states in conflicts in which they are unlikely to be successful. Indeed, as noted above, the deaths of the 241 U.S. Marines at the Beirut Marine barracks in October 1983 caused such consternation among the American electorate that President Reagan was forced to begin thinking about withdrawing U.S. troops from the conflict, an action that he took just a few months later. When comparing this case to the Croatia case, it becomes easy to imagine that if the United States had hired a PSC to intervene militarily in Lebanon (as was done in Croatia), the domestic pressure to withdraw U.S. support following such an attack would likely have been much less. This is particularly so because many fewer Americans would have likely been aware of U.S. involvement via the PSC to begin with. Indeed, few Americans appeared to know of the U.S. support of MPRI's activities in Croatia, as indicated by the lack of any U.S. public outcry despite the correlation of MPRI's activities in Croatia with the American public's lack of support for the commitment of ground troops in the former Yugoslavia.

SANDLINE IN SIERRA LEONE:
A PSC USED AS A PROXY INTERVENING FORCE
TO SUPPLY WEAPONS TO A FACTION IN A CIVIL WAR

Britain founded Sierra Leone, one of the most tumultuous states in West Africa, in 1787 as a homeland for freed British slaves. By 1792, this homeland, known as "Freetown," became one of Britain's first colonies in West Africa. Britain introduced a unitary constitution for Sierra Leone in 1951, providing for universal suffrage. The Sierra Leone People's Party (SLPP), led by Milton Margai, won the first elections. A decade later, in 1961, Sierra Leone gained independence, though it retained close ties with Britain.[82] Soon after gaining independence, the economy began to stagnate, despite Sierra Leone's rich mineral deposits of diamonds, bauxite, and rotile (titanium oxide).[83] In March 1967, the All-People's Congress (APC) led by Dr. Siaka Stevens gained the majority of seats. However, a military coup prevented Stevens from taking office, foreshadowing a pattern of military takeovers of civilian politics for the ensuing years.[84]

On April 30, 1992, Captain Valentine Strasser and a group of soldiers seized power in a coup, forcing President Joseph Saidu Momoh to flee to Guinea. Originally, Strasser's government promised to return Sierra Leone to civilian rule within a year but in 1993 changed the date for transformation to 1996. Meanwhile, the Strasser government was challenged by the Revolutionary United Front (RUF), which had launched its first attacks against the Sierra Leone government in 1991. Holding positions near Sierra Leone's diamond mining centers, the RUF was able to threaten the principal source of the nation's wealth, and the war with these revolutionaries continued through 1995.[85]

Sierra Leone's history with PSCs began when President Strasser met with representatives from the South African–based private military firm Executive Outcomes in April 1995, asking the firm to intervene in the civil war in Sierra Leone.[86] Executive Outcomes' involvement in Sierra Leone was a significant precursor to Sandline's involvement, as EO achieved key tactical and strategic successes in fighting the RUF and had multiple ties to Sandline. In fact, some critics argue that Sandline was a mere reincarnation of EO and that each company was a member of the Branch-Heritage Group (a British-based mining company).[87] The deployment of EO fighters and trainers to Sierra Leone led to the recapture of key diamond mining areas by August 1995. EO also helped to establish a militia of "Kamajor" fighters who were loyal to the central government, collected intelligence on rebels, and defended local towns from RUF attacks. Strasser promised to hand over power to a democratically elected president in January 1996 but was himself ousted by a coup on January 16, 1996, and replaced by his deputy, Brigadier General Julius Maada Bio.

By March 1996, EO had secured enough of the country to make possible the first free elections in Sierra Leone since 1967.[88] The country went forward with elections for a return to civilian rule, and Ahmad Tejan Kabbah became president. Bio handed power over to Kabbah, who signed a peace agreement with the RUF in November 1996. Throughout this entire period—from 1990 up through EO's departure from Sierra Leone in January 1997—the British government took little interest in the country's military problems, even refusing the local government's request for military support in May 1991.[89] This was a clear instance in which a sovereign nation hired a PSC of its own accord, with no interference by the international community.

Upon Executive Outcomes' exit from Sierra Leone—following a dispute regarding the firm's contract—the firm warned Kabbah's administration that a coup would occur within ninety days without EO's presence to maintain order in the country. Sure enough, on May 25, 1997 (eighty-nine days later), Kabbah was ousted by yet another coup mounted by junior officers.[90] Kabbah fled the country, and Major Johnny Paul Koroma declared himself head of state, abolishing the constitution and prohibiting the existence of political parties. The international community immediately condemned Koroma's coup, but lawlessness had spread through most of the country by June 1997.[91]

At an October 1997 meeting in Conakry, Guinea, with the foreign ministers of Cote d'Ivoire, Ghana, Guinea, Liberia, and Nigeria, Koroma agreed to restore power to Kabbah in April 1998. In return, he was promised immunity from prosecution. At this meeting, it was also promised that "foreign troops, private armies, mercenaries, and irregular troops" were to be banned from Sierra Leone, as a concession to the rebels. Meanwhile, prior to the 1997 coup, both Executive Outcomes and Sandline representatives had met with

Defense Intelligence Agency (DIA) officials in Washington at a workshop on the Privatization of National Security in Sub-Saharan Africa.[92] In March 1998, the *London Observer* revealed that Britain's High Commissioner to Sierra Leone, Peter Penfold, had held talks with Sandline. The British Foreign Office admitted that this was true but justified the talks as occurring under "extraordinary circumstances."[93] Also in March 1998, Kabbah was restored to power with help from Nigerian-led Economic Community of West African States Monitoring Group (ECOMOG) forces.[94]

Then, in May 1998, the extent of Sandline's involvement in the region began to come to light, starting with a massive arms shipment to war-torn Sierra Leone that Sandline arguably had made in defiance of a U.N. Security Council embargo on the shipment of arms to any of Sierra Leone's warring factions. Security Council Resolution 1132, paragraph 6, states:

> [The Security Council] decides that all states shall prevent the sale or supply to Sierra Leone, by their nationals or from their territories, or using their flag vessels or aircraft, of petroleum products and arms and related materiel of all types, including weapons and ammunition, military vehicles and equipment, paramilitary equipment and spare parts for the aforementioned, whether or not originating in their territory.[95]

Due to the wording of this paragraph, specifically the reference to "Sierra Leone" instead of to the parties involved in the conflict, much confusion arose in the aftermath of the so-called Sandline Affair regarding whether the provision of arms by Sandline was prohibited by the arms embargo.[96] Sandline had shipped approximately 1,000 AK-47 rifles, 60 mm mortars, light machine guns, and ammunition to Sierra Leone, where they were handed over to Nigerian peacekeepers, who later distributed the weapons. The Nigerians replaced some of their own older equipment with equipment from the Sandline shipment as well.[97]

Sandline president Timothy Spicer then made a statement directly implicating Britain in the affair, saying that he "understood and still believed that we were acting with the approval of Her Majesty's Government in assisting to restore President Kabbah."[98] When further details emerged, it became clear that Sandline's military consultants had met with Foreign Office officials, led by the deputy head of the Africa Department, on at least three separate occasions.[99] At least one of these meetings took place in the Foreign Office prior to Sandline's dispatch of arms to Sierra Leone. Sandline's lawyers sent a letter to the British Foreign Secretary in April 1998, providing further clues as to British involvement in hiring Sandline.[100] It states, in part:

> As you will be aware, the coup in Sierra Leone which removed President Kabbah was roundly condemned . . . and you, Sir, were widely reported as offering President Kabbah the full support of Her Majesty's Government in restoring the lawful government to power in Sierra Leone . . . At the suggestion of your High Commissioner in Freetown, Mr. Peter Penfold, President Kabbah asked our clients to provide [military] assistance. Thereafter negotiations proceeded with President Kabbah and . . . full briefings were given both personally and by telephone to representatives of Her Majesty's Government . . . our clients were led to believe that clearance was given at the Head of Department level . . . Our clients were assured . . . that the operation had the full support of Her Majesty's Government.[101]

This revelation proved to be an embarrassing scandal for the British government, whose Foreign Secretary, Robin Cook, had earlier insisted that he wanted Britain to pursue an "ethical" foreign policy.[102] In response, Cook initiated an inquiry, denying that ministers were involved in the decisionmaking process that led to Sandline's involvement in Sierra Leone.[103] This inquiry resulted in the "Report of the Sierra Leone Arms Investigation," otherwise known as the "Legg Report," which found that "The [Foreign and Commonwealth Office (FCO)] should have explained the arms embargo imposed by the U.N. Resolution more effectively within Government and to the public, and especially its application to President Kabbah's government," and that, "as a result of these shortcomings in communications, officials and Ministers outside the FCO in London could not be expected to realise that to supply arms to President Kabbah's government without a license would be a breach of the arms embargo and a criminal offence."[104]

With regard to the actions of the British High Commissioner in Sierra Leone, Peter Penfold, the Legg Report concluded that "Mr. Penfold was given no warning of the scope of the arms embargo, and he did not realise that the supply of arms to President Kabbah's government was illegal."[105] Yet, it also concluded that, "At their lunch together on 23 December, Mr. Penfold knew that Mr. Spicer's project included supplying arms to President Kabbah, and he left Mr. Spicer with a reasonable belief that he supported the project. To this extent, Mr. Penfold gave it a degree of approval. He had no authority to do so."[106] Mr. Penfold was pulled out of Sierra Leone against his wishes in April

2000, amid speculation that Foreign Secretary Robin Cook was retaliating against him for his role in what had become known as the "Sandline Affair," also called the "Arms to Africa Affair."[107]

Meanwhile, the U.S. government was informed of Sandline's activities in Sierra Leone as well, as the Sandline lawyers made clear:

> At the same time, our clients kept informed the U.S. State Department at the highest level, including John Hirsch, the U.S. Ambassador to Sierra Leone, Charles Snyder, Director, Office of Regional Affairs and Dennis Linskey, Chief, West and Southern Africa Division. Furthermore, following support having been given for the proposed operation by both the U.S. Department of State and the U.S. Department of Defence (represented by Alan Holmes, Assistant Secretary of Defence for Special Operations), we understand that Michael Thomas, the Country Desk Officer for Sierra Leone at the U.S. Department of State met with Phillip Parham, the Africa Watcher at the British Embassy in Washington indicating the U.S. Government's full support for Sandline International's involvement, which was no doubt reported back to [the British Foreign Secretary's Office] in London.[108]

In the end, President Kabbah was restored to power pursuant to the Conakry agreement, but Sandline had supplied the weapons carried by the Nigerian force supporting his return, with the apparent knowledge and approval of high-level officials in both Britain and the United States.

Impact on Military Effectiveness and the Democratic Advantage

Both Executive Outcomes and Sandline were effective at promoting democracy and/or restoring the democratic regime to power in Sierra Leone, and thus both can be said to have improved the effectiveness of military components friendly to the democratic regime and outside democracies. Sandline improved the *quality* and *skill* of the force in question by supplying it with weapons and training, as evidenced by the fact that this Nigerian force was able to successfully restore President Kabbah to power (Proposition 1). In the case of Executive Outcomes, the firm improved military effectiveness by creating a militia of Kamajors loyal to the central government and directly fighting the RUF to restore order in Sierra Leone. EO troops thus acted as force multipliers to improve *quality* and trained Kamajors to improve *skill* and, in doing so, improved the *responsiveness* of the entire force fighting the RUF (Proposition 1). The extent of EO's impact on military effectiveness is illustrated by the fact that another coup followed EO's departure from the country, as predicted by EO officials.

Both Sandline and EO therefore increased the likelihood that the aims of outside democracies involved (Britain and the United States, primarily) would be reached by improving the military effectiveness of the pro-democracy forces in this case. However, the Sierra Leone case once again clearly illustrates the process through which major democracies seek to use private military and/ or security firms as proxies to intervene in conflicts against the will of the domestic public or the international community. The fact that Sierra Leone was under a U.N. arms embargo when Sandline attempted to import large quantities of weapons into Sierra Leone, with the knowledge and support of both British and U.S. government officials, is an illustration of private military and security firms being used as conduits for backdoor assistance in contravention of internationally imposed restraints. The domestic backlash in Britain following the media's revelation of the British government's involvement in the Sandline Affair suggests that the public would likely not have supported the British involvement in Sierra Leone—either directly through British military assistance or indirectly through Sandline—had they been aware of it at the time. Such a conclusion is reinforced by the fact that then-Prime Minister Tony Blair came under criticism from the British domestic public several years later due to his commitment of British troops to Sierra Leone to support the U.N. Mission in Sierra Leone (UNAMSIL).[109] The domestic backlash following the Arms to Africa affair is also significant in its indication that while PSCs may allow democratic governments to become covertly involved in outside conflicts without public scrutiny, if the domestic public should somehow learn of the PSC deployment, the public backlash may be equal to or worse than the electoral repercussions that would have resulted if the regular military had been overtly deployed instead of a PSC in the first place.[110]

Therefore, while force privatization may support the democratic advantage when the private firms in question bolster military effectiveness—as was seen when Sandline equipped the Nigerian force in question to successfully restore Kabbah to power—the Sandline case also illustrates that these private firms enable democracies such as Britain to circumvent the political constraints on conflict involvement that are at the core of democratic advantage theory's "selection effects" argument. By reducing the likelihood that the public will become aware of the democratic government's involvement in the conflict, the use of PSCs decreases the prospects that the democratic policymakers in question will allow a concern with electoral repercussions to guide their se-lection of conflicts in which to become involved. Yet, if PSC involvement is eventually exposed in public discourse, this negative impact on the selection effects side of the democratic advantage is mitigated, for democratic leaders will be punished by the electorate and forced to reassess their conflict involve-ment decisions in a manner consistent with public opinion.

COUNTERFACTUAL #2:
THE IRAN-CONTRA AFFAIR

The very public controversy sparked by the exposure of Sandline's involve-ment in Sierra Leone demonstrates how the populations of democracies can react to the perception that their governments are "going behind their backs" by covertly using unofficial channels to achieve ethically questionable mili-tary objectives. How then might such publics react in response to the covert use of *official* channels for the realization of ethically murky objectives? The Iran-Contra affair indicates that the reaction may be equally forceful, suggest-ing that the use of PSCs to substitute for covert official military or government involvement can—*when it succeeds in remaining covert*—allow democratic leaders both the invisibility and plausible deniability of involvement in a particular conflict.[111] When such covert PSC actions do not remain covert, however, as indicated by the Sierra Leone case, they can entail similar elec-toral repercussions to those experienced through the exposure of covert use of regular government or military forces.

The Iran-Contra affair comprised two convoluted arms deals that, when they came to light in the U.S. public in 1986, became a full-scale political scan-dal that seriously undermined the hitherto popular presidency of U.S. Presi-dent Ronald Reagan. The first part of the affair consisted of senior members of the Reagan administration facilitating the shipment of U.S. arms to Israel, who then sold the weapons on to an allegedly moderate Iranian faction. The Iranian faction in turn agreed to do their utmost to secure the release of U.S. hostages being held principally by the Shi'a Islamic militant group Hezbol-lah in Lebanon. The second part of the affair developed subsequently, when Lieutenant Colonel Oliver North, a military aide to the National Security Council, negotiated large mark-ups on the original price of weaponry sold to the Iranians. A percentage of the profit was then channeled to covertly fund anti-Communist Nicaraguan counterrevolutionaries (known collectively as the *contras*, or *anti-Sandinistas*).

Both parts of this deal were politically explosive from multiple angles.

At the time, Iran was engaged in a protracted war against Iraq and was subject to a U.N. arms embargo.[112] On the whole, the United States took a dim view of both of these belligerents, with Henry Kissinger famously remarking that it was "a pity they both can't lose."[113] Nonetheless, Washington did to some extent accept the view promulgated within the Sunni Islamic world that Iraq represented a bulwark against the extremist tendencies of revolutionary Shi'ism in Iran. President Reagan reportedly decided that "the United States could not afford to allow Iraq to lose the war with Iran" and issued a National Security Decision Directive to this effect in June 1982.[114] As a result, the United States provided Iraq with substantial military equipment and technological aid during the war. In 1984, Saddam initiated the "Tanker War" by attacking Iranian oil tankers, in the hopes of aggravating Iran into closing the Straits of Hormuz, which are vital to the transportation of global oil supplies. Such a move on Iran's part, he knew, would draw in Western powers. Iran did not take the bait, and the Straits of Hormuz remained open, but the United States, sufficiently alarmed, did indeed reiterate its support for Iraq.[115]

U.S. partisanship toward Iraq was subsequently scrutinized when it emerged that Saddam Hussein had employed chemical weapons in contravention of the Geneva Conventions against both the Iranian enemy and against his own Kurdish citizens during and immediately after the war. At the time, however, the policy brought into stark relief the U.S. president's decision to allow weapons to be sold via Israel to Iran, albeit to allegedly moderate elements. Despite Israel's role as the middleman broker in this deal—which reinforced National Security Advisor Robert McFarlane's initial efforts in 1985 to distance the United States from the perception that it was providing the revolutionary theocratic Iranian government directly with arms—in time the arrangement evolved, and the sales were in fact made to moderate members of the Iranian military and then to the government itself.

In January 1986, under McFarlane's successor John Poindexter, the arms deal took on a new dimension. On Lieutenant Colonel North's suggestion, Israel was cut out of the equation, and weapons began to flow directly from the United States to Iran at hugely inflated prices.[116] In total, between August 1985 and October 1986 the United States provided Iran with over 2500 TOW missiles, in addition to Hawk anti-aircraft missiles and spare parts.[117]

When the story broke in the United States, it was perceived starkly as an arms-for-hostages deal, and, indeed, President Reagan eventually publicly admitted that this was what it amounted to. Most humiliatingly, there was limited evidence that the policy achieved its intended effect. Of the seven U.S. hostages held by Hezbollah in Beirut, five were eventually released in 1985 and 1986, but one died while being held hostage and another was executed, and during that time three more were abducted by another Lebanese militant group.[118] In addition, Islamic Jihad (a branch of Hezbollah) claimed responsibility for downing a U.S. aircraft containing nearly 250 U.S. servicemen.[119]

The Nicaraguan side of the affair was equally contentious. The Sandinista National Liberation Front (FSLN) was the socialist political party who established pro-Marxist rule in Nicaragua in 1979 and remained in power until 1990.[120] Initially part of a junta that overthrew the previous government, the Sandinistas were elected by popular vote in 1984. In 1981, the various factions of "contras" established themselves in opposition to Communism, setting up a number of death squads to pursue this purpose and garnering significant covert support from the CIA in the early 1980s (albeit without the authorization of Congress).

In 1983, the Boland Amendment was applied to the Defense Appropriations Act. It is described in the *Thomas Bill Summary and Status* as:

> An amendment to prohibit covert assistance for military operations in Nicaragua and to authorize overt interdiction assistance. The overt interdiction assistance consists of assistance furnished by the President on terms he may dictate to any friendly country in Central America to enable that country to prevent the use of its territory for the transfer of military equipment from or through Cuba or Nicaragua or any other country. The assistance must be overt. For this overt aid $30,000,000 is provided for FY83 and $50,000,000 is provided for FY84.[121]

In spite of this regulation, when Admiral John Poindexter replaced Robert McFarlane as national security advisor in December 1985, Oliver North—in addition to proposing the direct sale of arms to Iran—implemented a $15 million "markup" on the asking price, which he then arranged to use to both fund the delivery of arms to the Nicaraguan contras and to negotiate with third countries to undertake acts of sabotage against the Nicaraguan Marxist government. North suggested to Poindexter that the United States should provide the Panamanian leader Manuel Noriega with $1 million "from 'Project Democracy' capital raised from the sale of U.S. arms to Iran for the Panamanian leader's help with destroying Nicaraguan economic investments."[122]

President Reagan himself does not appear to have been involved in this initiative, although his opposition to the Sandinistas was clearly established. In December 1981, Reagan had signed a "Finding" authorizing the CIA's paramilitary war against Nicaragua in the interests of U.S. national security.[123] In June 1984, the president discussed with top aides how to fund third countries to oppose the Communist Nicaraguan government, in order to circumvent congressional opposition to the CIA's activities in Nicaragua.[124] In September 1986, Oliver North met with the Panamanian ruler Manuel Noriega to negotiate an end to U.S. pressure on Panama for its drug smuggling activities in return for Panama undertaking to conduct sabotage operations against Nicaraguan targets.[125]

The U.S. public became aware of these proceedings after the Nicaraguan government shot down a plane carrying U.S. weapons bound for the contras. The sole survivor of the crash, Eugene Hasenfus (a CIA contractor and freight handler), was captured by the Sandinistas and told his part of the story.[126] A Lebanese journal subsequently broke the news internationally after an Iranian national, Mehdi Hashemi, leaked the Iranian side of the bargain.

North publicly bore the brunt of public and official accusations of wrongdoing, but, in reality, scores of senior officials in the Reagan administration, and particularly members of the National Security Council, played active parts in the Iran-Contra affair. This shocked the U.S. public, and attempts by North to destroy some of the evidence in the aftermath of the revelation only fueled the scandal. Fourteen officials were eventually charged with crimes, including then-Secretary of Defense Caspar Weinberger, Robert McFarlane, and John Poindexter, and eleven others were convicted (although six were subsequently pardoned by President George H. W. Bush).[127] Although President Reagan himself was not charged with any crimes, the Independent Counsel of the Prosecution found:

> As the White House section of this report describes in detail, the investigation found no credible evidence that President Reagan violated any criminal statute. The OIC could not prove that Reagan authorized or was aware of the diversion or that he had knowledge of the extent of North's control of the contra-resupply network. Nevertheless, he set the stage for the illegal activities of others by encouraging and, in general terms, ordering support of the contras during the October 1984 to October 1986 period when funds for the contras were cut off by the Boland Amendment, and in authorizing the sale of arms to Iran, in contravention of the U.S. embargo on such sales.[128]

Public opinion told its own story, as Reagan's popularity saw a dramatic 16 percent drop, according to the Gallup polls of December 4 and 5, 1986, a dip from which he never recovered.[129]

Impact on Military Effectiveness

This much of Iran-Contra affair is well known, largely because the U.S. press treated the issue as one of political scandal as opposed to an international policy affecting U.S. national security.[130] Less is known of how the provision of arms to Iranian and Nicaraguan factions affected their respective militaries' effectiveness. As with Sandline's role in Sierra Leone, in neither Iran nor Nicaragua were U.S. military forces deployed on the ground to fulfill a combat role (although CIA operatives were known to be active in Nicaragua). Rather, the focus was on covertly delivering arms to factions within the countries.

In the Iranian case, the precise identity of the recipients of U.S. arms has proven remarkably difficult to establish, possibly because Reagan's officials themselves did not know who they were.[131] The initial arrangement was supposedly with political "moderates" believed to favor better relations with the West. An Iranian expatriate, Manucher Ghorbanifar, brokered the deal in 1985, claiming to speak for leading factions in Iran whom he alleged wanted better relations with the West. These included the prime minister, Shi'a religious leaders, and the speaker of Parliament. But even if it was the case that these individuals genuinely sought dialogue with the United States and were not particularly enthusiastic about the existing theocracy in Iran, this in no way suggested that they were particularly democratic in their outlook, and the fact that they clearly exercised influence over Hezbollah in Lebanon was itself indicative of their own willingness to negotiate with groups undertaking terrorist acts.[132]

When assessing whether the United States was effective in achieving its military objectives, we face the difficulty of identifying its overall objective: Was it the promotion of Iranian moderates who could counter the revolutionary regime, or was it the release of U.S. hostages in Lebanon? In neither case can the outcome be assessed as fully, or even at all, successful. Ayatollah Khomeini was not replaced, nor were all of the hostages released. The irony was that the Iranian side almost certainly did not use the weapons supplied for either of these purposes but rather for Iran's war against Iraq, whom the United States was militarily supporting. The impact of the U.S. weaponry sold to Iran under the Iran-Contra deal cannot have been extensive given the scale of the Iran–Iraq War, though the weapons undoubtedly strengthened the

Iranian military's *quality* to at least a limited extent, or they would not have been valued—and hence purchased—by Iran.[133] Furthermore, since the United States was not involved in training or professionalizing the Iranian army in any way, the United States cannot be said to have improved the latter's *skill*.

The effect of U.S. support to the efficiency of the Nicaraguan contras is more difficult to judge. In 1986, support from the U.S. administration to the contras was nothing new. The contras were a disparate collection of anti-Sandinista factions whose own ideological intentions differed, although two major fronts emerged among them as a result of the merger of smaller factions: the Nicaraguan Democratic Force based in Honduras and the Democratic Revolutionary Alliance based in Costa Rica.[134] Since their formation in 1981, the contras had enjoyed considerable U.S. backing for a guerilla war waged against the Sandinista government, in which an estimated 40,000 were killed.[135] The Boland Amendment outlawed direct covert U.S. funding to the contras, although funding to third parties who were sheltering contras and/ or engaged in anti-Sandinista activities was allowed to continue, with conditions.[136] Even after the Sandinistas won 67 percent of the popular vote in 1984, the latter type of U.S. funding continued, but the scandalous element of the Iran-Contra affair was that Oliver North authorized diverted funds for providing weapons *directly* to the contras once again, as well as to third parties.

It is unclear precisely what the contras got in terms of weaponry during the period under review. In addition to shipments arranged through North, the CIA channeled Soviet-type munitions that Israel had confiscated from the PLO in 1982 and the United States had subsequently acquired.[137] Assessing the quantity of arms provided, Lumpe notes that:

> Although the full extent of covert arms aid to the contras has never been established, the available documentation suggests that it was substantial. In one memo sent to CIA Director William Casey in July 1986, retired Major General John Singlaub (a key figure in the covert supply operation) discussed a pending delivery of 10,000 Kalashnikov AKM assault rifles, 200 RPG-7 rocket launchers, 200 60mm mortars, 50 82mm mortars, 60 112.7mm machine guns, 50 SA-7 portable surface to air missiles, and related ammunition. Other evidence of large arms shipments comes from the transcripts of radio communications between the contras and their contacts at the CIA. On April 12, 1986, for instance, a rebel field commander radioed a CIA official to acknowledge that his forces had received an airdrop of 20,000 pounds of military equipment, including German type G3 assault rifles, rifle magazines and ammunition,

RPG-7 rockets, grenades, and grenade launchers. Because supply operations of this type were conducted on a regular basis for several years, it is clear that substantial quantities of small arms and other light weapons were given to the contras during this period. These supply operations would have continued had not an Enterprise-owned Fairchild C-123K cargo plane been shot down on October 5, 1986 . . .[138]

The military *quality* of the contras was clearly enhanced through the provision of such weaponry. Furthermore, U.S. military aid to the contras did not in fact end with the exposure of the Iran-Contra affair; in June 1988, Congress approved a further $100 million in funding for the contras.[139] In sum, U.S. contributions to the contras were undoubtedly vital to the latter's ability to sustain a guerilla war against the FSLN throughout most of the 1980s, including the period of the Iran-Contra affair. Although the contras never succeeded in militarily overthrowing the Nicaraguan government, they did drive the FSLN leader Daniel Ortega to political reconciliation with them, which eventually led to a 1990 election in which the U.S.-backed Violeta Barrios de Chamorro won.[140] In this sense, the U.S. arms can be said to have improved the *responsiveness* of the contras, while covert CIA support in training and tactics may have improved both their *quality* and *responsiveness*.

Impact on the Democratic Advantage

In terms of the democratic advantage, the Reagan administration clearly desired to keep its weapons sales to Iran and its aid to the contras out of the public view, seeking to bypass the electoral constraints on conflict selectivity that are hypothesized to give democracies an inherent advantage in warfare. The fact that it failed to do so indicates the difficulty that democratic governments have in keeping such actions covert; hence the incentive for democracies to hire PSCs to carry out covert or relatively covert missions for them, as exemplified by MPRI's role in Croatia. Yet, the fact that the Sandline affair explored earlier in the chapter was similarly exposed and resulted in electoral repercussions illustrates that PSCs are not always flawless when it comes to conducting covert operations either. Certainly Reagan's administration portrayed the contras as the democratic alternative to the Marxist Sandinistas, attempting to rename them the "Democratic Resistance" as opposed to the rather more negative or reactionary sounding "contras." But for many years within Nicaragua itself, much of the populace *did* see the FSLN as a democratic option; so much so that 67 percent of the popular vote went to the FSLN in 1983. At the same time, the guerilla tactics employed by the contras were often brutal and sadistic. It was often claimed that they were guilty of terrorizing Nicaraguan citizens by raping, torturing, and dismembering supporters of the government. Such humanitarian abuses, even when perpetuated by a state or faction portrayed by U.S. policymakers as the democratic alternative to communist forces in the region, carried a risk for U.S. leaders seen as supporting the state or faction in question. If the public were to learn of direct U.S. support to these factions, there was a distinct risk of severe electoral repercussions or at least a major public outcry against the political party in question. That such an outcry ensued following the disclosure of the Iran-Contra affair and resulted in an irreversible drop in President Reagan's approval ratings proves this point. While the exposure of the British government's involvement in the Sandline affair led to a similar public outcry, the notion that PSC involvement is less likely to be exposed—and, if exposed, the connection between the PSC and the democracy might be plausibly denied—means that PSC involvement is therefore less likely to result in such public electoral repercussions, making PSCs an attractive alternative to policymakers seeking to involve their states in conflicts of which the public might disapprove.

Interestingly, however, this outcry did not result in the termination of U.S. support to the contras. Indeed, while both the Iranian and the Nicaraguan ends of the affair were roundly condemned when they were publicly revealed and the scandal saw an end to the arms deals with Iran, funding to the Nicaraguan contras continued steadily for several years in one form or another following its public exposure.

This continuation of funding in itself arguably demonstrates U.S. public opinion at the time in general. Military support to Iran seemed utterly unjustifiable. The bloody 1979 Iranian revolution that overthrew the shah, a staunch U.S. ally, was fresh in the memory of the U.S. public; the support that revolutionary Iran lent to the terrorist Lebanese Hezbollah was well known; and the principle of non-negotiation with terrorist groups was, in 1986, an established U.S. dictum. In short, the Iranian theocracy was entirely alien and hostile in the eyes of the American public.

By contrast, the plight of the contras in Nicaragua was somewhat more appealing to many Americans. At the height of the Cold War, the threat of international Communism appeared very real, and the U.S. media regularly echoed this fear. The Reagan administration fully embraced this position in order to demonize the Sandinistas and champion the contras. Even after the international community, including the International Court of Justice, had issued successive condemnations of the CIA's role in the Nicaraguan civil war, funding continued. The very implementation of the Boland Amendment was not so much an expression of blanket disapproval of funding to the contras as it was a bitter complaint that the administration, and particularly the CIA, had circumvented the powers of Congress to provide this funding. When the Iran-Contra story broke, it was the perception of sneakiness on the part of so many senior officials that the press and the public seemed to find so distasteful, rather than the funding of the contras itself.

This is similar to the public's dismay in the Sandline case, a dismay that centered not so much on the provision of weapons to support the return of a democratic regime in Sierra Leone as it did on the government's covert acquiescence to the use of a private military firm to supply the weapons. Again, both cases therefore indicate that if the democratic electorate learns of actions intended to covertly involve their state in a conflict—regardless of whether such actions are perpetuated directly by the government or regular military or are conducted indirectly by a PSC substituting for the government or military—the resulting electoral backlash may be worse than if the action had been conducted in an overt fashion in the first place. Of course, if the public never learns of such actions, or if they are minimized in public discourse (as occurred in the MPRI case), they have a negative impact on democratic leaders' conflict selectivity and thus a negative impact on the democratic advantage. If Reagan administration officials had hired a PSC, one could imagine, hypothetically, that this might have minimized the Reagan administration's risks in the Iran-Contra dealings by improving the odds that the dealings would have remained covert and/or that the administration could have plausibly denied its involvement in the scandal if it did become public. However, the use of a PSC is clearly not foolproof in terms of assuring secretiveness.

CONCLUSION

This chapter has analyzed two different cases involving a PSC hired in place of the regular military, as well as two counterfactual cases in which direct U.S. involvement occurred. In Croatia, a third party (the United States) brokered a deal to hire MPRI to train the Croatian military. In the Lebanese Civil War, by contrast, the U.S. military intervened directly to train the Lebanese Armed Forces. In Sierra Leone, British and American officials approved the actions of a PSC in funneling weapons to friendly actors in contravention of a U.N. arms embargo, the approval of which led to a scandal in Britain when it was later revealed. In the Iran-Contra affair, U.S. government officials directly arranged for the transfer of arms to Iran in exchange for hostages and to support the Nicaraguan anti-communist contras.

Though their facts vary, these cases—when taken as a whole—indicate that PSCs deployed in place of the regular military often bolster the tactical, operational, and/or strategic military effectiveness of the host nation actors they are tasked with assisting, as long as the long-term strategy underlying the entire operation is sound in the first place. Notably, however, it is difficult to conclusively argue based on the facts of these cases that PSCs have a *better* impact on the military effectiveness of the host nation's military than would the democratic intervening state's regular military, if it were deployed in place of a PSC. There is one possible exception to this, as indicated by a comparison of the Croatian and Lebanese cases: PSCs may be more likely to have a beneficial impact on military effectiveness than are regular military forces in situations of counterinsurgency due to their potentially heightened ability to evade the laws and norms of international humanitarian law. Because IHL non-compliance correlates with increased military effectiveness in both the Croatian and Lebanese cases, they both seem to provide support for the draining-the-sea approach as opposed to the hearts-and-minds approach to counterinsurgency warfare. Significantly, however, it is difficult to draw a conclusive causal link between non-compliance and increased effectiveness in either case.

The democratic advantage also suffers in both cases of PSC employment examined here, as hiring PSCs in place of the regular military allows states to engage in military actions outside the public eye. This hinders the electorate's capability to limit their government's involvement in risky conflicts and, according to the reasoning of the selection effects argument, makes it less likely that democratic governments hiring PSCs in this manner will tend to enter into "winnable" conflicts. However, a comparison of the Sandline and Iran-Contra cases shows that—while it might be less likely to be exposed in the first place and carries with it the possibility of plausible deniability for the democratic policymakers in question—if covert, government-supported PSC involvement *is* ultimately exposed, it can lead to a public backlash against the democratic leadership similar to the backlash experienced when direct, covert democratic military or government involvement is exposed.

5 HISTORICAL INSIGHTS
Mercenary and Auxiliary Forces
Integrated into National Militaries

THE CASES EXAMINED in the past two chapters were all relatively recent cases of modern private security companies acting as middlemen between the state and individual soldiers-for-hire. As explored in Chapter 3, one critical issue determining the degree to which modern PSCs have a beneficial impact on military effectiveness is the degree to which PSCs are required to work alongside regular military forces and the extent to which the two groups are able to work together harmoniously. The purpose of this chapter, therefore, is twofold: It seeks both to illustrate that recent uses of mercenary-like forces have a long historical trajectory preceding them and to explore the question of what it would take to make modern PSCs and the military work together well. To that end, and in an effort to generate insights relevant to modern instances of PSC employment, this chapter examines two historical cases that suggest relationships between certain uses of mercenary and auxiliary forces and particular outcomes. The analysis below explores the cases of the condottieri hired by the Italian city-states from the thirteenth through fifteenth centuries and the Hessian Army hired to fight for the British in the American Revolution from 1776 through 1783.

These cases were selected for several reasons. Aside from constituting examples of successful integration of mercenary or auxiliary forces and regular forces, both cases entail a grouped, foreign (and, in the case of the condottieri, profit-motivated) force analogous in many ways to a modern PSC. Indeed, as noted in Chapter 1, while PSCs are not mercenaries per se, both they and auxiliary forces are more mercenary-like than are regular military forces; therefore, these historical cases of mercenary and auxiliary force employment hold significant lessons to inform future uses of PSCs.[1]

Questions of compliance with normative expectations of humanitarian conduct arise in both cases as well. Furthermore, the Hessians were engaged in counterinsurgency warfare to at least some extent in the conflicts examined, fighting on the part of a major power seeking to put down a rebellion in its colonies. The style of warfare seen in this case is therefore comparable to the other cases explored in this study. Taken together, these two cases are therefore model cases from which to extrapolate lessons relevant to the study at hand and modern situations of PSC use. Both of these cases provide unique insight into the major theoretical issues probed in this study: the impact of private security companies on military effectiveness and the democratic advantage, the impact of force privatization on the state, and the relevance of structural and identity-based factors in defining PSC–military relations. Of primary importance, though, they provide insight into the policy-relevant questions examined here, particularly the overarching question of how best to insure that PSC deployment has a beneficial impact on military effectiveness and, by extension, the democratic advantage.

With these contributions in mind, the remainder of this chapter proceeds first with an exploration of the condottieri, followed by an examination of the Hessian case. Finally, the chapter examines the relationship of the state to the force in question in these two cases, with the aim of comparing this relationship with the state's role in the cases explored in Chapters 3 and 4. Through this analysis, it becomes clear that structurally integrating a mercenary or auxiliary force into the regular military can be quite effective in helping the overall force to overcome its identity differences with the mercenary or auxiliary force, improving the prospects that the mercenaries and auxiliaries will improve rather than harm military effectiveness. Yet, such a strategy is not foolproof, as illustrated by the Hessian case and the case of Sir John Hawkwood's White Company fighting alongside the Pisans against the Florentines in 1364. The chapter's overall message, therefore, is that both structural and identity variables are significant in determining a hired force's impact on overall military effectiveness. The cases in this chapter also indicate that: (a) regular military forces may be no more likely to comply with humanitarian norms than are mercenary or auxiliary forces; and (b) the structural constraints argued by democratic advantage theorists to be unique to democracies—and to lead to the theorized propensity for democracies to be disproportionately victorious in their conflicts—might, in fact, occur in some non-democracies as well.

THE CONDOTTIERI AND THE ITALIAN CITY-STATES

Background

The history of the mercenaries, or condottieri,[2] in the Italian city-states spanned the era of the Italian Renaissance, extending over three centuries. The records of the prominent fifteenth- and sixteenth-century politician and strategist Niccolo Machiavelli have famously maligned the influence of the condottieri:

> You must understand that the empire has recently come to be repudiated in Italy, that the Pope has acquired more temporal power, and that Italy has been divided up into more states, for the reason that many of the great cities took up arms against their nobles, who, formerly favored by the emperor, were oppressing them, whilst the Church was favoring them so as to gain authority in temporal power: in many others their citizens became princes. From this it came to pass that Italy fell partly into the hands of the Church and of republics, and, the Church consisting of priest and the republic of citizens unaccustomed to arms, both commenced to enlist foreigners.[3]

Machiavelli's writings immortalize some of the most damning criticisms about mercenaries: that they are either cowardly or scheming; that they charge exorbitant fees; that they have no patriotic allegiances; that they are quick to avoid war and slow to die in their employer's cause. There are various examples of these qualities recorded in chronicles from the thirteenth through fifteenth centuries. However, Machiavelli's criticisms hide the sheer diversity of condottieri roles over three centuries: the conditions of their employment, their individual and group identities, and their military strategies. For most of the period in question, Italian princes did not have the means to raise armies purely from among their own citizens. As a consequence, the weaponry and strategies brought to the battlefield by the condottieri played a large part in determining the modes of war fighting during the Italian Renaissance.

While the exploits of the Free Companies in the fourteenth and fifteenth centuries brought fame and notoriety in equal measure to the condottieri en masse, mercenary companies had been used in Italy since at least the early twelfth century, and on a purely individual basis for much longer. In the

Middle Ages, when war was common but standing armies were an unfamiliar concept and emergency armies difficult to raise on short notice, mercenaries were used all over Europe. In Italy, however, the tradition ran particularly strong. There are several related explanations for this. The central papal states divided Italy's north from its south around 1100, and Italian lands were broken down into feudal entities ruled by knights. Joseph Jay tells how, with the growth of commerce, flourishing self-administered towns known as *communi* arose under the influence of successful merchants who resisted the influence of both the Church and the Holy Roman Empire. Merchants, unlike noblemen, had no training in arms and were thus obliged to hire their soldiers.[4] The Church, for its part, while eager to continue increasing its wealth and its territories, did not have the army to do so. It therefore also resorted to mercenaries.[5] Aside from the lack of military training, the lack of any one central authority in the Italian city-states that could muster forces that might overwhelm those of any "self-made adventurer" was another reason for the city-states' heavy reliance on mercenaries.[6]

This is not to say that the communes and city-states of the twelfth and thirteenth centuries made no attempts to raise their own armies in times of need. Daniel Waley's book on Italian city-republics describes how communes called on their nobles and other wealthy citizens to keep a horse suitable for cavalry service: "By 1162 if not earlier, three hundred Pisan milites had to swear that they would provide war-horses."[7] As for the infantry, these were drawn from the remainder of the adult male population.[8] However, it seems clear that the majority of the larger commerce-based states also had recourse to mercenaries—whether through necessity because they lacked the prerequisite cavalry and trained infantry, for convenience due to speed of preparedness, or due to the misgivings of rulers about arming their own local population.[9]

There are multiple accounts of Italian rulers contracting mercenary and/or what Machiavelli would later term "auxiliary" forces—that is, the forces of another ruler—over the course of the thirteenth century. For instance, in 1216 the commune Rimini paid the counts of Montefeltro to raise 300 odd cavalry and infantry, and in 1225 Genoa contracted the Count of Savoy to send 200 cavalry for two months at a rate of 16 lire per man per month.[10] These mercenary forces appear for the most part to have supplemented, or in some cases to have led, the remainder of the state's forces or local militia in battle.

By the late thirteenth century, therefore, some states had abandoned the idea of raising their own armies, focusing instead on hiring mercenary armies.

Although the employment of foreign ad hoc forces was initially done via contracts with other rulers of feudal leaders, mercenary forces began to band together of their own accord as the practice of hiring them became more widespread.[11] The age of the so-called Free Companies in the fourteenth century developed following the signing of the Treaty of Bretigny between Britain and France in 1360. The sudden end to the war signaled by the treaty's signing left thousands of unemployed soldiers in its wake, many of whom were reluctant to give up the fight and go home. As a result, they rebanded with a new set of objectives: "The Free Companies spread all over France like the plague that had preceded them only a few years earlier."[12] In addition to English and French soldiers, these companies included Germans, Flemish, and Gascons.

Several of the largest companies found their way to Italy. The Free Companies were fluid: They fought for whomever would pay them, their members came and left on a regular basis, and at times of relative peace they were semi-dissolved, although the larger city-states such as Florence frequently contracted condottieri for defensive roles in peacetime.[13] Often, it seems, the city-states' main objective in such peacetime contracting was to prevent the mercenaries from selling their services to rival states.

The fifteenth century saw the gradual decline of the fortunes of the Free Companies. Despite the fact that these mercenaries fought centuries prior to the development of the Westphalian state system, some sovereigns began to view these mercenary armies as a threat to their own security as early as the fifteenth century and thus began to subsume individual mercenaries into their own armies.[14] By the middle of the century, some states (including Milan) had already begun to build up their own professional armies, and condottieri became increasingly tied down to long-term contracts lasting a year or longer, designed by city-state rulers to standardize their fighting forces.[15]

Eventually, the evolution of warfare in Europe as a whole gradually diminished the prospects and influence of private mercenaries. War became a far more expensive endeavor, with the cost of heavy artillery and armaments that were increasingly used in battles in the sixteenth century rising above the purchasing power of condottieri companies. A professionalized infantry began to develop, and war became the preserve of states rather than mercenaries.[16]

Judging by existing historical accounts, then, the characteristics of the *condottieri* evolved over the course of the thirteenth through fifteenth centuries. One can identify four rough phases in their evolution, based primarily on the extent to which they served as individuals, were integrated into cohesive companies, and/or were integrated into the regular military forces alongside which they served. During the first period, the condottieri emerged as a prevalent force and were used individually alongside city-state militias. Then, primarily in the fourteenth century, the condottieri system maintained fairly permanent companies of armed military specialists. It was during this second stage, the era of the Free Companies, that the condottieri really became established as a predominant military force. The third stage followed the demise of the Free Companies in the fifteenth century and was signified by the rising prominence of condottieri commanders of Italian noble blood in place of foreigners. In the final stage, the condottieri started to be replaced by standing armies akin to modern state armies, and were integrated into them to a greater or lesser extent. During this fourth stage, individual condottieri became increasingly involved in politics as well.[17]

The development of mercenary companies in the Italian city-states was therefore what one historian has called a "spasmodic affair," but it is clear that by the middle of the thirteenth century the condottieri were accepted as a regular feature of Italian life.[18] These foreign, profit-motivated forces had a varying impact on the battles in which they fought over the extended course of their existence, but more often than not they were successful in battle due to their superior organization, numbers, and weaponry. When serving individually, the condottieri acted principally as force multipliers. They remained under the control of the ruling commander and in this sense did not significantly differ in function from fighters drawn from the *communi* and the militias.

Serving as companies in the fourteenth century, however, they were organized with a clearly delineated command structure that led them to develop an esprit de corps among themselves and a sound basis for working together, just as in a standing army. The discipline, esprit de corps, and tactics pursued became decisive factors during this period. Their foreign quality could also be beneficial if it meant that they brought new and successful weaponry and tactics with them, as was the case with the primarily English White Company that is explored in greater detail below. This was not a given, however, because not every foreign culture had novel warfare tactics to contribute. The condottieri could also hinder military effectiveness in that their private, profit-motivated nature meant that they were open to bribery. Indeed, on more than one occasion the condottieri were known to switch sides in a battle when bribed to do so. During the War of the Eight Saints (1375–1378), for instance, a company of Breton mercenaries split apart, unsure as to whether they would receive payment from their papal employers. One faction went north to fight for Pisa, another stayed with the pope, and a third remained in the Sienese *contado* to loot and pillage.[19]

The loyalty of the condottieri companies was often therefore in question until late in the fourteenth and fifteenth centuries, when governments began to develop more permanent ties with the condottieri and to subsume them into state armies. The structure of condottieri deployments and the variance in condottieri identities, both of which are explored in greater detail in the following pages, were therefore quite significant.

A Broad Range of Condottieri Identities

Given the vast numbers of condottieri employed during the Renaissance period by the Italian city-states, it is not surprising that they displayed a wide range of identity characteristics apart from their nationalities. As Geoffrey Trease notes,

> In disposition, tastes, and ambitions, these men were as diverse as their backgrounds. Sigismondo Malatesta was reckoned a master of depravity, his neighbor and professional adversary, Federigo of Urbino, a pattern of humanity: both were passionate art-lovers and lavish patrons. Some condottieri, like [Sir John] Hawkwood, hoped for nothing but a peaceful and comfortable old age . . . yet other mercenary captains, by contrast, were consumed by lust for power. They risked and sometimes lost their lives in bids to seize the signoria, or lordship, of a city and establish their own dynasty . . . So there were treacherous condottieri and honest ones, avaricious and open-handed, illiterate and cultivated, calculating and impetuous . . .[20]

Of particular relevance to the study at hand is the issue of ethical behavior in condottieri warfare. Varying accounts exist on this issue; some claim that the condottieri were excessively humane, at least at the top levels of leadership, working out truces among themselves prior to battles and therefore shedding little blood on the actual battlefield.[21] Others claim that these accounts of bloodless battles are grossly exaggerated, but that many battles resulted in only lower-level personnel being killed in relatively small numbers, with condottieri leaders often murdered only outside of battle due to their political involvements.[22] Such accounts claim that these attempts at humane behavior were not respected by states at the time because inhumanity in warfare was the accepted norm:

> Indeed warfare in Italy, fought between condottieri who knew and to a certain extent respected each other, became more and more stylized. Carmagnola in

his later days fought a great battle against Piccinino and captured 5,000 horse-men and 5,000 footmen: no one was killed, though the slaughter of horses was incredible . . . *These later condottieri were the most civilized and humane of all war-makers, but the modern nation states, accustomed like tribal barbarians to reckon the seriousness of war by the slaughter it involves, would sneer foolishly at such proofs of civilization* (emphasis added).[23]

Still others remind us that the condottieri were famous for pillaging and marauding the countryside during peacetime and for forcing Italian cities to either fight them or to bribe them to forestall their raids.[24] While non-merce-nary forces were reportedly no less brutal during wartime, mercenary armies did not wait for the outbreak of war to engage in such misdemeanors:

In 1394 the mercenary captain and lord of Perugia, Biondo Michelotti, wrote to Siena with the news that his men were short of money and might turn their attention to the Sienese *contado* to remedy the situation; indeed, the records of Siena for the later 14th century are full of laments of the damage done to rural communities by the two "plagues" of disease and mercenary soldiery.[25]

Furthermore, the brutality of the condottieri at times was spurred on by at-tempts to avenge the killings of mercenary forces associated with these regular forces:

First at Faenza in 1376 and then at Cesena in 1377, the papal mercenaries car-ried out massacres of the civilian populations which were to be permanent stains on the records of Italian warfare. In both cases it was the papal officials who were as much to blame as the soldiers, and particularly the legate, Cardi-nal Robert of Geneva, who at Cesena demanded the blood of the entire popu-lation in revenge for the murder of some of his mercenaries.[26]

At times, these raids led the condottieri to be challenged and defeated militar-ily, thus indicating that their inhumane behavior decreased overall military effectiveness. As Michael Mallet notes:

Despite its size and experience, the Great Company was by no means invin-cible. Twice during these years it was humiliated by the army of Florence. In July 1358 when the Company had been called southwards to help Siena against Perugia, Conrad of Landau negotiated with Florence a free passage for his troops through the valleys of the Apenines on the eastern frontiers of the Florentine state. But the mercenaries got out of hand and began to despoil the countryside, so the Florentines quickly took action against them . . . The German and Hungarian cavalry were helpless against the hail of stones and crossbow bolts directed at them from the slopes above, and the majority were killed or captured. The Company, however, soon reformed in the Romagna and, joined by Bongarten, made an attempt the next year to revenge itself on Florence . . . But the Florentine captain general, Pandolfo Malatesta, was waiting for them with a powerful mercenary army and put them to flight at Camp delle Mosche.[27]

Such a recounting of events provides evidence to support the notion that mercenaries' non-compliance with the ethical norms preceding modern-day international humanitarian law decreases military effectiveness by undermining attempts to co-opt the citizenry, thus decreasing military *responsiveness* (Proposition 2b).

Therefore, while it is difficult to draw generalized conclusions regarding the comparative adherence of condottieri and regular military forces at the time to moral standards due to the fact that warfare during this period was often brutal and uncivilized, it appears that—at least in some cases—the condottieri companies' foreign, private nature made them willing to ravage the countryside in a manner that eventually led them to be targeted by regular forces and defeated militarily. Furthermore, we can distinguish among levels of ethical behavior at several different stages in the evolution of the condottieri, as it appears that many of the Free Companies were formed in the fourteenth century with the objective of pillaging and looting the countryside. The condottieri employed by these companies had made a living from war in the past and did not know what else to do with themselves once the major wars had subsided. Once the condottieri system became a more rooted part of the establishment in the fifteenth century, however, condottieri leaders became increasingly politically involved and, as such, had less inclination to ravage the countryside. Furthermore, by the fifteenth century condottieri commanders were predominantly Italian. Though they were often exiles from rival states, they later became embedded in the society itself. For instance, the pope's own son, Cesare Borgia, was in his time a cardinal, duke, condottiere, and employer of other condottieri. Meanwhile, Muzio Atendolo Sforza went from being a condottiere to being grand constable of the Kingdom of Naples, including a salary of 8,000 ducats and lordship of several castles. His son Francesco later became duke of Milan.[28] Such integration into formal political society reduced the appeal of inhumane behavior.

Aside from issues of ethical behavior in warfare, identity characteristics of certain condottieri companies led to direct tactical and operational benefits that increased military effectiveness. The White Company, later commanded by Hawkwood, was known for the large numbers of Englishmen in its ranks, its well-polished armor, its formation (men-at-arms at the front, pages holding horses to the rear), its use of crossbow and longbow, the impressive stature and physique of many of its men, its considerable esprit de corps, and greater levels of discipline in battle than were normal in the mercenary companies. Its practices, furthermore, portrayed a level of determination and willingness to fight unusual among the mercenary companies: "They were accustomed to riding at night and fighting deep into the winter, and—unlike most mercenary troops—they were equipped for siege warfare, carrying with them special collapsible scaling ladders and bombards."[29]

Other condottieri displayed high levels of professional pride and individualized tactical innovations:

> Possibly the condottieri's professional pride would have resisted any attempt made to form them into a regular and subservient army. Militarily, as this pride grew each condottiere developed and refined his own tactics. Alberigo de Barbiano was the first to protect his horse with long tanned leather coverings, painted and decorated. His two pupils, Sforza and Braccio, formed their own schools of war: the "bracceschi" of the "scuola braccesca" were renowned for the impetus of their assault, and the "sforzeschi" for their tactical cunning and skill in manoeuvering. The later condottieri were all formed in one or the other of these schools, though each developed his own military style. Indeed, warfare in Italy, fought between condottieri who knew and to a certain extent respected each other, became more and more stylized.[30]

The tactical innovations developed within these unique, stylized forms of condottieri warfare were defining identity characteristics that had a direct impact on their military effectiveness, often leading them to victory.

A Military Command Structure and Integration with Regular Forces: The Battle of Campaldino and Hawkwood's Fight against Florence

The structure of condottieri deployments over the course of their evolution varied in a similar fashion to their broadly ranging identities. As noted above, condottieri in the thirteenth century were employed on more of an individual basis than were those in the fourteenth century, when the Free Companies reigned. Throughout the thirteenth century, a "sprinkling" of mercenaries were integrated into the militia armies of the Lombard and Tuscan leagues, acting as force multipliers to strengthen the militia ranks:[31]

> The typical army now taking the field on behalf of a commune was a mixed force. Genoa went to war in 1248 with 400 Genoese cavalrymen and the same number of mercenary horse recruited at Piacenza, in addition to 600 of her own crossbowmen and big Genoese garrisons in her fortresses: she also had no less than 32 galleys on a war footing. Mutatis *mutandis*, the Florentine forces arrayed against Pistoia half a century later (1302) comprised the same sort of combination; the 500 cavalry were all Florentines, whereas 1,000 of the 6,750 foot were mercenaries.[32]

This integration of individual condottieri and regular forces eventually evolved into the company structure seen in the form of the Free Companies, as it became recognized that hiring out entire companies of mercenaries to fight together was sensible because they fought better if they knew each other and had experience fighting together. As Mallett notes:

> Once large numbers of mercenaries were an accepted part of the Italian military system, their formation into organized companies under recognized leaders was inevitable. It was both easier for states to recruit whole companies, and their military efficiency was likely to be improved by long experience of fighting together. Thirteenth century warfare and its innovations demanded an increased sophistication of tactics and disciplined collaboration among the troops, which an experienced mercenary company at least offered the hope of achieving.[33]

Yet this was a rocky evolution at times, with the integration of individual condottieri and regular forces known to cause confusion and disorganization among the ranks on occasion. The Florentines relied on "temporary officials" as late as the Pazzi War, with the result that the Milanese and Venetian troops sent to Tuscany to support them complained bitterly about the administration of the combined army. As a commander in the Milanese lanze spezzate, Gian Jacopo Trivulzo, wrote at the time:

> These Florentine troops are so badly organized that it disgusts me; the men-at-arms are spread out in confusion, often with squadrons mixed up together in a way which seems to conform to no plan, and squadrons as much as a half a mile apart. The soldiers are billeted all over the place without any provision for

pioneers or other essential auxiliaries; there are very few infantry, about 700, of which 150 only are properly armed although I have made constant protests about this . . .[34]

While integration of condottieri and regular forces could therefore result in decreased military effectiveness due to a negative impact on the *integration* and *quality* of the overall force, at times such integration also benefited military *quality* through its force multiplying effects. This was shown, for instance, at the Battle of Campaldino in 1289, when the Tuscan Guelf League led by Florence handily defeated the Ghibellines led by Arezzo. The Guelf army consisted of 1,600 cavalry and approximately 10,000 infantry. It included 1,000 cavalry provided by Florence, nearly half of whom were mercenaries led by Amauri of Narbonne and his Angevin knights. The Ghibelline army was smaller, comprising about 800 cavalry and 8,000 infantry. The force multiplying effects of the Guelf army's mercenaries played a decisive role in their victory, as the Ghibelline army found itself caught in a crossfire from the wings of crossbowmen, leading the Ghibelline reserve to panic and flee while the Guelf reserve swept around the flanks and came in on the rear of the trapped enemy. The result was a complete Guelf victory, as over half of the Ghibelline army was killed or captured.[35]

Nearly a century later, one of the most widely reported exploits of the White Company under Sir John Hawkwood's command was its role in the services of the Pisans in their 1364 war against Florence. Again, this case appears to suggest that successful integration in battle boosted the success of the mercenaries and the regular forces alongside which they fought. Hawkwood's force was calculated at about 3,500 horsemen and 2,000 infantry, "his own company being combined with the rest of the Pisan forces."[36] The Pisans nevertheless struggled against the Florentine enemy, who for their part had appointed numerous German mercenaries, until Hawkwood's side was joined by another senior condottiere, Annechin Bongarden, together with 6,000 German and Swiss men at arms, giving Pisa the upper hand.[37]

Meanwhile, the Free Companies and the later predominantly Italian-led condottieri forces of the fifteenth century not only worked alongside regular militaries at times but were themselves often structured similar to standing armies, having regular command positions with specific units falling under those commanders. These units included both cavalry and infantry. For instance, Mallett notes, "Piero Gianpolo Orsini in papal service in 1437 had 800 cavalry and 200 infantry. His company was divided into six squadrons, including his own, and two of the squadron leaders were also members of the Orsini family."[38]

The presence of such command and unit structures, and the fact that many companies employed the same men for extended periods of time, insured that the foreign, profit-motivated mercenaries fighting in the companies were well integrated among themselves. This often benefited the companies' military effectiveness through its impact on their ability to communicate well with each other and therefore to be *responsive* militarily. This command structure also insured that condottieri were positioned in a manner that would use their skills as efficiently as possible, thus enhancing the *skill* of the entire company.

The Impact of the Condottieri on Military Effectiveness and the Processes Relevant to the Democratic Advantage

As the preceding analysis illustrates, both structural and identity characteristics of the individual condottieri and the associated Free Companies hired by the Italian city-states from the thirteenth through fifteenth centuries had an impact on these forces' abilities to be effective militarily. A tendency toward inhumane behavior led the mercenary companies of the fourteenth century to be both targeted and defeated militarily at times, thus decreasing their chances for overall military effectiveness (Proposition 2b). Yet, high levels of professional pride led to tactical innovations that in many cases led to victory for condottieri forces. The primarily English White Company, in particular, demonstrated numerous identity characteristics that impressed the Italians and aided its ability to be militarily effective, including a willingness to travel at night and to fight well into the winter months, a tendency to be well-armed and equipped, and high levels of discipline in battle (Proposition 1). Meanwhile, structural innovations such as the tendency to integrate individual condottieri into regular armies had a variable impact on military effectiveness, depending on the extent to which this integration was well organized and the resulting force was well equipped for the task at hand. The well-defined command structure of many of the Free Companies, however, clearly had a beneficial impact on military effectiveness.

The question of the condottieri's impact on the processes relevant to the democratic advantage is an interesting one because the Italian city-states during the period in question constituted a feudal society that was a far cry from today's democratic systems. Yet lessons relevant to the democratic advantage can nonetheless be gleaned from this case. As the condottieri often had a beneficial impact on military effectiveness due to their force-multiplying effects, their tactical innovations and military command structure, by extension they had a beneficial impact on the likelihood that those city-states hiring them would be victorious in their conflicts. Furthermore, the political involvement of many condottieri leaders, particularly later in the fifteenth century, led them to encourage conflict involvement from which they might benefit economically. Their economic interest in sustained periods of warfare is illustrated in a short vignette about John Hawkwood:

> Once, two friars greeted Hawkwood with the customary phrase "God give you peace!," to which he retorted . . . "God take from you your alms!" The friars said they meant no offense. "How," said Hawkwood, "when you pass by me and pray that God would make me die of hunger? Do you not know that I live by war and that peace would ruin me?"[39]

While this does not exactly mimic the electoral considerations of the democratic advantage's "selection effects" dynamic as it is generally theorized, it does speak to the issue of mercenaries impacting conflict selectivity through the combination of their political involvement and their economic interest in sustained warfare.

Another indication of the impact of the *condottieri* on the processes relevant to the "selection effects" side of the democratic advantage is illustrated by the agreement of most of the surviving literature on the Free Companies of the fourteenth and fifteenth centuries that despite—or perhaps because of—the specific skills of the condottieri, rulers' reliance on them contributed toward a failure to achieve conclusive victories or to reach lasting settlements. This made rulers less selective regarding the conflicts into which they entered, as there was an expectation that wars would be relatively minor and inconclusive. With regard to the major Free Companies, Mockler notes that "Pisa, Florence, Siena, Perugia and Lucca employed all of these companies, with varying fortune but no long-lasting results, against each other."[40] It is difficult to discern whether this state of affairs had more to do with the inherent mercantile characteristics of the Italian city-states at the time (whose trading tradition precluded imperialistic empire building), or with the nature of condottieri companies—namely, their professional ambitions to live to fight another day and their stylized fighting and overreliance on the cavalry resulting from such ambitions. Both factors were interrelated. It does seem that the inability of any of the city-states to establish primacy perpetuated constant warfare between them on a relatively minor scale, and the tactical maneuvers of the condottieri made it even more difficult for Italian rulers to inflict crushing defeats. For this reason, "they were rated by their critics as inferior to other European armies, and battles like Agincourt stunned Italians with their ferocity and casualties."[41]

Therefore the use of the condottieri could be said to increase both the need and the likelihood of rulers to engage in warfare, even if the outcome was far less bloody than it might have been had only *communi* forces (whose allegiances were arguably more closely connected to the city-states) been used. Italian rulers' conflict selectivity was thus negatively impacted by their ability to hire condottieri. The fact that the Italian city-states were not democracies at this time, however, means that this case provides evidence to refute democratic advantage theory, for it illustrates that the processes argued by democratic advantage theorists to be unique to democracies may actually be present in non-democracies as well. A similar dynamic is present in the Hessian case, which is explored in the following pages.

THE HESSIAN FORCES IN THE AMERICAN REVOLUTION, 1776–1783

Background

On June 16, 1775, Britain sustained huge losses at the Battle of Bunker Hill while striving to put down its American colonists' rebellion. The British government subsequently began to panic regarding its military capabilities to quell the rebellion in America. Fearing that the colonists could field 50,000 militiamen against the 30,000-man British Army (half of which was otherwise engaged in Ireland), the British proposed to hire 20,000 Russian auxiliaries from Catherine the Great. Catherine, however, refused to hire out any of her soldiers on grounds of principle "simply to calm a rebellion which is not supported by any foreign power."[42] The British then made an attempt to hire the Scots Brigade from the Dutch, but the States General offered to hire it out only "on condition that it should not be used outside Europe."[43] As a last resort, Britain turned to the German provinces for auxiliary forces.

Though the first few German princes refused the British request, in the end six different German rulers sold their troops to Britain to join the approximately 16,500 British soldiers fighting in the American Revolution at that point: Frederick II, Landgrave of Hesse-Cassel sent 16,992 troops; Duke Charles I of Brunswick sent 5,723 troops; Count William (Frederick II's son) of Hesse-Hanau sent 2,422 men; Margrave Charles Alexander of Anspach-Bayreuth sent 2,353 men; Prince Frederick of Waldeck sent 1,225 troops; and Prince Frederick Augustus of Anhalt-Zerbst sent 1,160 men.[44] Because Hesse-Cassel was the largest single contributor of the Germans deployed to America, the entire German auxiliary force deployed to America was and is commonly referred to as "Hessians."[45]

It has been argued that many of the Hessian soldiers deployed to America were forcibly recruited into the Hessian army to fill the quota of soldiers promised to Britain, though such claims are disputed. Joseph George Rosengarten, for instance, notes that the Hessian government republished an order directly following the Hessian parliament's conclusion of its 1777 treaty with Britain, stating:

> Officers guilty of enlisting men by force or unfair means will be dismissed from the service; non-commissioned officers and privates for the like offence will receive corporeal punishment, and the orders of their superiors will not protect them. Soldiers enlisted by force or trick shall be released at once without expense to them or any charge for food or pay, which shall be collected from the officer responsible for such illegal enlistment.[46]

Rosengarten therefore concludes, "No foreign subject was ever retained in the Hessian service against his will."[47] By another account, however, Hessian recruiters either successfully delivered the recruit to the place of deployment or shot him; desertion was *not* considered acceptable, whether or not you were caught.[48] Another account notes several instances in which deserters were brutally punished but not killed. In his diary, Hessian officer Johann Ernst Prechtel—when listing deserters—notes, "Private Schaeffer, of the first recruit shipment was brought back to the regiment and punished by having to run the gauntlet twelve times a day for two days in a row."[49] On another occasion, Prechtel notes that on February 17, 1780, "Private Katzenwinkel, who deserted on 10 March 1778, was not punished for his desertion, but because he had used the false name Major Ernst von Reitzenstein for a time, he was made to run the gauntlet twelve times."[50]

These two characteristics of the Hessian deployment call into question whether the Hessian soldiers were motivated to fight wholeheartedly in the American Revolution. Indeed, this was a foreign conflict in which they had no personal stake, and many did not want to be there to begin with. Some analysts and historians have argued that because of their lack of personal stake in the conflict, the Hessians were "reluctant soldiers at best."[51] The following discussion demonstrates that because the Hessian troops were structurally integrated into the British military as auxiliaries, they could benefit the British force without the risk that *integration* problems between the Hessian and British troops would hamper the prospects for success.[52] More beneficial than this, though, was the Hessians' impact as force-multipliers for the British military. Yet, despite these structural pre-conditions for success, identity variables—namely, the Hessian reputation for unwonted cruelty—as well as the forcible recruitment structure for these forces, led them to have an overall impact on British military effectiveness ranging from negligible to negative.

"The Most Militarized Society in All Germany"

Mercenaries were prevalent in most European conflicts in the seventeenth and eighteenth centuries, many of them employed by the Prussian Army of Frederick the Great. After the Seven Years' War ended in 1763, Frederick's foreign mercenaries returned home, causing the German princes to realize that they had a major war-fighting force available for export at a time when they faced financial difficulties.[53] The treaty concluded between Frederick II of Hesse-Cassel and Britain on January 31, 1776, followed almost a year of negotiations between the two states and was easily the most lucrative of the six treaties that Britain entered into with German rulers for the provision of troops. This was partly due to the fact that the British expected that quick dispatch of the Hessian forces would end the revolt in one or two campaigns and thus agreed to pay Frederick II twice the rate per soldier agreed on by the other German rulers until at least one year beyond the end of hostilities. Furthermore, the British agreed to indemnify Hesse-Cassel for the destruction suffered during its last war, backdated the treaty by two weeks in order to give Hesse-Cassel a large amount of cash up front to stimulate recruitment efforts, and pledged military assistance to Hesse-Cassel in case of an attack against its territory. Significantly for the military deployment, the British promised not to break up the Hessian forces or to commit them outside of North America and allowed them to be led by their own Hessian commanders.[54]

Frederick II anticipated that the treaty would allow him to reduce the country's taxes and otherwise improve its economy by bolstering the Hessian weapons and war-provisions industries and increasing soldiers' pay. Recent crop failures had aggravated the country's dual burdens of food shortages and rural overpopulation, and he hoped that this treaty could alleviate these problems. Therefore, while the individual Hessian soldiers' motivation may not have been primarily economic, the entire deployment can be said to have been motivated by profit considerations on the part of Frederick II.

The fact that Hesse-Cassel was clearly the most heavily militarized state in Europe certainly helped to cement the deal. The country maintained a 12,000-man field army, and another 12,000 militia served in garrisons; in other words, there was one soldier for every fifteen citizens, a ratio double that of Prussia's soldier-to-civilian ratio. It was relatively easy to maintain the military at these levels, as both economic and cultural incentives kept recruitment levels high. The many rural and urban poor in Hesse-Cassel often enlisted in the army to avoid starvation, and military families were exempt from paying income taxes. Furthermore, Hesse-Cassel's history of war against the Catholics and the French had instilled in the citizenry a general sense of obligation to defend the country. Enthusiasm for military life grew out of the high esteem in which the military was held, and the popular mythology of military adventure passed between generations.[55]

A Hessian officer returning from America noted that this military identity was not limited to Hesse-Cassel but was pervasive throughout the German states:

> Historians of all ages and peoples combine on this very point, that they portray the Germans as a very pugnacious and warloving people. Even envy of the meanest sort has never disputed their reputation for valour; it is woven into the spirit of the nation and stems from its very origin . . . This warlike spirit still prevails amongst the people into our present age; it is the distinguishing feature of their character.[56]

Hesse-Cassel's entire identity was so enveloped in its military presence that one traveler described it as "the most militarized society in all Germany," and another noted "before I came to Hesse I hardly knew what a military nation was."[57] This military identity stemmed from Hesse-Cassel's relationship with the outside world as well as the previously noted domestic influences, for its military was undisputedly the country's primary export industry.

When the time came to recruit additional soldiers to send to America, however, public support for the maintenance of a large military were in many cases subjugated to personal concerns of losing family members overseas in a conflict in which Hesse-Cassel itself had no stake. Indeed, many deserters were more concerned with the perils of the ocean crossing and the American wilderness, as well as the inevitable separation from their families, than they were opposed to fighting a foreign war. This is not to say, however, that deserters outnumbered volunteers signing up for the American deployment. Many joined the army specifically hoping to start a new life in America, a trend that the government could do little to forestall, as it was desperate to recruit the soldiers promised to Britain. Recruiters were also successful in their efforts by recruiting non-German citizens. Such soldiers came much closer to the traditional definition of "mercenaries" than did their Hessian "auxiliary" counterparts. Regardless of these nominal distinctions, however, all components of the Hessian force deployed to America were foreign to the conflict in which they were fighting, which had ramifications for their levels of motivation and morale.

Hessian Forces' Impact on Military Effectiveness and the Democratic Advantage

Both identity and structural factors were relevant in determining the Hessian forces' impact on British military effectiveness. Three structural factors were significant: the fact that the Hessian troops were allowed to remain in their own units under their own commanders, the fact that they were simultaneously integrated into the British military as auxiliary forces, and the fact that many of the Hessians were forcibly recruited to serve in this war in which they had no personal stake. They acted as a massive force multiplier, thus increasing the *quality* of the British deployment (Proposition 1). Furthermore, the fact that they were themselves a structured military force and were included in the structure of the British forces meant that the Hessian troops knew their position in the chain of command and thus did not harm the *integration* of the overall British force. Yet, the possibility that some may have been forcibly recruited meant that they may not have been motivated to fight to the best of their abilities, which may have lowered their demonstrated level of *skill* (Proposition 2). In fact, a large proportion of the 17,313 surviving German auxiliaries at the end of the war had been wounded or captured without winning a single battle in which Hessians or other Germans were pitted exclusively against Americans.[58]

The key identity factor was, as already mentioned, the Hessian military identity (a constitutive norm). Faith in this aspect of their identity likely contributed to the Hessians' few military successes in the American Revolution. Yet another identity characteristic recognized early on by the other parties to the conflict—the Hessians' tendencies for unwonted cruelty—led them to become the subject of ridicule by other parties to the conflict, and, ironically, to subsequently become much less feared by the other parties to the conflict.[59]

Hessian soldiers' journal entries from the American Revolution provide some indication of the Hessian forces' alleged cruel tendencies. Johann Georg

Zinn, auditor and regimental quartermaster of the Hesse-Cassel von Donop Regiment, noted in his journal during the Battle of Long Island in August 1776, "Another patrol from our regiment brought in many prisoners, however." The translator of Zinn's journal and an expert on Hessian forces in the Revolution, Bruce Burgoyne, notes following this statement "[Code—Many high ranking individuals at this time shed their ideas of being heroes. The prisoners who knelt and sought to surrender were beaten.]"[60] Another journal entry by Carl Friedrich Rueffer, an ensign and later a lieutenant in the Hesse-Cassel von Mirbach Regiment, writes of Hessian treatment of suspects in a string of arson incidents during the Battle of Harlem Heights in September and October 1776:

> There was a great fire behind our front at twelve o'clock at night, which we assumed to come from New York, and which we found to be the case as soon as it was light. About 100 rebels, who had remained hidden in the empty houses and cellars, set the fire and even though the English garrison, which consisted of three battalions, turned out at once, two churches and 400 houses to windward were laid in ashes. One of these criminals was thrown into the fire, another hung by the legs and burned . . . Several other suspicious persons were now and again thrown into the flames.[61]

The rebel forces wrote of the Hessians' cruelty in more descriptive terms. In a letter to the editor published in the *New York Times* in 1819, an anonymous writer quoted a "letter written by one John A. Gillett to his wife:"

> I was prisoner by the 27th day of August by a people called heshens (Hessians) and by a party called Gagers (Yagers or Jagers) the most Inhuman of all mortals. I can't give Room to picture them here; but thus much I at first Resolved not to be taken but by the Impertunity of the Seven taken with me and being surrounded on all sides by numbers I unhappily surrendered; would to God I never had then I should never (have) known their unmerciful cruelties; they first disarmed me they plundered me of all I had, watch Buckles money and sum clothing after which they abused me by bruising my flesh with the Butts of their (guns). They knocked me down. I got up and they (kept on) beating me almost all the way to there (camp) where I got shot of them—the next thing was I was almost starved to death by them . . . After giving you a small sketch of myself and troubles, I will Endeavor to faintly lead you into the poor situation the soldiers are in, especially those taken at Long Island, where I was; in fact, there cases are deplorable and they are Real objects of pity—they are still

confined and in houses where there is no fire—poor mortals, with little or no cloths, perishing with hunger . . . occasioned for want of food their natures are brook and gone, some almost loose their voices and some their hearing. They are crowded into churches and there guarded day and night. I can't paint the horrible appearance they make—it is shocking to human nature to behold them. Could I draw the curtain from before you there expose to your view a lean Jawd mortal . . . surrounded with tattered garments, Rotten Rags close beset with unwelcome vermin.[62]

Such actions likely did not contribute to British military effectiveness, as American defeats of primarily German forces handily outnumbered German victories in the American Revolution, as detailed in the following discussion. Looking to the British experience in the Boer War as an indication of the mechanisms related to cruelty in colonial wars, one might argue that the Hessians' inhumane treatment of civilians was counterproductive in achieving both its immediate and long-term goals because it resulted in opposition both within the British—and possibly even Hessian—ranks, as well as among public opinion in Britain and the American colonies.[63] Of particular importance in terms of battle outcomes were the Hessian defeats at Trenton, Bennington, and the attempted Springfield, New Jersey, raid of Knyphausen.[64]

Americans at the time noted that British regulars were also apt to act with unnecessary cruelty toward civilians on occasion, often alongside the Hessians:

The Regulars and Hessians together Robed and Plundered two wealthy farmers (that were brothers) of the Greatest part of their moveable Estates About four or five miles from Princetown, and not only took away their Cretures but robed their Houses and ript open their Beds and turned out the feathers and took away the Ticken and left the owners but very little to cover them, or even to live on . . . They go out late in the night and Steal and Kill Sheep and cattle Even Milch Cows and skin them, leave their skins and hides and take away the meat.[65]

The same colonist notes, however, that the Hessians had a tendency to ride through town and abuse civilians directly following British regulars who had offered protections to the same civilians:

On the same day the 8th of December there followed the Regular Army a Parcel of Hessians and took away four Horses from the People to the westard of the town, One of them was said to be valued at 100 pound, and commited

Several other Outrages the same day In pulling of mens hats from their heads, Though the Regular Officers had given them Protections as they went before, In these Words or near it, Viz., Let no Man Presume to Injure A; B. In his Person or Property. Yet these men had no Regard to it But Directly to the Contrary Injured the Protected Men both in their Persons and Propertys, by Insulting their Persons and by Robing them of their Propertys.[66]

Such stories indicate that while the Hessians were by no means the only forces to act with disregard for ethical standards at times, they may have done so more frequently than the regular forces.

This is not to say that the Hessians had a consistently negative impact on British military effectiveness. They were a significant force-multiplier, if nothing else. The impact of the number of Hessians troops is recounted by nineteenth-century historian Edward J. Lowell, who notes that a German magazine editor during this period remarked that many letters from Hessian officers printed in newspapers ascribed a great deal of the victory in the Battle of Long Island in August 1776 to themselves, and that, in view of the "well-known valor of the Hessian soldiery, they undoubtedly deserve it," but that they understate the fact that the British and Hessians together outnumbered the Americans by a ratio of five or four to one (20,000 British and Hessians to 4,000 or 5,000 Americans).[67] It is notable that this battle occurred almost immediately following the arrival of the first dispatch of Hessians to America and that they numbered approximately 8,000, thus substantially increasing the size of the British forces available for the Battle of Long Island.[68] Thus, these auxiliary forces clearly improved military effectiveness in certain cases through their force-multiplying impact on the *quality* of the entire British force (Proposition 1).

The Hessian forces failed, however, to assist the British in outmaneuvering the Americans at all junctures. Indeed, on December 26, 1776, George Washington's army attacked the main force of 1,400 Hessians in Trenton, on the Delaware River. Washington's troops achieved a significant level of surprise, killing thirty Hessians and capturing over 900 Hessian prisoners, using them through the winter as free labor.[69] A week later, Washington again surprised the British and Hessian forces in Princeton, New Jersey, killing or capturing 400. These two battles shocked those back home in Britain, who had expected that with Hessian troops they would be able to quickly put down the colonists' rebellion.[70] The Hessians' overall impact on British military effectiveness thus appears to range from negligible to negative. Although the Hessians did act as force-multipliers and increased military effectiveness in limited instances, their relative lack of motivation and reputation for unreasonable cruelty ultimately decreased military effectiveness by reducing *skill* and *responsiveness*. The case therefore appears to provide greater support for the logic of Proposition 2 than that of Proposition 1, even though the components of military effectiveness found to be most significant in this case (*skill* and *responsiveness*) do not completely match those hypothesized in Proposition 2 (*integration* and *skill*).

Although international humanitarian law was not established by the time of the American Revolution, the fact that large numbers of non-Hessian forces ridiculed the Hessians for their unwonted cruelty indicates that the normative anathema regarding unethical behavior in warfare was pervasive during this period. This case can therefore be said to also provide support for the notion underlying both Proposition 1a and Proposition 2b: that ethical behavior in warfare is more likely to benefit military effectiveness than is unethical behavior due to the impact of such behavior on the war for the hearts and minds of the civilian population.

Hessian Forces' Impact on the Democratic Advantage

Neither Hesse-Cassel (or any of the other German provinces) nor Britain were democracies at the time of the American Revolution. Nonetheless, the process of hiring Hessian auxiliaries sheds light on decisionmaking relevant to democratic advantage theory. The key question is whether British officials purchased military services from the Hessians for the explicit purpose of reducing domestic political opposition to the war. Such data would indicate that the Hessian forces allowed the British government to be less selective in its conflict choices, as without them the government might have been forced by domestic political will to pull out of the war or to avoid war through compromise. This would provide evidence against democratic advantage theory, for it would indicate that there is nothing special about democracies in this regard. Indeed, as in the case of the condottieri, the following analysis provides a preliminary indication that some of the structural constraints argued by democratic advantage theorists to be unique to democracies may, in fact, occur in non-democracies as well.

Britain's motives for hiring the Hessian forces are central to the analysis at hand because its role as the hiring state is roughly analogous to the situation of modern states hiring PSCs. The parliamentary debate regarding the treaties with Germany showed that proponents of hiring the Hessian and other German forces justified doing so on grounds of necessity. On February 29, 1776, Lord North argued in Parliament that the German troops would:

> be the best and fastest means of reducing America to a proper constitutional state of obedience, because men could be readier had and upon much cheaper terms in this way than they could possibly be recruited at home . . . and that the force which this measure would enable them to send to America would be such as, in all human probability, must compel that country to agree to terms of submission, perhaps without further effusion of blood.[71]

Even more telling is Lord Barrington, who reluctantly conceded that recruits could be "obtained on no other terms," and that while the bargain was not advantageous to Britain, it was the best possible.[72]

The notion that recruits could not be obtained in any other way than—or at least, not as inexpensively and quickly as—by hiring foreign forces indicates that the ability to hire the Hessians and other German troops allowed Britain to be less selective than it might otherwise have been with regard to whether and how to continue fighting the American colonists. It is clear that hiring the Hessians alleviated the direct military burden on the British citizenry, thus making them less likely to express any criticisms about the conflict in America. If Britain had been a democracy at the time, the selection effects argument of the democratic advantage would tell us that hiring the Hessian troops likely caused Britain to continue the war longer than it would have otherwise. Because Britain was not a democracy, however, this case provides evidence to contradict the basic assumption of democratic advantage theory, for it indicates that *both* democracies and non-democracies can experience the processes that democratic advantage theory insists are unique to democracies.

HISTORICAL MERCENARY AND AUXILIARY FORCES: THEORETICAL CONTRIBUTIONS

The historical cases in this chapter contribute theoretical leverage and policy-relevant knowledge to the overall study in four ways: (1) by illustrating the significance of structural force integration for military effectiveness; (2) by illustrating particular relationships between the state/city-state and foreign or profit-motivated forces; (3) by indicating that the structural constraints argued by democratic advantage theorists to be unique to democracies may, in fact, be present in non-democracies as well; and (4) by indicating that regular military forces may be as likely as mercenary or auxiliary forces to violate the norms of humanitarian conduct in war. Both the condottieri at various points from the thirteenth through fifteenth centuries and the Hessians in the American Revolution were irregular, profit-motivated and/or foreign forces deployed alongside regular, state-sanctioned military forces. Yet they were either structurally integrated at least occasionally into the regular forces alongside which they were deployed or were organized into companies with a distinct, military-like command structure. These cases thus illustrate that by structuring private, foreign, or profit-motivated forces in a manner similar to the military, and/or by integrating their structure into the structure of the regular forces alongside which they fight, the identity cleavages between these forces and the regular military are not as apparent or potentially divisive as they are in situations where the two types of forces are not structurally cohesive. Yet, as illustrated by both cases, structural integration cannot always overcome the disturbing identity characteristics of a mercenary or auxiliary force, particularly when those characteristics include unethical behavior in warfare. Because PSCs are more mercenary-like than are regular forces, the lessons of these cases provide insight into how to ensure that modern PSCs work together well with regular military forces.

The second critically important theoretical contribution of these two cases is apparent when one considers the position of the state (or city-state) in these cases as opposed to its position in the cases examined in Chapters 3 and 4. The state/city-state's role in the historical cases examined in this chapter is a central one; it is the seller, buyer, and—in the Hessian case—the creator of mercenary military services. Furthermore, the state's role in the international arena during the time period examined in the Hessian case was also quite central. Transnational activity was apparent in the late eighteenth century but was much less pronounced than it has been in recent decades. The state, then, figured much more prominently in the Hessian case, both in general and in its direct involvement in the military actions discussed here. In contrast, and in a fashion quite reminiscent of the system of the Free Companies during the era of the condottieri, modern-day private security companies act as middlemen between the sovereign or intervening state and the individual who desires to sell his military abilities for a profit. Figure 5.1 illustrates the evolution of the state's role in force provision.[73]

The chapter's third theoretical contribution, as already noted, is its illustration of the presence in non-democracies of the structural constraints argued

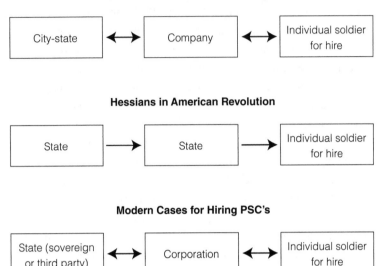

Figure 5.1. Conceptual map of the evolution of the state's role in force provision.

by democratic advantage theorists to be unique to democracies. In both the condottieri and Hessian cases, such structural constraints were apparent despite the fact that neither case involved a democracy.

Finally, these two cases illustrate that regular military forces may be just as likely to perpetrate humanitarian abuses as are mercenaries. This was shown in the papal forces' involvement in the massacre of civilians in Faenza and Cesena in 1376 and 1377 and in the British mistreatment of American colonists during the American Revolution.

CONCLUSION

As noted in the preceding discussion, the condottieri fighting for the Italian city-states both individually and in companies and the Hessian troops fighting as British auxiliaries in the American Revolution contributed to the military effectiveness of the regular militaries with which they were deployed, primarily by acting as force-multipliers and increasing the forces' *quality*. This benefit was often not overshadowed by *integration* problems because, despite the identity differences between these foreign forces and the militaries with which they were deployed, they were often either structurally integrated into the military such that they were able to communicate and coordinate with the regular military effectively, or they were structured into companies with a command structure reminiscent of a standing army. Both cases thus indicate the importance of effectively structuring and/or structurally integrating modern private forces into the professional military with which they are often deployed. However, both the Hessian case and the case of the Florentine army defeating the Great Company in 1358 due to the Great Company's unethical destruction of the Florentine countryside illustrate that structural measures are not always sufficient to overcome identity-related issues detracting from the hired force's impact on military effectiveness. Clearly, both identity and structural variables must be considered when assessing a hired force's potential impact on overall military effectiveness.

Furthermore, special attention must be paid to issues of unethical behavior in warfare, as these can have a significant impact on military effectiveness. In some instances, non-state or foreign actors such as mercenary or auxiliary forces might be more likely to perpetrate such abuses. The case of the papal forces working alongside condottieri to massacre civilians in Faenza in 1376 and Cesena in 1377, however, provides evidence that non-mercenary military forces are also prone to violations of humanitarian norms. Evidence of British soldiers' mistreatment of American colonists and their possessions during the American Revolution supports this notion. One final insight from this chapter focuses on the state/city-state's evolving role in force provision in the condottieri and Hessian cases. Seeking to expand on the various theoretical and policy implications of all three of the case study chapters, the next chapter summarizes lessons learned and develops policy and regulatory recommendations to inform future uses of private military and security forces.

6 CONCLUDING LESSONS AND RECOMMENDATIONS

AS THE PREVIOUS CHAPTERS HAVE ILLUSTRATED, contracting of military functions occurs to an unprecedented extent in the United States at present and shows little indication of tapering off in the near future. Such extensive contracting practices occur for numerous reasons. Primarily, it is argued to be less expensive and more efficient over the long term to hire a contractor to perform a soldier's job: contractors require very little to no training (and so can be deployed immediately) and require no retirement plan, pension, health care, or related long-term benefits. This viewpoint reflects the worldwide tendency toward the outsourcing of government functions that began in the 1980s. Despite ever-increasing calls for increased regulation of and transparency within the industry, the historical pervasiveness of mercenarism and the modern industry's strong position vis-à-vis contracting states both indicate that the private military and security industry is here to stay for the foreseeable future. What remains to be determined is the manner in which this industry can and should best be used to support democratic endeavors.

Numerous government, academic, and media reports over the past several years have assessed the various effects of the private military and security industry on the militaries of the United States and its partners, as well as on U.S. operations and U.S. legal and moral accountability both at home and abroad. More theoretical accounts have assessed the impact of the modern private military and security industry on the future of the Westphalian state as we know it, pointing to the rise of the modern industry as a sign of the decline of the state's monopoly on legitimate violence. However, little analysis of private security contractors' impact on democracies' military effectiveness and conflict selectivity across different deployment scenarios and different types of operations has been conducted up to this point. Because PSCs are primarily based in and hired by democratic states in the modern era, this analytical void is a significant one.

Seeking to fill this void, the preceding chapters have assessed the impact of private security companies on democracies' military effectiveness and on their propensity to be victorious in conflicts across various deployment situations. Chapter 1 places the issues at hand into the global historical and political context of mercenarism and the outsourcing of violence and other governmental functions. From this contextual setting, it becomes clear that violence has been outsourced throughout history and across the globe to both supplement the capacity of state militaries and to allow states to distance themselves from normatively undesirable conduct. The modern private security industry is similarly employed according to this logic of capacity and normative logic. Chapter 1 also outlines the study's overall goals: (1) to compare different situations of privatized force employment to illustrate PSCs' potential effects on military effectiveness, and, by extension, on the theory of the democratic advantage; and (2) to understand the different effects of structure and identity on the effectiveness of military forces composed of national armies combined with PSCs, with an eye to providing prescriptions for current U.S. policy.

Chapter 2 places these goals in a theoretical context, drawing on relevant tenets of state theory, democratic advantage theory, and various theories of military effectiveness. Chapter 2 also elaborates upon the structure-identity debate in the social sciences, noting this debate's significance for the underlying determinants of PSC-military coordination problems and for attempts to devise well-targeted policy recommendations. Using each of these bodies of theoretical literature, the chapter develops several propositions that are explored throughout the remainder of the study.

In looking at recent situations of PSC–military co-deployment primarily through the lens of Operation Iraqi Freedom, Chapter 3 deconstructs PSC–military coordination problems. To do so, it assesses original and existing interview data to determine the relative salience of two competing explanations for such problems: the argument that they are caused primarily by structural variables versus the argument that they are caused primarily by identity-based variables. Chapter 3 thus has two important theoretical and policy-relevant contributions. It contributes first to the military effectiveness literature by analyzing the causes and consequences of PSC–military coordination problems when PSC and military personnel are co-deployed. The findings derived from this analysis indicate that PSC–military coordination problems, caused by a combination of structural and identity-related variables, lead PSCs to have a negative impact on the military's *integration, responsiveness,* and *skill* when the two groups are co-deployed in the field. Yet, by acting as (often well-equipped) force multipliers in such co-deployment situations, PSCs do have a beneficial impact on *quality.*

Chapter 3's second theoretical and policy-relevant contribution speaks to the ongoing debate in the social sciences regarding structure versus identity, speculating that structural variables are causally prior to identity-based variables in situations of PSC–military coordination. In other words, deployed private security company and military personnel turn first to the structure guiding their interactions when determining how to coordinate, relying on both perceived and actual identities when structural variables are either not available to guide their interactions or are indeterminate with regard to how those interactions should proceed.

Finally, Chapter 3's analysis of the Fallujah case indicates that contractor deaths may in some instances decrease conflict selectivity and the prospects for the democratic advantage. In such cases, contractor deaths would prompt the electorate to push for conflict involvement based mainly on a desire for revenge as opposed to rational considerations of the likelihood of victory.

Chapter 4's exploration of cases in which PSCs are deployed in place of a national military force depicts the ease with which democratic statesmen can use PSCs to involve their country in a foreign conflict, bypassing the electoral restraints on such involvement and thus decreasing the prospects that the state in question will enjoy the democratic advantage. This impact on the "selection effects" side of the democratic advantage operates only as long as the PSC deployment remains covert, however; if it is unveiled to the democratic public, it can entail electoral repercussions similar to those that would be experienced if the government or military had been directly involved, rather than a PSC.

On the other hand, the chapter demonstrates that when involved in a conflict in place of a national military, PSCs can often have quite a positive impact on military effectiveness by benefiting the *skill, responsiveness,* and *quality* of the foreign forces they are sent to assist. It is by no means clear, however, that PSCs are more effective than the democratic intervening state's regular military would be in such situations. There is one potential exception to this: PSCs' beneficial impact on military effectiveness can come at the cost of conducting the conflict in accordance with the international laws of war. This may allow these private forces to have a more beneficial impact on military effectiveness than regular democratic military forces would have had in some cases, because PSCs are able to perform the "dirty jobs" argued by some to be necessary to win in certain types of conflicts. While it is difficult to conclusively prove that national militaries would be more likely to comply with IHL in every situation, one can—at the very least—reasonably conclude that the use of private firms to carry out traditionally military tasks carries with it the risk that these tasks will not be achieved in accordance with international laws of war, due to the relative dearth of public oversight of such deployments.

Chapter Five, in exploring the question of what it would take to make PSCs and the military work together well, examines two historical cases of profit-motivated, hired foreign forces, fighting at times alongside regular military forces. Although these are not instances of PSC employment per se, they illustrate the long history of the employment of mercenary-like forces, and point to various dynamics relevant to the deployment of foreign and/or profit-motivated mercenary or auxiliary forces. These two historical cases therefore suggest relationships between certain uses of PSCs and particular outcomes. In each case, the foreign and/or profit-motivated forces in question are either structured similarly to a regular military force, or are structurally integrated into the regular force, illustrating the potential for successful coordination between private and national forces when the appropriate structural boundaries are delineated. This chapter also, however, demonstrates the significance of both identity and structural variables in determining a hired force's impact on military effectiveness. Because both the Hessian case and the case of the *condottieri* fighting for the Italian city-states include some degree of infractions of the norms of ethical warfare, they provides insight into the question underlying the study's four IHL-related propositions: whether ethical behavior in warfare is more likely to benefit military effectiveness than is unethical behavior.

Each of the preceding chapters contains findings that are intended to speak to audiences both supportive and critical of the value of PSCs. Those taking for granted that PSCs are here to stay are most likely interested in the findings regarding how to use PSCs most effectively, many of which are elaborated in this chapter's policy recommendations. Meanwhile, those skeptical of the value of PSCs are likely most interested in two notable implications of the findings herein: (1) the critique of the democratic peace hypothesis posed by the evidence indicating that PSCs can and are being used by democratic leaders to avoid accountability to the citizenry for decisions to go to war; and (2) the fact that greater regulatory oversight of PSCs, as recommended below, is potentially so costly of a "solution" to the problems facing the private security industry at present as to render PSCs uneconomical.

OVERALL LESSONS

Six main lessons can be gleaned from the analyses of the preceding chapters, along with several related speculative findings deserving further research:

First, Chapter 3's analysis of the PSC–military co-deployments in Iraq and Afghanistan shows significant support for the idea that PSCs decrease military effectiveness (Proposition 2), indicating that co-deployment situations have a negative impact on military effectiveness. The robustness of this finding could be bolstered by further research involving cases other than OIF and OEF. This is related to the first lesson discussed above, as co-deployment situations primarily have a negative effect on *integration*. Such integration problems stem from both structural and identity-based causes: Among other structural gaps, a lack of adequate training pertaining specifically to PSC-military field interactions and a doctrinal weakness in specifying and clarifying security contractors' position in the chain of command play a large role in exacerbating the military's largely unfavorable perceptions of PSCs and vice versa. The tense PSC–military relations stemming from such problems have a negative impact on the entire co-deployed force's *integration* and, relatedly, its *responsiveness*. Co-deployment scenarios also have a negative impact on *skill*, both by hindering commanders' leadership capabilities and by risking a decrease in soldiers' motivation levels when deploying them alongside private contractors receiving much higher pay than the soldiers. The fact that many soldiers see PSC personnel as patriotically motivated does speak to the possibility that PSC and military personnel are similarly motivated. However, PSCs' higher wages and dwindling military retention rates in an era when co-deployment is common are enough to make one wary and to stimulate further research on PSCs' overall impact on soldiers' motivation levels.

However, the case studies examined in Chapters 4 and 5 demonstrate support for the notion that PSCs increase military effectiveness (Proposition P1), indicating that private or mercenary-type forces can have the best impact on military effectiveness in situations where they are either structurally integrated into the military force alongside which they operate or where they are deployed in place of a national military force. This is primarily because PSCs in such deployment situations have a positive impact on *quality* while avoiding a negative impact on military *integration*. Tense PSC–military relations are avoided, either through structural mechanisms that minimize resentment between the two groups or through the deployment of only one group to a particular combat zone.

Third, the analyses in the preceding chapters demonstrate that PSCs have a predominantly negative impact on the democratic advantage across deployment scenarios. In cases of PSC deployment in place of a regular military force, PSCs allow democratic policymakers to involve their countries in conflicts not approved by the electorate, thus making it less likely that the electorate will have any influence in "selecting" to engage only in those conflicts that the democracy is most likely to win. This has a negative impact on the selection effects mechanism of the democratic advantage. Furthermore, such uses of PSCs—to avoid democratic accountability to the electorate—pose a serious challenge to democratic peace theory.

In cases of co-deployment, moreover, PSCs act as force multipliers whose deaths do not have to be reported in official casualty statistics, thus allowing policymakers to deceive the electorate in such a manner as to disrupt the electorate's conflict selectivity. This, again, has a negative impact on the selection effects side of the democratic advantage. Furthermore, if gruesome contractor deaths are widely publicized, as occurred in the Fallujah case, the dynamics of the selection effects argument can be reversed, actually prompting electoral support of conflict involvement not based on considerations of the likelihood of victory. This, again, can decrease the prospects for the democratic advantage, though in a manner different from that which is typically theorized. Although PSCs do improve democracies' military effectiveness in some cases, their negative impacts on democracies' conflict selectivity tend to counteract any positive impact that they may have on the military effectiveness mechanism of the democratic advantage.

Related to this finding is the fact that the Hessian and condottieri cases provide evidence to refute the basic logic underlying democratic advantage theory. Several British lords made statements at the time of the parliamentary debates regarding the hiring of German troops to fight alongside the British in the American Revolution, indicating that British recruits could not be had on such terms, and that Britain was fairly dependent on these German troops if it wanted to bolster existing forces fighting in America. These statements would support the notion that the Hessian forces decreased Britain's conflict selectivity and thus its chances to experience the democratic advantage, but Britain was not a democracy at the time of the American Revolution. This case therefore illustrates that the processes argued by democratic advantage theorists to be unique to democracies are actually experienced by non-democracies as well, therefore weakening the logic underlying democratic advantage theory. The condottieri case displays similar mechanisms at work.

Fourth, as outlined above, Chapter 3's examination of the underlying reasons for PSC-military coordination problems illustrates the fact that a combination of structural and identity-based variables are at the root of poor PSC–military coordination. Drawing upon the OIF and OEF case study evidence, I argue that structural variables are more significant than identity-based variables in this regard. However, identity variables come into play where structural shortcomings exist. This finding is significant for policy, for it directs policymakers to first develop adequate structural mechanisms to guide PSC–military interactions and then to devise mechanisms to encourage the development of those identity characteristics beneficial to PSC–military relations.

The case studies in Chapters 3, 4, and 5, by providing empirical support for Propositions 1a and 2b, illustrate another lesson deserving further examination: that PSC compliance with the laws of war benefits military effectiveness across the spectrum of deployment situations. This preliminary finding provides support for the hearts-and-minds approach to civilian treatment in counterinsurgency warfare. It should be noted, however, that the case of MPRI in Croatia provides limited support for the draining-the-sea approach to civilian treatment, as it provides evidence to support Proposition 1b. Yet, it is difficult to establish a clear causal link between IHL non-compliance and military effectiveness in the Croatian case.

Finally, the sixth lesson evident in Chapters 1 through 5 is that the state remains a prominent actor in force provision, despite the growth of the private security industry and its increasing involvement in traditional military activities. The state maintains its prominence by maintaining state militaries, providing contracts to PSCs, arranging contracts between PSCs and other states (as the United States did between MPRI and Croatia, for instance), and devising and enforcing regulations pertaining to PSCs in the field. Interview data examined in Chapter 3 provide a preliminary indication that the professional jurisdiction of national militaries may not be exceedingly challenged by PSCs, as there appears to be a limit to the actions modern private security companies and their personnel will carry out for money, at least in some cases.[1] Thus, these data allow us to speculate that PSCs will not infringe on at least some professional military functions, therefore leaving open a continuing state role in the control of national forces. Yet, as outlined in Chapter 1, PSCs do appear to impact weak and strong states differently, particularly in terms of state-building activities. By hindering the development of a viable bureaucratic apparatus in weak states—whether employed directly by the leaders of those states or by stronger intervening powers—PSCs can narrow weak states' options for improving their systemic position in the long run. Simultaneously, PSCs can provide strong states that wish to intervene in regional conflicts and/or less-developed areas of the world with an expanded range of options for doing so. I argue that PSCs therefore have significant potential to alter the systemic organization of states within the international system.

Using these lessons, it is possible to devise a set of policy measures aimed at improving PSCs' impact on military effectiveness and, therefore, the likelihood that democracies will experience the democratic advantage.

RECOMMENDED POLICY INITIATIVES
AND IMPROVEMENTS

As Chapter 3 notes, the 2005 GAO Report on *Actions Needed to Improve the Use of Private Security Providers in Iraq* recommended that the U.S. Secretary of Defense enhance military procedures to reduce incidences of the military firing on security providers and provide training to U.S. military forces on the role of security providers. Yet, the 2006 follow-up report found that no action had been taken on the development of a pre-deployment training program and that PSCs continue to enter the battlespace without coordinating with the U.S. military.[2] Since then, limited attempts have been made by both PSC and military representatives to enhance military training regimens. Both the International Stability Operations Association (ISOA) and the Peacekeeping and Stability Operations Institute (PKSOI) of the Army War College have worked on this, resulting in the inclusion of a role for "contractors" into military readiness exercises (MREs).[3] The Department of Defense is also developing programs to improve training of uniformed personnel to manage contractors during contingency operations, and intends to introduce courses on contract support into the curriculum for non-acquisition personnel. Furthermore, DoD is developing an on-line course that offers pre-deployment training to personnel about planning for and working with contractors during military operations. Likewise, the Army is developing informational handbooks for military personnel who work with contractors regarding the contracting process and the roles and responsibilities of military personnel when working alongside contractors.[4] Notably, such measures only partially address the problem, only educating military personnel regarding contractors' roles in the field and failing to educate PSC personnel or to provide pre-deployment opportunities for the two groups to interact outside of the "fog of war." Indeed, five years after the GAO first made these recommendations, the *Washington Post* reported with regard to OEF that "officials are also considering whether private security firms that guard USAID contractors should coordinate with U.S. military units. At the moment 'they don't talk to each other,' a U.S. official said."[5]

The 2005 and 2006 GAO reports also focus heavily on the difficulties in conducting criminal background screenings when hiring PSC personnel, as well as the lack of U.S. or international standards for establishing private security provider and employee qualifications.[6] While the GAO reports' recommendations are substantial and represent a step in the right direction, they fail to highlight some of the information from the interviews conducted in preparing these reports. A more comprehensive approach to reforming the nature of PSC–military interactions in Iraq (and elsewhere, potentially) would build upon the GAO recommendations while recognizing and correcting their shortcomings.

The establishment of a standardized pre-deployment training program for both PSC and military personnel is of primary importance, to teach each group its respective roles and responsibilities with regard to other actors in the battlespace. In the United States, the Continental U.S. Replacement Centers (CRCs) provide potential venues for such a training program—at least for U.S. citizens—as contractors, soldiers, and military civilians already come together at the CRCs for administrative processing and related tasks prior to deployment.[7] Policymakers would need to establish similar programs at other venues in or near conflict zones to insure adequate training of local nationals and third-country nationals as well. Preferably, such training programs would bring together groups of PSC and military personnel for at least a few hours to conduct a training scenario in tandem and would include both classroom and practical training. Any PSC winning a government contract should be required to send all operators on its staff through such a program, although there should be variation in program levels to suit different types of contractors, given that PSCs use varying degrees of expatriates, third-country nationals, and local nationals in different security roles and positions.

The GAO reports fail to take into account the question of what party would be responsible for funding such a training program, but logic dictates that funding for training PSC operators could be deducted directly from PSCs' government contracts, with the contracting government covering the costs of soldiers attending such trainings. Companies could also be mandated by the laws of the country in which they are based to require each of their operators to participate in a PSC–military joint training program, with the costs to be covered by the firm employing the operators. This would ensure that the appropriate training reaches those PSC personnel operating under nongovernmental contracts (such as, for instance, PSC personnel guarding pipelines for an oil company in Azerbaijan). Because the passage of legislation on these issues may progress more slowly than desired, the Pentagon and other defense agencies worldwide may wish to pass rules mandating such training as an intermediate step prior to the passage of formal legislation.

Related to this notion of Pentagon-mandated rules, it is necessary to establish institutional mechanisms and clear, unambiguous military doctrine to guide PSC–military interactions, including the military's responsibilities to PSCs in the field and vice versa. For instance, doctrine should highlight the need for PSCs to report their location to the military commander when in or traveling through his or her AOR and should clearly define the chain of command with respect to contractors on the battlefield. The doctrine should apply to all contractors on the battlefield, regardless of the companies employing them and the actors holding the contracts with those companies. This doctrine must then be integrated into the pre-deployment training programs of both the military and PSCs, so that everyone is made aware of the rules. Progress is slowly being made to institute these doctrinal changes and develop institutional mechanisms to support them; for instance, DoD set up the Joint Contracting Command in both Iraq and Afghanistan to provide a more centralized management system and to enforce contracting support requirements during ongoing operations, and the congressionally mandated Joint Contingency Acquisition Support Office was established as a result of the FY2007 Defense Authorization Act to assist commanders in planning, supporting, and overseeing contracting activities during the early stages of contingency operations. Furthermore, the Chairman of the Joint Chiefs of Staff published Joint Publication 4-10, *Operational Contract Support*, in October 2008, elaborating doctrine for contract support and contract management during joint contingency operations. Then, in March 2009, Deputy Secretary of Defense

William J. Lynn issued a directive detailing who within DoD is responsible for the various aspects of contract management and oversight.[8] However, the pace of change needs to hasten to best insure that the growing numbers of PSCs accompanying military forces in modern warfare are improving—not detracting from—military effectiveness. Indeed, one official estimated that it could take up to three years to update policies and regulations, integrate contractors into operational planning, and implement appropriate training.[9]

Third, it is crucial to the success of military operations involving PSCs to standardize communications between the two forces. Ideally, this would result in interoperable radios being distributed to all verifiable PSC teams operating in a military unit's AOR. Such a proposition is risky, however, given the nature of modern warfare and the chance that insurgents or terrorists could penetrate PSC teams and thus intercept military communications. At the very least, it is necessary to establish an enforceable rule making it mandatory for *all* PSCs operating in a co-deployment scenario to participate in that particular theater's equivalent of the Reconstruction Operations Center (ROC) or Contractor Operations Center (CONOC). While such a rule was eventually announced with regard to OIF, the degree to which it is enforceable is questionable. This trend must spread beyond the boundaries of Iraq and Afghanistan as well, with the establishment of ROCs or CONOCs in all other theaters where PSC–military co-deployment occurs and a requirement that all companies and military units operating in those theatres use the ROC or CONOC.

Fourth, national legislation should be developed to require that any contractor employed by a U.S. government agency (or subcontracted thereto) require its staff to wear standardized uniforms with identifying insignia. Many firms do require this of their employees, but others do not. While some may see this as a trivial matter, the fact that uniforms allow military personnel to distinguish contractors from insurgents is extremely relevant to the issue of blue-on-white incidents and to overall PSC–military communication, coordination, and trust. Having to wear standard, identifiable uniforms will also bring PSC personnel one step closer to fitting the current IHL definition of "combatant," thus helping to clarify the status of PSC personnel under the international laws of war. As Chapter 3 mentions, this is a structural change that will assist all PSCs in aligning their identities with those most likely to demonstrate operational professionalism. On a related note, national legislation should be developed to mandate the use of armored vehicles, at least in all co-deployment scenarios. This will reduce the frequency of blue-on-white incidents by making contractors both more identifiable to friendly forces and less vulnerable to both enemy and friendly fire, therefore better ensuring overall contractor safety.

Regulatory Recommendations

Several recommendations pertaining to the legal regulation of the private security industry are relevant here as well. A number of international conventions define mercenaries and their rights and limitations under international humanitarian law (IHL). The two key questions in determining the legal status of PSC personnel under IHL are (1) whether they qualify as "mercenaries," based on the various IHL definitions of the term; and (2) whether they are (lawful or unlawful) "combatants," or "non-combatants," based on the definitions of the Geneva Conventions. If found to qualify as mercenaries, lawful combatants, or unlawful combatants under IHL, PSC employees' protected status under IHL would be altered, and in some cases they could be subject to criminal prosecution.

It is unlikely that the majority of PSC personnel would qualify as mercenaries under IHL. This is primarily because definitions of mercenaries in international law are filled with ambiguities and contradictions that make it difficult for *anyone* to qualify as a mercenary.[10] Notably, there is some debate as to whether third-country nationals would qualify as mercenaries under the Geneva Conventions' Article 47.2 definition of the term.[11] Regardless, however, in most cases where certain categories of PSC personnel might qualify as mercenaries according to one of the legal definitions, the laws in question do not restrict mercenary activities sufficiently to effectively regulate the behavior of PSC personnel. In the few cases where mercenary definitions are broad enough to encompass PSC activity and the laws in question impose strict penalties on mercenaries, states have chosen not to enforce the restriction on mercenary activity.

Employing the laws of international armed conflict to regulate the private security industry is therefore an unlikely prospect, at least as these laws currently stand. For instance, prisoner-of-war (POW) status is not a significant issue in practice; it applies only in international armed conflicts, which are rare in modern warfare. Furthermore, the Geneva Conventions do not draw distinctions between defensive and offensive operations, a fact that creates friction when attempting to apply these laws to actors defined in terms of their sole reliance on defensive capabilities.[12] The distinction between combatants and non-combatants is similarly filled with ambiguities when applied to the category of "contractors," requiring that each be assessed on an individual basis.[13] Finally, no international tribunal has jurisdiction to try contractors under IHL; enforcement therefore falls upon the state parties.[14]

Therefore, the first of these regulatory recommendations deals specifically with international regulation of the industry, recommending that the states party to the Geneva Conventions convene a meeting to devise an additional protocol to the Geneva Conventions that would provide detailed guidance on how states and the international community are to regulate the private security industry. At the very least, representatives at this meeting should revise existing IHL definitions of *mercenary* to account for modern private security actors. Due to the confusion regarding PSCs' classification under international law, the broad reach of the Geneva Conventions, and the transnational nature of the private security industry, this would be a necessary and useful way to begin the project of international regulation of the industry.

Second, with regard to domestic regulation of the industry in the United States, two potential legal regulatory mechanisms are commonly cited. The Uniform Code of Military Justice (UCMJ) was created in 1950 as the U.S. military's criminal code, providing for prosecution of military personnel to be entirely administered by the military, through the court-martial process.[15] U.S. Senator Lindsay Graham inserted an amendment to the UCMJ into the 2007 Defense Authorization Act, placing civilian contractors accompanying the armed forces in the field under court-martial jurisdiction during times of contingency operations, in addition to times of declared war. Thus, to convene a court-martial for a contractor, the contractor must be serving with or accompanying the armed forces in the field, and the trial must take place in time of war or contingency operations.

Unlike the UCMJ, the Military Extraterritorial Jurisdiction Act (MEJA) authorizes private contractors to be tried in U.S. federal courts. Originally passed in 2000 to target offenses committed overseas by private contractors employed by the U.S. Department of Defense, the MEJA was revised in 2004 to extend federal criminal jurisdiction to all contractors "supporting the mission of the Department of Defense."[16] The House of Representatives passed legislation in October 2007 to further extend MEJA jurisdiction to *all* contractors working in a contingency operation.[17]

Whether the UCMJ or the MEJA is a more appropriate vehicle for prosecuting contractor abuses is a hotly debated topic among policymakers, legislators, and industry insiders at this time. Yet the UCMJ would clash with the existing

contracting regime, which gives contracting authorities the power over contractors, and the U.S. government is unlikely to approve of a local commander
having the authority to order a PSC or PSC employee to do anything outside of
the scope of an existing contract. There is also some question as to whether the
language of the amended UCMJ applies to third-country nationals (TCNs)
working for PSCs; if not, firms could evade the regulatory oversight provided
by the UCMJ by simply relying more heavily on TCNs than on local nationals or U.S. citizens to comprise their workforce.[18] The UCMJ's applicability to
non-DoD contractors is also debatable. The MEJA is therefore likely to be the
easier of these laws to implement, and—once it is used regularly—the most
likely to prevent future contractor abuses. Indeed, at least one MEJA case has
been brought against Blackwater contractors, though it was dismissed in December 2009 due to prosecutorial misconduct.[19]

Because the MEJA is the most likely U.S. domestic law to be used against
private security contractors in an enforceable manner, U.S. policymakers
should consider the creation of an office within the U.S. Department of Justice
that would be tasked with investigating and trying war zone contractors under
the MEJA. The establishment of such an office would do much to remedy the
problem of the MEJA's minimal case history, creating norms of MEJA enforcement that would build on each other to establish a solid base from which
to regulate PSC abuses in the field. The establishment of such norms of MEJA
enforcement would also, it is hoped, alleviate the issues related to prosecutorial misconduct that were apparent in the case involving the five Blackwater
contractors implicated in the Nisour Square incident.

Domestic regulation of U.S.-hired PSCs *outside of* the United States is
also an option, as the host state on whose territory the PSCs operate can also
choose to impose regulations on PSC behavior. This is a complicated process,
as the hiring state, the supplying or "home" states (of which the contractors
in question are citizens), and the host state must all agree (at least implicitly)
that the PSCs are liable to the host country's regulations. However, if it can be
done, this option holds great potential for regulating PSC behavior. An example of this has been seen in Iraq since the January 2009 implementation of the
new Status of Forces Agreement (SOFA) between the U.S. and Iraqi governments. Under the new SOFA, all contractors operating in Iraq are subject to
Iraqi legal jurisdiction.[20] While some in the U.S. government and the private
security industry were concerned that this would limit the number of firms
willing to operate in Iraq due to the country's nascent judicial system and due

to questions regarding the ability of the country to bring fair and speedy trials for any contractors charged with crimes under Iraqi law, such concerns also work strongly to deter improper contractor behavior.

A fourth viable possibility for regulating PSC behavior and preventing PSC abuses in the field exists in the form of contract provisions, which could be used in a standard manner to regulate PSC behavior across various situations. As Michael Cottier notes, contracting parties should use the selection criteria, obligations specifications, monitoring mechanisms, and sanctioning aspects of contracts and the contracting process to regulate PSC behavior.[21] Using the contracting process in this way would enable purchasers of PSC services to create market-driven incentives for private security firms to: (a) possess all required authorizations; (b) follow adequate procedures and standards regarding the hiring, training, and vetting of employees; (c) possess rulebooks and follow standard operating procedures; (d) have internal oversight mechanisms; and (e) be a member of a reputable trade association, such as the International Peace Operations Association (discussed in further detail in the following paragraphs). Government oversight of companies and government agencies purchasing PSC services would enable the standardization of certain contract requirements across the industry and its range of services, thus standardizing regulation of the industry through market mechanisms. Section 862 of the 2008 National Defense Authorization Act initiated such an effort, including a provision requiring the insertion into each covered contract of a contract clause addressing the selection, training, equipping, and conduct of personnel performing private security functions under such contract.[22] Policymakers should do everything in their power to support such a program, although limited government regulation of contract provisions at first may be the most efficient and effective means of instituting such a system. A program that is established incrementally will allow policymakers to test out particular contract provisions on a small scale and to make corrections to them if necessary prior to large-scale implementation.

Finally, on a related note, policymakers around the globe should allot government funding to support PSC trade associations in their respective countries. One such trade association, the British Association of Private Security Companies (BAPSC), has argued that:

> for the industry, regulation is a vital issue for several reasons. Most importantly, it can enhance its respectability and legitimacy by putting its operations on a firm legal basis . . . It can be argued that the industry understands itself

better than the government and can therefore apply sanctions that are better targeted.[23]

The International Stability Operations Association (ISOA) in Washington, D.C., makes similar arguments for self-regulation of the industry. Serving as a trade association for U.S. and international private military and security firms, the ISOA was formed in 2001 as the International Peace Operations Association (IPOA) and now has over fifty member companies and its own code of conduct to regulate member behavior. While the code of conduct is open to critiques that it is vague and idealistic, it cites specific concepts from IHL for the ethical conduct of warfare and has survived numerous revisions to make it as comprehensive as possible. Membership in the association is limited, and the ISOA Standards Committee, composed of officials from member companies and ISOA staff, is responsible for independently investigating infractions of the code of conduct alleged to have been committed by member companies or their personnel. The Standards Committee is also responsible for determining an appropriate course of action if the company and/or employee in question are found guilty of the alleged abuse, ranging from requiring that the company fire the employee to expelling the company from the ISOA altogether.

This system is effective in terms of the market incentives that it creates for compliance with the ISOA Code of Conduct, as member companies benefit from the reputational effects associated with ISOA membership. Membership in ISOA signals to potential purchasers of the companies' services that these firms are committed to ethical operating practices and that their activities and company practices have been independently and thoroughly assessed for compliance with ethical norms. This is, quite simply, good for business—both for the supplier and the purchaser of security services. ISOA member companies thus have an incentive to comply with the code of conduct and remain a member of the ISOA. This is particularly true of those firms who intend to stay in business for the long term, for whom reputation is crucial.[24]

However, successful examples of self-regulation—outside of a more formalized regulatory system—are rare. Indeed, when abuses do occur, the ISOA's system reveals its flaws. For instance, when Blackwater USA was under investigation by what was then the IPOA following the September 2007 Nisour Square incident, Blackwater simply announced that it was putting its IPOA membership on hold: "We have decided to take a hiatus from the [association] . . . We, like many other organizations engaged in this type of work, are pursuing other aspects and methods of industry outreach and governance."[25] Though Blackwater received massive media coverage following this incident, very little of it mentioned the company's decision to withdraw from what was then the IPOA. Thus, the reputational effects of ISOA withdrawal, at least with regard to a firm as large and influential as Blackwater/Xe, have proven in this case to be negligible. Furthermore, the code of conduct and Standards Committee have no teeth in such situations, as there is nothing that ISOA can do to enforce the code aside from expelling a company who refuses to abide by it—and clearly, in this case, expulsion was irrelevant.

This is not to say that industry self-regulation is impossible or undesirable but rather that it should be pursued in combination with a legalistic regulatory approach, at least as far as the U.S. case is concerned. Both the BAPSC and ISOA are significant players in this process, and the system envisaged and developed by the ISOA in particular might be effective with slight revision and the establishment of state structures to support it. For instance, the ISOA Standards Committee has very few resources with which to investigate alleged abuses, particularly those occurring outside of U.S. territory. If U.S. and foreign governments were to provide financial support to the ISOA and/or similar trade associations, as well as mandate that any government-held contracts for security services were to be given only to companies who were members of these trade associations, the self-regulatory schemes outlined here could be much more effective. Indeed, allotting government funding to support such trade associations would allow them to encourage the development of enforceable industry standards without the undue financial influence of those firms that the standards are designed to regulate. If government regulations were to simultaneously push PSC purchasers toward hiring only those firms that belong to such trade associations, the result would be the efficient and effective use of government regulations to create market mechanisms—industrywide standards verified and enforced by trade associations—for the regulation of the industry and of contractor behavior.

All in all, the private security industry is clearly an influential player in domestic and international politics at present, and likely will be for the foreseeable future. As such, it has vast potential to affect military effectiveness and the likelihood of democratic victories in conflicts worldwide. It is therefore imperative that policymakers in key democracies—particularly in the United States—establish a clear structure to guide PSC activities and to ensure that these firms will work seamlessly alongside regular troops in conflict-ridden areas of the globe. The legal accountability of private security actors must similarly be more clearly defined, to ensure that PSCs do not have a detrimental impact on military efforts to win the hearts and minds of the civilian populations among which they operate. The preceding recommendations are intended to spur such legislative and policy changes, with the hope that they will assist in integrating these new war-zone actors into existing models of military activity.

NOTES

Chapter 1 Introduction

1. David Ivanovich, "Contractor Deaths Up 17 Percent across Iraq in 2007," *Houston Chronicle*, February 9, 2008. Retrieved on April 14, 2008, from: www.chron.com/disp/story.mpl/front/5528613.html. See also U.S. Congresswoman Jan Schakowsky, "Schakowsky Uncovers 1,001 Contractor Deaths in Iraq," Press Release (August 6, 2007); retrieved on September 4, 2007, from: www/house.gov/list/press/il09_schakowsky/pr_contractordeaths_080607.s. By December 2008, this figure had grown to 173,000 private military and security contractors operating in Iraq, compared to 146,000 U.S. troops. See Matthew Lee, "U.S. Contractors Lose Immunity in Iraq Security Deal," *The Seattle Post-Intelligencer*, November 20, 2008; retrieved on November 24, 2008, from: http://seattlepi.nwsource.com/national/1152ap_iraq_security_contractors.html. This ratio declined slightly by March 2009 but remained high nonetheless, with 132,610 contractors working for the U.S. Department of Defense (DoD) in Iraq compared to 141,300 uniformed U.S. military personnel in-country. These figures do not include those contractors employed by the U.S. Department of State or other governmental or private entities, however, so the ratio of contractors to regular military was actually higher during this time period. Indeed, earlier estimates put the numbers of contractors employed by the Department of State and the U.S. Agency for International Development in Iraq at approximately 5,000 each (Lee, 2008). See also Moshe Schwartz, "Department of Defense Contractors in Iraq and Afghanistan: Background and Analysis," *CRS Report for Congress* (August 13, 2009): 5; retrieved on September 2, 2009, from: www.crs.gov.

2. Schwartz, 2009: 6; Steve Fainaru, "Iraq Contractors Face Growing Parallel War," *The Washington Post* (June 16, 2007), A01. Retrieved on January 11, 2008, from: www.washingtonpost.com/wp-dyn/content/article/2007/06/15/AR2007061502602.html.

3. Schwartz, 2009: 8.175.

4. Kevin O'Brien, "PMCs, Myths, and Mercenaries: The Debate on Private Military Companies," *Royal United Services Institute Journal* (February 2002); retrieved on June 10, 2008, from: www.globalpolicy.org/nations/sovereign/military/02debate.htm. See also "Executive Outcomes," *SourceWatch*; retrieved on June 10, 2008, from: www.sourcewatch.org/index.php?title=Executive_Outcomes.

5. As Chapter 2 elaborates, the focus on democratic advantage theory is appropriate here because democracies dominate in the hiring and supplying of PSCs today.

6. David Forsythe's work supports this finding, illustrating that—in spite of their unwillingness to *openly* go to war against other democracies—democratic governments are very willing to attack other democracies covertly. Because PSCs offer an increased range of action for democratic policymakers seeking to pursue plausibly deniable covert activities, we can expect that increased PSC use and availability in the modern era might lead to an increase in the frequency with which democracies covertly attack other democracies. This, in turn, will have negative implications for the democratic peace. See David P. Forsythe, "Democracy, War, and Covert Action," *Journal of Peace Research* 29, 4 (1992): 385–395.

7. Gil Merom, *How Democracies Lose Small Wars* (New York: Cambridge University Press, 2003), 247.

8. "Making a Living with a Gun," *Fiji Times* (February 26, 2008); retrieved on June 3, 2008, from: www.fijitimes.com/print.aspx?id=82373.

9. Michael Lee Lanning, *Mercenaries: Soldiers of Fortune, from Ancient Greece to Today's Private Military Companies* (New York: Ballantine Books, 2005), 3–4.

10. Lanning, 2005: 9–10.

11. M. Dee Beutel, "Buying Our Decline: Mercenaries and Modernity." Paper Presented at the Annual Meeting of the International Studies Association's 49th Annual Convention, San Francisco, March 26, 2008.

12. Lanning, 2005: 31–32.

13. Lanning, 2005: 32.

14. Charles W. Ingrao, *The Hessian Mercenary State* (New York: Cambridge University Press, 1987).

15. Alexander Tabarrok, "The Rise, Fall, and Rise Again of Privateers," *The Independent Review* XI, 4 (Spring 2007): 567.

16. Tabarrok, 2007: 566.

17. U.S. Department of Defense Directive 3000.05, "Military Support for Stability, Security, Transition, and Reconstruction (SSTR) Operations" (November 28, 2005), Section 4.1, 2; retrieved on October 31, 2007, from: www.dtic.mil/whs/directives/corres/pdf/300005p.pdf. Notably, DoD Directive 3000.05 represents a profound shift from the U.S. Army's Capstone Doctrine of 1905, which defined the Army's two core missions as offense and defense.

18. U.S. Department of Defense Directive 3000.05, Sections 4.3–4.5.2, pp. 2–3. While some in the military may take issue with the claim that civilians could better perform stability operations tasks than could the military, this thinking reflects a doctrinal trend focused on increased civil–military cooperation in warfare and operations other than war (OOTW) that began in the late 1980s and gained substantial momentum in the post–Cold War era. See U.S. Department of the Army, *Civil Affairs Operations*, Field Manual 41-10, January 1993; U.S. Department of Defense Directive Number 3000.05, 2005: 3.

19. Merom, 2003: 18. Merom builds on the aforementioned notion regarding the limitations associated with policies of conscription in the context of the normative conduct of war as well: "The potential size and power of the anti-war coalition depends in large measure on the sort and number of people who are personally affected by the war—that is, the fate of the war depends on the nature and scope of military mobilization . . . In the long run, a greater reliance on conscription and reservists reduces the capacity of the state to act in the battlefield with unrestrained force, to pursue far-reaching objectives, and to win the war" (Merom, 2003: 21). Logically, reliance on private forces would allow the state to act with unrestrained force because it would not have a direct impact on the electorate.

20. Keith Harmon Snow, "Chloe's Blood Diamond: Angola Rock Sold for $16 Million to GUESS Jeans Founder," *Global Research* (November 24, 2007). Retrieved on June 3, 2008, from: www.globalresearch.ca/PrintArticle.php?articleid=7423.

21. Earl A. Reitan, *The Thatcher Revolution: Margaret Thatcher, John Major, Tony Blair, and the Transformation of Modern Britain, 1979–2001* (Lanham, MD: Rowman & Littlefield, 2003), 37–38.

22. Reitan, 2003: 78–79.

23. Reitan, 2003: 135.

24. James Carroll, "Outsourcing Intelligence," *The Boston Globe* (August 27, 2007). Retrieved on February 4, 2008, from: www.boston.com/news/globe/editorial_opinion/oped/articles/2007/08/27/outsourcing_intelligence/

25. "The Reagan Years: Reaganomics," CNN.com In-Depth Specials. Retrieved on February 4, 2008, from: www.cnn.com/SPECIALS/2001/reagan.years/whitehouse/reaganomics.html. See also William Greider, "The Education of David Stockman," *The Atlantic Monthly* (December 1981). Retrieved on March 21, 2008, from: www.theatlantic.com/politics/budget/stockman.htm.

26. Center for International Development at Harvard University, "Washington Consensus." Retrieved on April 23, 2008, from: www.cid.harvard.edu/cidtrade/issues/washington.html.

27. Anders Aslund, *Post-Communist Economic Revolutions: How Big a Bang?* (Washington, DC: The Center for Strategic and International Studies, 1992), 69.

28. Aslund, 1992: 83–84.

29. Aslund, 1992: 87.

30. Jeremy Scahill, *Blackwater: The Rise of the World's Most Powerful Mercenary Army* (New York: Nation Books, 2007), xvi. Halliburton received $3.9 million to write its initial report, and an additional $5 million to do a follow-up study. These reports offered a strategy for private enterprise to provide support to 20,000 troops. In August 1992, the U.S. Army Corps of Engineers selected Halliburton to do the work necessary to support the military over the next five years, in accordance with the plan the company itself had drawn up. Such an agreement speaks to both capacity gaps in the U.S. military at the time and to the political clout of Halliburton in the few years directly preceding Cheney's tenure as the firm's CEO. Notably, Cheney took $44 million in salary as Halliburton CEO from 1995–2000. See Jeffrey Steinberg, "Rohatyn, Shultz, Cheney 'Privatization' Scheme to Wreck U.S. National Security," *Executive Intelligence Review* (March 31, 2006). Retrieved on October 26, 2009, from: www.larouchepub.com/other/2006/3313rohatyn_privatiz.html.

31. Defense Science Board, *Report of the Defense Science Board Task Force on Outsourcing and Privatization* (August 1996), 3A. Retrieved on May 15, 2007, from: www.acq.osd.mil/dsb/reports/outsourcing.pdf.

32. Defense Science Board Task Force Report, 1996: 6A.

33. Defense Science Board Task Force Report, 1996: 6A.

34. U.S. General Accounting Office, "Outsourcing DOD Logistics: Savings Achievable but Defense Science Board's Projections Are Overstated," Publication No. GAO/NSIAD-98-48 (Washington, DC: December 1997), 13.

35. Quoted in Scahill, 2007: xiv.

36. Scahill, 2007: xv.

37. Donald H. Rumsfeld, "Transforming the Military," *Foreign Affairs* (May/June 2002).

38. Peter W. Singer, *Corporate Warriors: The Rise of the Privatized Military Industry* (Ithaca, NY: Cornell University Press, 2003), 93.

39. Singer, 2003: 92.

40. Singer, 2003: 95.

41. Singer, 2003: 97.

42. Eric Westropp (Director, Control Risks Group) in interview with the author, January 23, 2007.

43. Interview with high-level PSC official, January 24, 2007.

44. Jon W. Glass, "Blackwater Aims High with Unmanned Aircraft," *The Virginian-Pilot*, November 23, 2007. Retrieved on August 28, 2009, from: http://hamptonroads.com/node/433181.

45. Blackwater Foundation, "Kenya Rescue 2008." Retrieved on March 18, 2008, from: www.blackwaterusa.com/foundation/Kenya_Rescue.html. Blackwater Foundation, "Blackwater Worldwide Provides Relief within a Fire." Retrieved on March 18, 2008, from: www.blackwaterusa.com/foundation/Wildfire_Victim_Relief.html.

46. Deborah Avant, *The Market for Force* (New York: Cambridge University Press, 2005), 16.

47. Christopher Kinsey, *Corporate Solders and International Security: The Rise of Private Military Companies* (London: Routledge, 2006), 10.

48. Kinsey, 2006: 10.

49. Each of the typologies mentioned here has strengths and weaknesses, and any one may be better suited to use in certain analytical situations than would the others. The typology I develop in Chapter 3 is not intended to be a competing means of classifying the private security industry but rather to complement those outlined above.

50. Anthony Mockler, *The Mercenaries* (New York: Macmillan, 1969): 21; Janice Thompson, *Mercenaries, Pirates, and Sovereigns* (Princeton, NJ: Princeton University Press, 1994: 27.

51. Singer, 2003: 43.

52. Sarah Percy, *Mercenaries: The History of a Norm in International Relations* (Oxford, UK: Oxford University Press, 2007): 54.

53. Percy, 2007: 57.

54. Niccolo Machiavelli, *The Prince*, Chapter XIII (New York: Random House, 1950); Percy, 2007: 59.

55. Article 47.2 of Additional Protocol I defines a mercenary as any person who:

  (a) is specially recruited locally and abroad in order to fight in an armed conflict

  (b) does, in fact, take a direct part in hostilities;

  (c) is motivated to take part in the hostilities essentially by the desire for private gain and, in fact, is promised by or on behalf of a Party to the conflict material compensation substantially in excess of that promised or paid to combatants of similar rank and functions in the armed forces of that Party;

  (d) is neither a national of a Party to the conflict nor a resident of territory controlled by a Party to the conflict;

  (e) is not a member of the armed forces of a Party to the conflict; and

  (f) has not been sent by a State which is not a Party to the conflict on official duty as a member of its armed forces.

56. Acting almost like a non-governmental organization or think tank, Blackwater maintained and widely distributed a weekly electronic newsletter titled "The Blackwater Tactical Weekly," a collection of (usually conservative-minded) newspaper articles and other media reports pertaining to the Iraq War, the War on Terrorism, and other key U.S. national security issues. Even more notable was Blackwater's Global Peacekeeping and Stability Operations Institute (BW GPSOI), which sponsored its first annual two-day symposium in Washington, D.C., in December 2007. The symposium's theme, the "Public/Private Partnership in Peacekeeping," had as its goal to "look at those areas where the military and government can use private sector expertise to successfully accomplish security and reconstruction operations. To most

effectively and efficiently accomplish stability and reconstruction missions requires using the most appropriate skill sets. Frequently those skill sets reside in the private sector. To best use the taxpayer's resources may require leveraging the private sector." See the Blackwater Global Peace and Stability Operations Institute website, retrieved on October 22, 2007, from: http:/gpsoi.org/index.html. Whether elaborate lobbying tactics or public relations schemes to improve Blackwater's public image, these two examples illustrate the firm's interest in and proactive approach to influencing U.S. foreign and military policy. Having changed its name in an attempt to remake its public image, it is unclear to what extent Xe will continue these initiatives of Blackwater. Meanwhile, company founder Erik Prince acknowledged in October 2007 that Blackwater held over fifty U.S. federal contracts at that point in time. By the end of 2006, the total value of all Blackwater contracts was $1 billion. See "Blackwater by Numbers: A Statistical Index," *Mother Jones Blog* (October 3, 2007); retrieved on March 21, 2008 from: www.motherjones.com/cgi-bin/print_mojoblog.pl?url=http:// www. . . . archives/2007/10/5663_blackwater_by_numbers_a_statistical_index.html. As of late 2006, the company had 450 permanent employees, and a contractor database of thousands more ready to be called into service (Ken Silverstein, "Revolving Door at Blackwater Causes Alarm at CIA," *Harper's Magazine* [September 12, 2006]; retrieved on March 21, 2008, from: www.harpers.org/archive/2006/09/sb-revolving-door-blackwater-1158094722.

57. Doug Brooks (President, International Peace Operations Association), in interview with the author, April 3, 2007.

Chapter 2: Democratic States, Their Militaries, and Security Privatization: Theoretical Considerations

1. James Cockayne, "The Global Reorganization of Legitimate Violence: Military Entrepreneurs and the Private Face of International Humanitarian Law," *ICRC Review* 88, 863 (September 2006): 460–461; David Held, "Central Perspectives on the Modern State," in David Held et al., eds., *States and Societies* (New York: New York University Press, 1983), 34–38; Paul G. Lewis, "Introduction," in David Held et al., eds., *States and Societies* (New York: New York University Press, 1983), 413.

2. Max Weber, "Politics as a Vocation," in H. H. Gerth and C. W. Mills, eds., *From Max Weber* (Oxford, UK: Oxford University Press, 1972), 8.

3. Stephen D. Krasner, "Westphalia and All That," in Judith Goldstein and Robert O. Keohane, eds., *Ideas and Foreign Policy* (Ithaca, NY: Cornell University Press, 1993), 235.

4. Krasner, 1993: 236.

5. Janice E. Thomson, *Mercenaries, Pirates, and Sovereigns* (Princeton, NJ: Princeton University Press, 1994), 3.

6. Thomson, 1994: 6.

7. General Rupert Smith, *The Utility of Force: The Art of War in the Modern World* (London: Penguin Books, 2006): 269.

8. Smith, 2006: 301. This idea that state force is in decline due to decreasing military size and due to contemporary arguments regarding the sole legitimacy of multinational forces is not entirely original. See Martin van Creveld, *The Rise and Decline of the State* (New York: Cambridge University Press, 1999).

9. Avant, 2005b: 7. See also Joakim Berndtsson, "Private Military Companies and the Privatisation of Violence and Security: Rethinking the Monopoly of Violence and the Role of the State," *Paper presented at the Annual Meeting of the International Studies Association* (San Diego: March 2006).

10. Avant, 2005b: 258. See also Berndtsson, 2006.

11. Charles Tilly, "War Making and State Making as Organized Crime," in Peter B. Evans, Dietrich Rueschemeyer, and Theda Skocpol, eds., *Bringing the State Back In* (New York: Cambridge University Press, 1985).

12. Avant, 2005b: 255.

13. Avant similarly notes the existence of this phenomenon: "In strong states, privatization has often brought new security tools in ways that opened the way for a broader variety of functions, sometimes at increased cost and with still uncertain effects on professionalism within the military (and thus the long-term military effectiveness)." See Avant, 2005b: 256.

14. Rebecca Ulam Weiner, "Peace Corp.," *Boston Globe*, April 23, 2006. Retrieved on July 2, 2007, from: www.boston.com. See also Olivia Allison and Martha Clark Dunigan, "Ensuring Effective Use of Private Forces: Domestic, International, and Transnational Regulatory Options in the Face of Changing Warfare," in Isaiah Wilson III and James J. F. Forest, eds., *Handbook of Defence Politics* (London: Routledge, 2008): 106.

15. Tilly, 1985: 184.

16. The 2007 *State of the Peace and Stability Operations Industry Annual Survey* reported that North America was the base of operations for 61 percent of the private security industry's companies, with 52 percent of the world's companies based in the United States at that time. Operationally, companies had their largest presence in Iraq and Afghanistan, with 70 percent and 65 percent of companies operating in those countries, respectively. The companies operating in these theaters were employed to a large extent by U.S. and coalition governments and companies. Over 65 percent of the companies surveyed similarly operated in the European Union. The private security industry also had a sizable presence in the Middle East, Central Asia, North and East Africa, and non-EU Europe during this period. See J. J. Messner and Ylana Gracielli, *State of the Peace and Stability Operations Industry: Second Annual Survey* (2007), Peace Operations Institute, International Peace Operations Association. Retrieved from www.ipoaonline.org.

17. David A. Lake, "Powerful Pacifists: Democratic States and War," *The American Political Science Review* 86, 1 (March 1992): 24–37.

18. Dan Reiter and Allan C. Stam III, "Democracy and Battlefield Military Effectiveness," *The Journal of Conflict Resolution* 42, 3 (June 1998): 271–272; Reiter and Stam, *Democracies at War* (Princeton, NJ: Princeton University Press, 2002), 27, 193.

19. Reiter and Stam, 2002: 70.

20. Author's interview with two anonymous high-level PSC officials, London, January 24, 2007; author's interview with anonymous PSC operator and trainer, Washington, DC, April 26, 2007. Deborah Avant's experimental research likewise indicates that "Americans see the motivations of private security personnel as more monetary than patriotic," though Americans also feel that they and the U.S. government are just as responsible for contractor deaths as for U.S. military deaths in Iraq. See Deborah Avant, "After Blackwater, Four Fundamental Questions About Our Democracy," *San Francisco Chronicle* (October 8, 2007). Retrieved on November 14, 2007, from: www .pacificcouncil.org/pdfs/Avant_10.08.pdf.

21. Kenneth A. Schultz and Barry R. Weingast, "The Democratic Advantage: The Institutional Sources of State Power in International Competition," *International Organization* 57, 1 (Winter 2003): 3–42.

22. Erik Gartzke, "Democracy and the Preparation for War: Does Regime Type Affect States' Anticipation of Casualties?" *International Studies Quarterly* 45, 3 (September 2001): 467–484.

23. See Bruce Bueno de Mesquita, *The War Trap* (New Haven, CT: Yale University Press, 1981); Bruce Bueno de Mesquita, "The War Trap Revisited: A Revised Expected Utility Model," *American Political Science Review* 79, 1 (1985): 156–177; Bruce Bueno de Mesquita and D. Lalman, *War and Reason, Domestic and International Imperatives* (New Haven, CT: Yale University Press, 1992); R. M. Siverson, "Thinking about Puzzles in the Study of International War," *Conflict Management and Peace Science* 15, 2 (1996): 113–132.

24. Sven Chojnacki, "Democratic Wars and Military Interventions, 1946–2002: The Monadic Level Reconsidered," in Anna Geis, Lothar Brock, and Harald Muller, eds., *Democratic Wars: Looking at the Dark Side of Democratic Peace* (New York: Palgrave, 2006): 26.

25. Thomas Risse-Kappen, "Democratic Peace—Warlike Democracies? A Social Constructivist Interpretation of the Liberal Argument," *European Journal of International Relations* 1, 4 (1995): 491–517; Harald Muller, "The Antinomy of Democratic Peace," *International Politics* 41, 4 (2004: Special Issue: The Dynamics of Democratic Peace): 494–520; Chojnacki, 2006: 27.

26. Deborah Avant, "The Implications of Marketized Security for IR Theory: The Democratic Peace, Late State Building, and the Nature and Frequency of Conflict," *Perspectives on Politics* 4 (2006): 507–528.

27. Examining both the historical record and Reiter and Stam's methodological approach, Desch argues that five explanations other than those based on regime type more plausibly explain how states perform in war: (1) an advantage in military power; (2) the nature of the conflict; (3) nationalism; (4) a spurious correlation between democracy and victory; and/or (5) the degree of regime consolidation. See Michael C. Desch, "Democracy & Victory: Why Regime Type Hardly Matters," *International Security* 27, 2 (Fall 2002): 7. Brooks argues that Reiter and Stam do not give adequate attention to a variety of aspects of tactical activity that affect battlefield success, nor to the broader strategic and operational plans and decisions that are essential to victory, and that they conflate culture and institutions, lump together all autocratic states, fail to control for confounding variables, and code "level of democracy" problematically. See Risa A. Brooks, "Making Military Might: Why do States Fail and Succeed? A Review Essay," *International Security* 28, 2 (Fall 2003): 167, 172–177. Another critique of this literature questions whether regime type is the root cause of the unit-level factors causing victory in wars, or whether those unit-level factors actually cause regime type. See Stephen Biddle and Stephen Long, "Democracy and Military Effectiveness: A Deeper Look," *The Journal of Conflict Resolution* 48, 4 (August 2004): 525–546.

28. See Jessica L. Weeks, "Autocratic Audience Costs: Regime Type and Signaling Resolve," *International Organization* 62 (Winter 2008), 35–64.

29. Merom, 2003: 15.

30. Risa A. Brooks, "The Impact of Culture, Society, Institutions, and International Forces on Military Effectiveness," in Risa Brooks and Elizabeth Stanley, eds., *Creating Military Power: The Sources of Military Effectiveness* (Stanford, CA: Stanford University Press, 2007), 7–8.

31. See for instance John Mearsheimer, *The Tragedy of Great Power Politics* (New York: W. W. Norton & Company, 2001); Kenneth Waltz, *Theory of International Politics* (Reading, MA: Addison-Wesley, 1979); Stephen M. Walt, *The Origins of Alliances* (Ithaca, NY: Cornell University Press, 1987); Hans J. Morgenthau, "Alliances in Theory and Practice," in Arnold Wolfers, ed., *Alliance Policy in the Cold War* (Baltimore: Johns Hopkins Press, 1959); Robert Jervis, "Cooperation under the Security Dilemma," *World Politics* 30, 2 (January 1978): 167–214.

32. See for instance Stephen Van Evera, *Causes of War: Power and the Roots of Conflict* (Ithaca: Cornell University Press, 2001); Sean M. Lynn-Jones, "Offense-Defense Theory and Its Critics," *Security Studies* 4, 4 (1995): 660-691; Charles L. Glaser and Chaim Kaufmann, "What is the Offense-Defense Balance and Can We Measure It?," *International Security* 22, 4 (Spring 1998): 44-82; Stephen Biddle, "Rebuilding the Foundations of Offense-Defense Theory," *The Journal of Politics* 63, 3 (August 2001): 741-774.

33. Rosen argues that social structures can influence the generation of military power in two ways: (1) people in a political unit can identify themselves with social structures in ways that can create divisive loyalties within the political unit, thereby

reducing the military effectiveness of the unit as a whole; and/or (2) the social structures that create fissures in the unit may extend to the military organizations of that unit. While these are useful concepts for the purposes of this study, Rosen does not employ a very nuanced or detailed view of what constitutes military power, and by extension, military effectiveness. His conception of military power depends on the enemy's strength in any given situation, focuses only on territory lost and gained, and is measured in terms of relative capabilities, weapons, and equipment. See Stephen Peter Rosen, *Societies and Military Power: India and Its Armies* (Ithaca, NY: Cornell University Press, 1996), ix.

34. Stephen Biddle, *Military Power: Explaining Victory and Defeat in Modern Battle* (Princeton, NJ: Princeton University Press, 2004), 193.

35. Biddle and Long, 2004: 528.

36. Smith, 2007: 269.

37. See for instance Max Boot, "The Lessons of a Quagmire," *The New York Times* (November 16, 2003), retrieved on February 8, 2008, from: http://query.nytimes.com/gst/fullpage.html?res=9803E5DD1038F935A25752C1A9659C8B63&sec=&spon=&pagewanted=print; Max Boot, "An Iraq To-Do List: How We Can Help the Surge Succeed," *The Weekly Standard* 12, 34 (May 21, 2007), retrieved on February 8, 2008, from www.weeklystandard.com/Utilities/printer_preview.asp?idArticle=13643&R=139501DB68; Benjamin Valentino, Paul Huth, and Dylan Balch-Lindsay, "'Draining the Sea': Mass Killing and Guerilla Warfare," *International Organization* 58 (Spring 2004): 375–407; Alexander B. Downes, "Desperate Times, Desperate Measures: The Causes of Civilian Victimization in War," *International Security* 30, 4 (Spring 2006): 152–195.

38. LTC Isaiah Wilson III and Jason Lyall, "Rage against the Machines: Explaining Outcomes in Counterinsurgency Warfare," *International Organization* 63 (2009): 67–106. See also John A. Nagl, *Learning to Eat Soup with a Knife: Counterinsurgency Lessons from Malaya and Vietnam* (Chicago: University of Chicago Press, 2002).

39. Joseph H. Felter, "Taking Guns to a Knife Fight: Effective Military Support to Counterinsurgency," Draft Paper, U.S. Military Academy (February 16, 2007).

40. Brigadier Nigel Aylwin-Foster, "Changing the Army for Counterinsurgency Operations," *Military Review* (November-December 2005). Retrieved on May 1, 2009, from: www.army.mil/professionalwriting/volumes/volume4/february_2006/2_06_1_pf.html.

41. Valentino et al., 2004: 376; Downes, 2006: 155–156.

42. Allan Millet, Williamson Murray, and Kenneth Watman, "The Effectiveness of Military Organizations," *International Security* 11, 1 (Summer 1986): 37.

43. Brooks, 2007: 9–10.

44. Brooks, 2007: 10.

45. Brooks, 2007: 11.

46. Brooks, 2007: 12.

47. Brooks, 2007: 13.

48. Reiter and Stam, 1998: 265.

49. Millet, Murray, and Watman, 1986: 38.

50. Stephen Biddle, "Explaining Military Outcomes," in Risa A. Brooks and Elizabeth A. Stanley, eds., *Creating Military Power* (Stanford, CA: Stanford University Press, 2007): 207.

51. Norms of just war include non-combatant immunity, military necessity, utility, and proportionality, among others. For a comprehensive analysis of the principles underlying just war theory see Michael Walzer, *Just and Unjust Wars: A Moral Argument with Historical Illustrations* (New York: Basic Books, 1977).

52. See for example Robert Jervis, *Perception and Misperception in International Politics* (Princeton, NJ: Princeton University Press, 1976).

53. This practice is far from unprecedented in the social sciences. The structure–identity debate applies to many levels of analysis other than that of the state and international system, as shown in sociological and psychological works incorporating these concepts at the individual and small group levels. See Henri Tajfel, "Aspects of National and Ethnic Loyalty," *Social Science Information* 9 (1970): 119–144; Henri Tajfel, *Human Groups and Social Categories* (Cambridge, UK: Cambridge University Press, 1981); John C. Turner, "Social Categorization and the Self-Concept: A Social Cognitive Theory of Group Behavior," in E. J. Lawler, ed., *Advances in Group Processes, Vol. 2*, 77–121 (Greenwich, CT: JAI Press, 1985); John C. Turner et al., *Rediscovering the Social Group: A Self-Categorization Theory* (New York: Blackwell, 1987).

54. Wendy Pullan, "Structuring Structure," in Wendy Pullan and Harshad Bhadeshia, eds., *Structure in Science and Art* (New York: Cambridge University Press, 2000): 8.

55. structure. (n.d.). *Dictionary.com Unabridged (v 1.1)*. Accessed February 1, 2007 at http://dictionary.reference.com/browse/structure

56. structure. (n.d.). *WordNet 3.0*. Princeton University. Retrieved on February 8, 2008, from: http://dictionary.reference.com/browse/structure.

57. Waltz, 1979: 82.

58. Rawi Abdelal et al., "Identity as a Variable," *Perspectives on Politics* 4 (2006): 1.

59. Abdelal et al., 2006: 7–16.

60. Abdelal et al., 2006: 5–6. Note here the distinction between the "rules" cited in the definition of structure versus those mentioned in the definition of constitutive norms. The rules making up the structure of PSC–military co-deployments are formal, institutionalized rules defining what each type of actor is allowed to do (for instance, rules of engagement); these rules exist whether or not they are followed in practice. These structural rules in turn define actors' roles, which, when acted out repetitively over time, become the constitutive norms defining each group. The rules making up constitutive norms, then, are both formal and informal rules that are actually used in practice.

61. Abdelal et al., 2006: 6.

62. Abdelal et al., 2006: 17. While this study focuses more on identity content than levels of contestation regarding identities, it should be noted that contestation—particularly among PSC personnel—is ever present. The variety of services that PSCs provide, as well as the various means they employ to perform these services, are both symptoms and causes of this contestation.

63. Samuel P. Huntington, *The Soldier and the State* (Cambridge, MA: Belknap Press, 1959), 7–8.

64. Huntington, 1959: 7.

65. Huntington, 1959: 15.

66. Huntington, 1959: 16.

67. Abbott defines *career* in this context as "the idea of a single occupational skill or identity characterizing individuals for their entire working lives." Andrew Abbott, "The Army and the Theory of Professions," in Don M. Snider and Gayle L. Watkins, eds., *The Future of the Army Profession* (Boston: McGraw-Hill, 2002), 530–531.

68. Andrew Abbott, *The System of Professions: An Essay on the Division of Expert Labor* (Chicago: University of Chicago Press, 1988): 2.

69. Richard Lacquement, "Mapping Army Professional Expertise and Clarifying Jurisdictions of Practice," in Don M. Snider and Lloyd J. Matthews, ed., *The Future of the Army Profession* (Boston: McGraw Hill, 2005), 226. See also Abbott, 2002: 534–535.

70. Deborah Avant, "Losing Control of the Profession Through Outsourcing?" in Don M. Snider and Lloyd J. Matthews, eds., *The Future of the Army Profession* (Boston: McGraw Hill, 2005a), 272.

71. Lacquement, 2005: 226. A related question exists regarding how such a takeover of the military's professional jurisdiction by the private military and security sector would affect U.S. civil–military relations. Theoretically, it would appear that this competition—if the end result were a decrease in military professionalism and a strengthening of the private sector's professional hold over formerly military functions—could decrease objective civilian control over the U.S. military. This could be a fruitful avenue for future research.

72. David Phinney, "Marines Jail Contractors in Iraq: Tension and Confusion Grow Amid the 'Fog of War,'" *CorpWatch* (June 7, 2005), retrieved on December 13, 2005, from: www.corpwatch.org/article?php.id=12349; John M. Broder and James Risen, "Contractor Deaths in Iraq Soar to Record," *The New York Times* (May 19, 2007), retrieved on May 19, 2007, from: www.nytimes.com/2007/05/19/world/middleeast/19contractors .html?hp=&pagewanted=print; Christopher Spearin, "Special Operations Forces a Strategic Resource: Public and Private Divides," *Parameters* (Winter 2006-07): 59–65.

73. Doug Brooks, "Hope for the 'Hopeless Continent': Mercenaries," *Traders: Journal for the Southern African Region* 3 (July–October 2000); Derek Wright, "Point of View: PSCs Like Saito Key to Peace," *The Asahi Shimbun* (July 15, 2005), retrieved on November 14, 2007, from: http://ipoaonline.org/php/index.php?option=com_content& task=view&id=64&Itemid=82&date=2007-08-01; Deborah Avant, "Private Security

and the Prospects for Institution Building and Democracy in Transitional States," Paper presented at the annual meeting of the American Political Science Association, Washington, DC (September 1, 2005c), retrieved on November 14, 2007, from: www .allacademic.com/meta/p41783_index.html.

74. U.S. Government Accountability Office, "Rebuilding Iraq: Actions Needed to Improve Use of Private Security Providers," Publication No. GAO-05-737 (Washington, DC: July 2005); U.S. Government Accountability Office, "Rebuilding Iraq: Actions Still Needed to Improve Use of Private Security Providers," Publication No. GAO-06-865T (Washington, DC: June 13, 2006).

75. These reports indicate that PSCs lower military skill by weakening officers' abilities to competently execute tactics and to seize the initiative when opportunities present themselves.

76. The Associated Press, "Legal Avenues against Blackwater Murky," *The New York Times* (October 3, 2007), retrieved on October 3, 2007, from: www.nytimes.com/ aponline/us/AP-Blackwater-Legal.html?pagewanted=print; Alissa J. Rubin and Paul von Zielbauer, "Blackwater Case Highlights Legal Uncertainties," *The New York Times* (October 11, 2007), retrieved on October 11, 2007, from: www.nytimes.com/2007/10/11/ world/middleeast/11legal.html?_r=1&hp=&oref=slogin&pagewanted=print; "Blackwater Christmas Eve Shooting and Immunity" (September 12, 2007), retrieved on October 14, 2007, from: www.blackwaterblogger.com/2007/09/accountability1.html; Mark Hemingway, "Blackwater's Legal Netherworld: Private Contractors Are Subject to Military Justice—Or Are They?" *National Review Online* (September 26, 2007), retrieved on September 26, 2007, from: http://article.nationalreview.com/?q=MmYzMTkwMzQ 2OTVhNGY2MGQzMDYoMTJiM2ExYmY3YmY=; David Stout and John M. Broder, "Report Depicts Recklessness at Blackwater," *The New York Times* (October 1, 2007), retrieved on October 1, 2007, from: www.nytimes.com/2007/10/01/washington/01cnd-blackwater.html?_r=1&hp=&oref=slogin&pagewanted=print; James Glanz and Alissa J. Rubin, "From Errand to Fatal Shot to Hail of Fire to 17 Deaths," *The New York Times* (October 3, 2007), retrieved on October 3, 2007, from: www.nytimes.com/2007/10/03/ world/middleeast/03firefight.html?hp=&pagewanted=print; David Johnston and John M. Broder, "F.B.I. Says Guards Killed 14 Iraqis without Cause," *The New York Times* (November 14, 2007), retrieved on November 14, 2007, from: www.nytimes.com/2007/11/ 14/world/middleeast/14blackwater.html?_r=1&hp=&pagewanted=print.

77. See for instance Boot, 2003, 2007; Valentino et al., 2004; Downes, 2006.

78. On the issue of future wars being fought in multinational coalitions, see Smith, 2007, 303–307.

79. Avant, 2005b: 38.

80. There are three variables at play in the propositions elaborated above. Each of the cases is selected on the independent variable for the two main propositions (P1 and P2), which is the use of private security companies in conflicts. The dependent variable is military effectiveness, measured as detailed above. There is a second independent

variable at play in the four propositions related to IHL: level of PSC compliance with international laws of war. As noted by King, Keohane, and Verba, "the best 'intentional' design selects observations to ensure variation in the explanatory variable (and any control variables) without regard to the values of the dependent variables" (Gary King, Robert O. Keohane, and Sidney Verba, *Designing Social Inquiry* [Princeton, NJ: Princeton University Press, 1994], 140).

81. While most of these interviews were conducted in person, approximately 30 percent of the interviews—mostly on the military side—were conducted as online, asynchronous, in-depth interviews. These are semistructured interviews conducted via e-mail, involving multiple e-mail exchanges between the interviewer and interviewee over an extended period of time. This technique has several benefits, particularly given the sensitive nature of the topic at hand in this study, and the busy schedules and geographic distance separating many of the relevant interview participants from the researcher. This method has been shown to cost considerably less to administer than in-person interviews, allowing researchers to invite the participation of geographically dispersed samples of people and enabling researchers "to study individuals or groups with special characteristics or those often difficult or impossible to reach or interview face-to-face or via telephone." See Lokman I. Meho, "E-Mail Interviewing in Qualitative Research: A Methodological Discussion," *Wiley Interscience* (May 25, 2006): 2, 5, retrieved on October 20, 2007, from: www.interscience.wiley.com.

Owing to the bureaucratic constraints hindering formal U.S. military approval to interview military personnel for a study on a relatively sensitive topic, this method was found to be especially appropriate for this study. Some potential weaknesses with this method should be noted, however. For instance, it is easier in an e-mail interview for respondents to give false responses, deceiving the researcher. Furthermore, there is a related risk that e-mail interviews lack the media richness of in-person interviews, owing to both parties' inability to pick up on visual or non-verbal cues. Yet there is evidence that "in many cases e-mail facilitates greater disclosure of personal information, offering further benefits to both the researcher and participants." See N. Bowker and K. Tuffin, "Using the Online Medium for Discursive Research about People with Disabilities," *Social Science Computer Review* 22, 2 (2004): 228–241.

82. Sarah Cotton, Ulrich Petersohn, Molly Dunigan, Q Burkhart, Ed O'Connell, and Michael Webber, *Hired Guns: Views about Armed Contractors in Operation Iraqi Freedom* (Santa Monica, CA: RAND Corporation, MG-987, 2010).

Chapter 3: Brothers in Arms? PSCs Deployed Alongside the National Military

1. Lee, 2008.

2. Ivanovich, 2008. See also Schakowsky, 2007.

3. Congressional Budget Office, *Contractors' Support of U.S. Operations in Iraq.*, August 2008; retrieved on December 23, 2008, from: www.cbo.gov/ftpdocs/96xx/doc9688/08-12-IraqContractors.pdf.

4. Lee, 2008.

5. Congressional Budget Office, 2008.

6. Testimony of Ambassador Richard J. Griffin, Assistant Secretary of State, Bureau of Diplomatic Security, Department of State, "Private Security Contracting in Iraq and Afghanistan," House Committee on Oversight and Government Reform, October 2, 2007; retrieved on October 5, 2008, from: http://oversight.house.gov/documents/20071002145249.pdf.

7. Testimony of Ginger Cruz, Deputy Special Inspector General for Iraq Reconstruction, "The Role of the Department of Defense in Provincial Reconstruction Teams," House Committee on Armed Services, Subcommittee on Oversight and Investigations, September 5, 2007. Retrieved on December 23, 2008, from: http://armedservices.house .gov/pdfs/OI090507/Cruz%20_Testimony090507.pdf.

8. U.S. Government Accountability Office, July 2005: 20.

9. U.S. Government Accountability Office, 2006.

10. Office of the Special Inspector General for Iraq Reconstruction, *Field Commanders See Improvements in Controlling and Coordinating Private Security Contractor Missions in Iraq*, SIGIR 09-022, July 28, 2009: 2-3, retrieved on October 19, 2009, from: www.sigir.mil/reports/pdf/audits/09-022.pdf.

11. Office of the Special Inspector General for Iraq Reconstruction, 2009: 2–3.

12. Office of the Special Inspector General for Iraq Reconstruction, 2009: 4.

13. Office of the Special Inspector General for Iraq Reconstruction, 2009: 5–7.

14. U.S. Government Accountability Office, "Rebuilding Iraq: DOD and State Department Have Improved Oversight and Coordination of Private Security Contractors in Iraq, but Further Actions Are Needed to Sustain Improvements," Publication No. GAO-08-966 (Washington, DC: July 2008): 4.

15. See for instance David Barstow, "Security Companies: Shadow Soldiers in Iraq," *The New York Times* (April 19, 2004); Eric Schmitt, "Accord Tightens Control of Security Contractors in Iraq," *The New York Times* (December 5, 2007).

16. U.S. Government Accountability Office, 2006: 1.

17. This study uses original interview data to answer these questions, drawing on interviews that I conducted between September 2006 and December 2007 with academic experts, high-level private security company officials, private security company operators (lower-level personnel), and U.S. Army and U.S. Air Force soldiers of various ranks, ranging from non-commissioned officers to colonels. I conducted further interviews with one U.K. military officer and four U.K. PSC officials, to research any potential differences in PSC–military relations between the United States and the United Kingdom. Seventeen of the eighteen PSC interviewees were former military. Four had British military experience, one had New Zealand military experience, and the remainder had U.S. military experience. Altogether, fourteen military and eighteen PSC personnel were interviewed specifically for this study, for a total of thirty-two respondents with direct field experience. Twenty-three of the thirty-two total interviewees

had OIF experience (twelve PSC and eleven military personnel), five had OEF experience (two PSC and three military personnel), and four had been deployed to both OIF and OEF (three PSC interviewees and one military interviewee). Their dates of service in Iraq and Afghanistan ranged from 2002 to 2007, with some interviewees deployed more than once to these theaters.

The analysis below also draws on a series of twenty-four separate individual and small group interviews conducted between July 2004 and March 2006 by the GAO in writing its 2005 and 2006 reports on "Actions Needed to Improve the Use of Private Security Providers." The transcripts reflect a mixture of structured and semi-structured interviewing techniques, and I obtained them in October 2006 through a written request to the GAO. All of the figures cited below are drawn from my own analysis of the GAO transcripts. For more on these transcripts, see Chapter One.

These interview data are bolstered by large-n military survey data collected by researchers at the RAND Corporation in 2008, and pertaining specifically to Operation Iraqi Freedom during the 2003–2008 time period. RAND surveyed 249 military personnel and 892 State Department personnel with OIF deployment experience from 2003 to 2008, seeking to assess the impact of armed contractors on the U.S. military's ability to achieve its mission in Iraq. These data also reflect a range in respondents' levels of experience with armed contractors. In the analysis that follows, I explicitly note when I am considering the entire pool of RAND survey respondents, and when I am considering only those who had experience or a lack of experience interacting with armed contractors.

18. Interview with colonel, U.S. Army, October 10, 2006; interview with high-level PSC official, December 2006; John Nettles (former Army Special Forces; Trainer, Olive Security Training Center), in interview with the author, April 2007.

19. Interview with lieutenant colonel, U.S. Air Force, October 31, 2007.

20. Interview with colonel, U.S. Army, Ret.; employed at time of interview as high-level PSC official, July 7, 2007.

21. Military *skill* and *quality* are also affected in situations of PSC–military co-deployment, though neither is linked to PSC–military coordination per se. *Skill* is affected by the impact of PSCs' higher pay on soldiers' motivation, while *quality* is affected by the force-multiplying effects of PSCs. Both phenomena are discussed in further detail later in this chapter.

22. It is worth noting here that, for the purposes of this project, Operation Enduring Freedom does not differ significantly from the situation in Iraq, although there is a different ratio of PSC to military personnel in Afghanistan and the development of structural measures to assure smooth communications (that is, ROCs or CONOCs) has occurred at a slower pace there than in Iraq.

23. Interestingly, the Reconstruction Operations Center is managed by Aegis Defence Services, Inc., a private intelligence company owned by former Sandline owner Tim Spicer, whose activities in Sierra Leone are discussed in detail in Chapter 4. The

Washington Post reports that Aegis won the largest single contract for private security in Iraq—a three-year, $293 million U.S. Army contract—for its management of the ROC. Steve Fainaru and Alec Klein, "In Iraq, a Private Realm of Intelligence-Gathering," *The Washington Post* (July 1, 2007), retrieved on December 18, 2007, from: www.washingtonpost.com/wp-dyn/content/article/2007/06/30/AR2007063001075_pf.html.

24. The ROC Watch Officer originally produced these charts. I would like to thank Colonel Timothy Cornett of USSOUTHCOM and the Peacekeeping & Stability Operations Institute of the U.S. Army War College for providing me with access to these data, which Colonel Cornett presented at the Combat Training Center Commander's Conference at the Combined Arms Center at TRADOC on September 26–27, 2006.

25. It is difficult to grasp the frequency of blue-on-white incidents relative to other friendly fire incidents, as no centrally collected figures exist of friendly fire incidents between regular military forces (so-called blue-on-blue incidents) in Operation Iraqi Freedom. However, one report suggests that thirty-two blue-on-blue incidents involving British and coalition vehicles occurred in southern Iraq in 2004. See Mark Townsend, "Why Won't the US Tell Us How Matty Died?," *The Guardian*, February 4, 2007, retrieved on June 10, 2008, from: www.guardian.co.uk/2007/feb/04/iraq.military/print.

26. Human Rights First, *Private Security Contractors at War: Ending the Culture of Impunity* (Washington, DC: Human Rights First, 2008), 13.

27. Human Rights First, 2008: 16.

28. Human Rights First, 2008: 16. Note that the aforementioned regulatory policies instituted in 2007 and 2008 by the DoD and the State Department may alleviate some of the problems associated with self-reporting, as these newer measures *were* instituted, at least in part, for the purpose of monitoring PSC personnel.

29. Cotton et al., 2010.

30. Interview with colonel, U.S. Army, Ret.; employed at time of interview as high-level PSC official, July 7, 2007.

31. Interview with private security contractor employed by Triple Canopy in Iraq, April 17, 2007.

32. Alan Brosnan (director, Olive Security Training Center) and Todd Taylor (instructor, Head of Law Enforcement Training Division, Olive Security Training Center), in interview with the author, April 10, 2007.

33. Eric Westervelt, "Profile: Confusion in Iraq over Alleged Incident between Marines and Private Contractors," *National Public Radio: Morning Edition* (June 13, 2005), retrieved on March 8, 2007, from: www.npr.org.

34. Phinney, 2005

35. Phinney, 2005: 4.

36. Interview with U.S. Army major, November 26, 2007.

37. Interview with private security contractor employed by Triple Canopy in Iraq, April 17, 2007.

38. Cotton et al., 2010.

39. Cotton et al., 2010.

40. Westervelt, 2005: 2.

41. Abdelal,et al., 2006: 5, 6.

42. Interview with high-level British PSC officials, January 24, 2007.

43. Interview with U.S. Army colonel, July 12, 2007.

44. Major Royce Edington (U.S. Army), in interview with the author, July 10, 2007.

45. Charles "Chuck" S. Mahan Jr. (Lieutenant General, U.S. Army (Ret.), and General Manager, Law Enforcement and Security and Government Services, DynCorp International), in interview with the author, November 7, 2007.

46. Reiter and Stam, 2002: 61.

47. Peter W. Singer, "Should Humanitarians Use Private Military Services?" *Small Wars Journal*, retrieved on February 11, 2008, from: http://smallwarsjournal.com/documents/petersinger.pdf.

48. Cotton et al., 2010. Because the RAND survey was not specific with regard to how respondents should measure and define morale, it is unclear whether this can be equated with Reiter and Stam's measurement of morale in terms of patriotism.

49. Cotton et al., 2010.

50. Cotton et al., 2010.

51. See for instance Robert Young Pelton, *Licensed to Kill: Hired Guns in the War on Terror* (New York: Crown Publishers, 2006), 119; Associated Press, "Blackwater Blamed for Fallujah Bloodshed," *Newser* (September 28, 2007), retrieved on January 9, 2008, from: www.newser.com/story/8370.html.

52. Bill Sizemore and Joanne Kimberlin, "Blackwater: When Things Go Wrong," *The Virginian-Pilot* (July 26, 2006).

53. Bing West, *No True Glory* (New York: Bantam, 2005), quoted in Sizemore and Kimberlin, 2006.

54. Roy McCarthy, "Uneasy Truce in the City of Ghosts," *The Guardian* (April 24, 2004), retrieved on February 11, 2008, from: www.guardian.co.uk/Iraq/Story/0,2763,1202163,00.html.

55. Pelton, 2006: 138–139.

56. Pelton, 2006: 131.

57. U.S. House of Representatives, Committee on Oversight and Government Reform, Majority Staff, "Private Military Contractors in Iraq: An Examination of Blackwater's Actions in Fallujah," (September 2007): 3, 11.

58. Sizemore and Kimberlin, 2006.

59. Pelton, 2006: 119.

60. Glanz and Rubin, 2007; James Glanz and Alissa J. Rubin, "Blackwater Shootings 'Murder,' Iraq Says," *The New York Times* (October 8, 2007), retrieved on January 9, 2007, from: www.nytimes.com/2007/10/08/world/middleeast/08blackwater.html?scp=1&sq=nisour+square+blackwater; Richard A. Oppel Jr. and Michael R. Gordon, "U.S.

Military and Iraqis Say They Are Shut Out of Inquiry," *The New York Times* (October 11, 2007), retrieved on January 9, 2008, from: www.nytimes.com/2007/10/11/world/middleeast/11blackwater.html?scp=3&sq=nisour+square+blackwater; Johnston and Broder, 2007; Lara Logan, "Interview with Erik Prince," *60 Minutes* (October 13, 2007a).

61. "Blackwater 5: Case Dismissed," *The Washington Post* (January 6, 2010): 14; August Cole, "Blackwater Dismissal Risks Hurting Iraq Relations," *The Wall Street Journal* (January 2, 2010): 7.

62. Daniel Luban, "Blackwater Pays Price for Iraqi Firefight," *Asia Times* (September 19, 2007), retrieved on December 30, 2008, from: www.atimes.com/atimes/Middle_East/II19Ak04.html.

63. Interview with U.S. Army colonel, October 11, 2007.

64. Interview with U.S. Army major, November 26, 2007.

65. Kevin McNeill (former New Zealand Army Infantry and Special Air Services, Personal Security Detail operator for Control Risks Group in Iraq, and Security Consultant/Trainer for Background Asia Risk Solution in the Malacca Straits; at time of interview, employed by BLP to train the Iraqi National Police), in interview with the author, April 19, 2007.

66. Interview with U.S. Army colonel, July 12, 2007.

67. Cotton et al., 2010.

68. See, for instance, Spearin, 2006–2007: 58–70.

69. While the selection effects argument theorizes that the democratic public will wish to involve its country only in wars that it is predisposed to win, the Fallujah case indicates that highly publicized and gruesome contractor deaths may drive the democratic public and policymakers toward a desire for revenge that overrides more rational considerations regarding the likelihood that greater involvement will result in victory. Such a notion, if borne out in future research, has the potential to weaken or at least alter the theorization of democratic advantage theory's selection effects argument.

70. Abdelal et. al., 2006: 5–6. For a further explanation of these measurement rubrics, refer to Chapter 2.

71. Interview with lieutenant colonel, U.S. Army, October 11, 2007.

72. Interview with lieutenant colonel, British Army, January 22, 2007.

73. Interview with lieutenant colonel, British Army, January 22, 2007.

74. GAO interview with U.S. military personnel, May 9, 2005. Transcript acquired from the U.S. Government Accountability Office, October 2006.

75. GAO interview with U.S. military personnel, March 27, 2006. Transcript acquired from the U.S Government Accountability Office, October 2006.

76. GAO interview with PSC personnel, August 31, 2004. Transcript acquired from the U.S. Government Accountability Office, October 2006.

77. GAO interview with U.S. military personnel, March 27, 2006. Transcript acquired from the U.S. Government Accountability Office, October 2006.

78. GAO interview with military official from the 1st Armored Division, U.S. Army, December 9, 2004. Transcript acquired from the U.S. Government Accountability Office, October 2006.

79. GAO interview with U.S. military personnel, March 27, 2006. Transcript acquired from the U.S Government Accountability Office, October 2006.

80. Interview with high-level PSC official, January 23, 2007.

81. Eric Westropp (Director, Control Risks Group) in interview with the author, January 23, 2007.

82. For more on the dynamic and mutually constitutive qualities of identities, see Peter J. Katzenstein, "Introduction," in Peter J. Kazenstein, ed., *The Culture of National Security* (New York: Columbia University Press, 1996), 5, 6, 26; Alexander Wendt, "Anarchy Is What States Make of It: The Social Construction of Power Politics," in Charles Lipson and Benjamin J. Cohen, eds., *Theory and Structure in Political Economy: An International Organization Reader* (Cambridge, MA: The MIT Press, 1999), 83, 95; Jeffrey Checkel, "Why Comply? Social Learning and European Identity Change," *International Organization* 55, 3 (September 2001): 553–588.

83. GAO interview with U.S. military personnel, March 27, 2006. Transcript acquired from the U.S Government Accountability Office, October 2006.

84. Abbott, 1988: 8.

85. Interview with high-level PSC official, January 25, 2007.

86. This, in turn, could have the effect of shaping an interventionist democracy's foreign policy in predictable ways. In other words, if an interventionist democracy becomes dependent on PSCs to serve particular functions, other state and non-state actors will begin to realize the limits to what the hired forces of this democracy are willing to do and thus the limits of what the democracy itself is able to do with the forces at its disposal.

87. GAO interview with PSC personnel, August 30, 2004. Transcript acquired from the U.S. Government Accountability Office, October 2006.

Chapter 4: Trading Places: Private Firms Hired in Place of National Militaries

1. It should be noted that MPRI considers itself to be a "Government Services Company," not a "PSC," because it does not provide personal security through armed protection means and programs. Yet because it does provide extensive military advice and training—and has been said to have provided operational planning support to the Croatian military, as detailed in this chapter—it will be considered here in the context of PSCs.

2. MPRI has expanded to include work in areas such as public health, law enforcement, commercial driver training, education, logistics, and international development. Interview with high-level MPRI official, April 2, 2007; Esther Schrader, "US Companies Hired to Train Foreign Armies," *The Los Angeles Times* (April 14, 2002), retrieved on January 16, 2008, from: www.globalpolicy.org/security/peacekpg/training/pmc.htm.

3. Leslie Wayne, "America's For-Profit Secret Army," *The New York Times* (October 13, 2002), 2. Retrieved on January 16, 2008, from: www.globalpolicy.org/security/peacekpg/training/mercenaries.htm.

4. Interview with high-level MPRI official, April 2, 2007.

5. Roger Cohen, "U.S. Cooling Ties to Croatia after Winking at Its Buildup," *The New York Times* (October 28, 1995), retrieved on January 18, 2008, from: http://query.nytimes.com/gst/fullpage.html?res=9503E5DB1F39F93BA15753C1A963958260&scp=1&sq=US+cooling+ties+with+croatia+after+winking+at+its+buildup.

6. Cohen, 1995: A1.

7. "Press Statement of Minister of Defense Mediu," retrieved on August 12, 2009, from: www.mod.gov.al/botime/html/revista/2007/5/faqe13.htm.

8. Ken Silverstein, "Privatizing War: How Affairs of State Are Outsourced to Corporations beyond Public Control," *The Nation*, August 4, 1997, 11.

9. Susan L. Woodward, *Balkan Tragedy: Chaos and Dissolution after the Cold War* (Washington, DC: The Brookings Institution, 1995), 198.

10. Woodward, 1995: 147–148.

11. Laura Silber and Allan Little, *Yugoslavia: Death of a Nation* (New York: Penguin Books, 1997), 322–323.

12. Ozren Zunec, "Civil–Military Relations in Croatia," in Constantine P. Danopoulos and Daniel Zirker, eds., *Civil–Military Relations in the Soviet and Yugoslav Successor States* (Boulder, CO: Westview, 1996), 222; Avant, 2005b: 99–101.

13. Silber and Little, 1997: 353.

14. Tim Ripley, *Operation Deliberate Force* (Lancaster, UK: Centre for Defence and International Security Studies, 1999): 81–82, 90; Christian Jennings, "Private U.S. Firm Training Both Sides in Balkans," *Scotsman* (March 2, 2001).

15. Avant, 2005b: 102.

16. Yves Goulet, "MPRI: Washington's Freelance Advisors," *Jane's Intelligence Review* 10, 7 (July 1998).

17. Schrader, 2002: 5.

18. Quoted in Silber and Little, 1997: 357.

19. Avant, 2005b: 104.

20. Avant, 2005b: 104; Schrader, 2002: 5.

21. Ken Silverstein, *Private Warriors* (New York: Verso, 2000), 172.

22. Schrader, 2002: 5.

23. Avant, 2005b: 107.

24. Avant, 2005b: 103.

25. Avant, 2005b: 103.

26. "Croatian Atrocities Being Forgotten," CBC Report, July 21, 2003, retrieved on September 1, 2009, from: www.globalresearch.ca/articles/CHO307D.html.

27. "Croatian Atrocities," 2003.

28. "A Nation Resolved to Overcome Its Tough Heritage," International Special Reports, *The Washington Times*, retrieved on January 16, 2008, from: www .internationalspecialreports.com/europe/01/croatia/anationresolved.html.

29. Michel Chossudovsky, "NATO Has Installed a Reign of Terror in Kosovo," Paper Presented to the Independent Commission of Inquiry to Investigate U.S./ NATO War Crimes Against The People of Yugoslavia, International Action Center, New York, July 31, 1999; see footnote 22. Retrieved on September 1, 2009, from: www .iacenter.org/warcrime/chossu.htm.

30. Quoted in Raymond Bonner, "War Crimes Panel Finds Croat Troops Cleansed the Serbs," *New York Times*, March 21, 1999.

31. Quoted in Bonner, 1999.

32. Bonner, 1999.

33. Bonner, 1999.

34. Silber and Little, 1997: 359.

35. Silber and Little, 1997: 360.

36. "Croatian Atrocities," 2003.

37. Mark Danner, "Operation Storm," *New York Review of Books*, Oct. 22, 1998.

38. Sam Vaknin, "Analysis: Private Armies—II," *United Press International*, July 18, 2002.

39. Danner, 1998.

40. Avant, 2005b: 106.

41. Schrader, 2002: 5.

42. William Norman Grigg, "Why Kosovo?" *New American* (May 10, 1999); Serbian National Federation, "Kosovo: An Unjust and Unnecessary War" (Serbian National Federation, 1999), retrieved on September 1, 2009, from: www.balkanstudies.org/wordfiles/ Kosovo/Aussie_Kosovo_Paper0899.htm.

43. Richard Sobel, "U.S. and European Attitudes toward Intervention in the Former Yugoslavia: *Mourir Pour la Bosnie?*" in Richard Henry Ullman, ed., *The World and Yugoslavia's Wars* (New York: Council on Foreign Relations, 1996): 146–148. Sobel consulted the following U.S. polls, each based on representative samples of about 1,000 respondents and conducted between 1992 and 1995: ABC/Washington Post Poll, CBS/New York Times Poll, the Gallup Poll, the Harris Poll, Los Angeles Times Poll, NBC/Wall Street Journal Poll, Opinion Research Memoranda, and Princeton Survey Research.

44. Silber and Little, 1997: 357, 360.

45. Interview with high-level MPRI official, April 2, 2007.

46. "Lebanon Civil War: 1975–1991," *GlobalSecurity.org*, retrieved on September 1, 2009, from: www.globalsecurity.org/military/world/war/lebanon.htm. Estimates of the number of fatalities start at 150,000 people, with some estimates considerably larger. See Edgar O'Ballance, *Civil War in Lebanon, 1975–1992* (New York: Palgrave, 2002).

47. O'Ballance, 2002.

48. Itamar Rabinovich, *The War for Lebanon, 1970–1985* (Ithaca, NY: Cornell University Press, 1985).

49. Antoine J. Abraham, *The Lebanon War* (Westport, CT: Praeger, 1996): xv.

50. O'Ballance, 2002: vii–viii. See also "Lebanon: World War I and the French Mandate, 1914–1941," retrieved on September 1, 2009, from: www.country-data.com/cgi-bin/query/r-7940.html.

51. Eyal Zisser, *Lebanon: The Challenges of Independence* (London and New York: I. B. Tauris, 2000): 7.

52. Thomas Collelo, ed. "Phalange Party," *Lebanon: A Country Study* (Washington, DC: GPO for the Library of Congress, 1987), retrieved on September 1, 2009, from: http://countrystudies.us/lebanon/85.htm.

53. "Lebanon," 2009.

54. For a discussion of the U.S. motives for action in Lebanon, see John H. Kelley, "Lebanon: 1982–1984," in Jeremy R. Azrael and Emil A. Payin, eds., *U.S. and Russian Policymaking with Respect to the Use of Force*, Chapter 6. Santa Monica, CA: RAND Corporation, 1996.

55. Paul E. Salem, "Superpowers and Small States: an Overview of American-Lebanese Relations," retrieved on August 31, 2009, from: www.lcps-lebanon.org/pub/breview/br5/psalembr5pt3.html. This is a revised version of an article that originally appeared in the June 1992 issue of *Cahiers de la Méditerranée*, published by the University of Nice, Sophia, Antipolis.

56. Salem, 1992.

57. Marius Deeb, *The Lebanese Civil War* (Santa Barbara, CA: Praeger Publishers, 1980): 135.

58. Deeb, 1980: 135.

59. Dov Yermiya, *My War Diary: Lebanon June 5–July 1, 1982* (London: Pluto Press, 1984): ix.

60. George W. Gawrych, "Siege of Beirut," *GlobalSecurity.org*, retrieved on September 1, 2009, from: www.globalsecurity.org/military/library/report/2002/MOUT Gawrych.htm; Mitchell G. Bard, *Myths & Facts: A Guide to the Arab-Israeli Conflict* (Chevy Chase, MD: American-Israeli Cooperative Enterprise, 2002).

61. Gawrych, "Siege of Beirut."

62. John Laffin, *The War of Desperation—1982–85* (Oxford, UK: Osprey Publishing Ltd, 1985): 175.

63. Laffin, 1985: 175.

64. This impression was all the more persuasive due to the French military deployment because France had a long colonial history of supporting the Maronite Christian community in Lebanon.

65. Ralph A. Hallenbeck, *Military Force as an Instrument of U.S. Foreign Policy (Intervention in Lebanon, August 1982–February 1984)* (New York: Praeger, 1991).

66. "Lebanon: The Lebanese Armed Forces in the 1980s," Library of Congress Country Studies, *CIA World Factbook* (Washington, DC: Central Intelligence Agency), retrieved on July 3, 2009, from: www.photius.com/countries/lebanon/national_security/lebanon_national_security_the_lebanese_armed_f~107.html.

67. U.S. Special Operations Command, "The History of the 10th Special Forces Group (Airborne)," retrieved on April 2, 2010, from: www.soc.mil/SF/history.pdf.

68. Benis M. Frank, *U.S. Marines in Lebanon: 1982–84* (Washington, DC: History and Museums Division, Headquarters, U.S. Marine Corps, 1987). Retrieved from: www.ibiblio.org/hyperwar/AMH/XX/MidEast/Lebanon-1982-1984/USMC-Lebanon82/USMC-Lebanon82-4.html#cn21

69. Jarrett Murphy, "Beirut Barracks Attack Remembered," *CBS News*, October 23, 2003. Retrieved on September 1, 2009, from: www.cbsnews.com/stories/2003/10/23/world/main579638.shtml.

70. See Nicholas Blanford, "U.S. Warship Stirs Lebanese Fear of War: The USS *Cole* Has Deployed off the Coast of Lebanon as That Nation's Political Crisis Deepens," *Christian Science Monitor* (March 4, 2008), retrieved on July 3, 2009, from: www.csmonitor.com/2008/0304/p01s01-wome.html; Charles D. Smith, *Palestine and the Arab Israeli Conflict* (Boston and New York: Bedford/St. Martin's, 2004): 383.

71. Murphy, 2003.

72. Hallenbeck, 1991.

73. "USMC Barracks Bombing," *The Patriotic Gentleman*, retrieved on September 1, 2009, from: www.thepatrioticgentleman.com/USMC-barracks-bombing/USMC-barracks-bombing.html.

74. Laffin, 1985: 187.

75. Thomas Hammes, "Foreword," in Eric Hammel, *The Root: The Marines in Beirut, August 1982–February 1984* (Osceola, WI: Zenith Press, 2005): xxiii; Agnes G. Korbani, *U.S. Intervention in Lebanon, 1958 and 1982* (New York: Praeger: 1991): 83.

76. Korbani, 1991: 92.

77. Compare, for instance, the relative success of MPRI's training efforts in Croatia with the questionable training record of DynCorp trainers working with Afghan police forces. See "U.S.-Trained Afghan Police Force Is Failing," *APS Diplomat News*, December 11, 2006, retrieved on September 28, 2009, from: www.thefreelibrary.com/US-Trained+Afghan+Police+Force+Is+Failing-a0155719639.

78. Hammes, 2005: xxiii–xxiv.

79. Hammes, 2005.

80. Laffin, 1985: 187.

81. Laffin, 1985: 187.

82. U.S. Department of State, Bureau of African Affairs, "Background Note: Sierra Leone," August 2009, retrieved on September 29, 2009, from: www.state.gov/r/pa/ei/bgn/5475.htm.

83. Lieutenant Colonel Tim Spicer, *An Unorthodox Soldier: Peace and War and the Sandline Affair* (London: Mainstream Publishing, 2000), 189.

84. Guy Arnold, *Mercenaries: The Scourge of the Third World* (London: MacMillan Press, 1999), 132.

85. U.S. Department of State, 2009.

86. William Reno, "Privatizing War in Sierra Leone," *Current History* 96, 610 (May 1997): 228.

87. David Shearer, "Dial an Army," *The World Today* (August/September 1997): 203–205.

88. Reno, 1997: 228–229.

89. Christopher Kinsey, *Corporate Solders and International Security: The Rise of Private Military Companies* (London: Routledge, 2006), 63.

90. William Reno, "The Clinton Administration and Africa: Private Corporate Dimension," *Issue: A Journal of Opinion* 26, 2 (1998): 25–26.

91. U.S. Department of State, 2009.

92. Reno, 1998: 26.

93. Arnold, 1999: 135.

94. U.S. Department of State, 2009.

95. U.N. Security Council Resolution 1132, Paragraph 6, October 8, 1997, p. 2, retrieved on September 28, 2009, from: www.customs.gov.sg/NR/rdonlyres/876D72D9-7B10-4881-9189-CC5E76B07CAC/24002/UNSCResolution11321997.pdf.

96. Kinsey, 2006: 75–77.

97. Kinsey, 2006: 79.

98. Arnold, 1999: 136; Nicholas Watt, Philip Webster, and Michael Evans, "Arms Scandal Engulfs Cook," *The Times of London* (May 9, 1998), 1–2, retrieved on January 16, 2008, from: www.times-archive.co.uk/news/pages/tim/98/05/09/timnwsnws01020.html?1621558.

99. Sir Thomas Legg KCB QC and Sir Robin Ibbs KBE, *Report of the Sierra Leone Arms Investigation*, Return to an Address of the Honorable the House of Commons (London: The Stationary Office: July 27, 1998): 27–28; Arnold, 1999: 136.

100. Watt et al., 1998: 1.

101. "Annex A: The Berwin Letter," in Sir Thomas Legg KCB QC and Sir Robin Ibbs KBE, *Report of the Sierra Leone Arms Investigation*. Return to an Address of the Honorable the House of Commons. London: The Stationary Office: July 27, 1998: 119–120.

102. Arnold, 1999: 135.

103. Arnold, 1999: 140.

104. Legg and Ibbs, 1998: 105.

105. Legg and Ibbs,1998: 105.

106. Legg and Ibbs, 1998: 106.

107. Fran Abrams and Alex Duval Smith, "Foreign Office 'Victimised' Penfold," *London Independent*, June 3, 2000.

108. "Annex A: The Berwin Letter": 120. All spelling original.

109. This deployment was not popular with the public, and the press chided the decision on the grounds that the British were overextended militarily with concurrent ongoing deployments in Northern Ireland, Bosnia, and Kosovo. When the mission changed from simple evacuation to a support role for UNAMSIL, the public feared another "Black Hawk Down" type involvement in an African civil war and the media criticized Blair's with terms like "mission creep" and "overstretch" to describe the decision to bolster UNAMSIL positions. See John Kampfner, *Blair's War* (London: The Free Press, 2003): 70; Patrick J. Evoe, "Operation Palliser: The British Military Intervention into Sierra Leone, A Case of a Successful Use of Western Military Interdiction in a Sub-Sahara African Civil War," Thesis Presented to the Graduate Council of Texas State University-San Marcos in Partial Fulfillment of the Requirements for the Degree of Master of Arts (San Marco, Texas: December 2008): 66–67.

110. Ironically, democratic peace theory argues that such overt action is unlikely to occur, at least between democratic governments. However, as noted in Chapter 1, David Forsythe's work illustrates that democracies are willing to undertake covert activities against other democracies despite their unwillingness to attack each other openly. His research reinforces this study's argument that PSCs may undermine the democratic peace in addition to the democratic advantage, by stimulating more covert activities between democracies. This is true regardless of whether the activity succeeds in remaining covert. See Forsythe, 1992: 385–395.

111. In the increasingly global democratic arena, the backlash against revelations of covert democratic government actions can occur both among the domestic electorate and among the publics of other democratic states affected by these activities. While the electoral repercussions relevant to the selection effects argument are most likely to feel the domestic impact of these activities, international reactions might have an indirect effect by influencing the views of the domestic public over time. New Zealanders' reaction to the French government's bombing of the *Rainbow Warrior* Greenpeace ship in 1985, as well as the British public's reaction to the Israeli Mossad's assassination operation in 2010 using the forged passports of twelve British citizens, are examples of negative international public reaction to revelations of democratic governments' covert operations. See Gillian Bradford, "20 Year Anniversary of the Bombing of the Rainbow Warrior," *ABC News*, retrieved on April 2, 2010, from: www.abc.net .au/am/content/2005/s1410516.htm; Rosa Prince and Adrian Massie-Blomfield, "David Miliband Attacks 'Intolerable' Israeli Cloning of British Passports," *London Daily Telegraph*, retrieved on April 2, 2010, from: www.telegraph.co.uk/news/newstopics/ politics/7506701/David-Miliband-attacks-intolerable-Israeli-cloning-of-British-passports.html.

112. The Iran–Iraq War lasted from 1980 until 1988. It was instigated by then Iraqi leader Saddam Hussein, who hoped to defeat the newly installed revolutionary Shi'a theocracy in Iran and to quash agitation among his own Shi'a and Kurdish citizens. However, neither side made any successful territorial gains, there was no conclusive victory, and Efraim Karsh describes the war as "a costly exercise in futility." See Efraim Karsh, *The Iran–Iraq War: 1980–1988* (Oxford, UK: Osprey, 2002): 84. Casualty figures are disputed. Nathan Brown notes that "Iran claimed to have lost 200,000 or fewer of its own citizens, while Iraq claimed to have killed 800,000 Iranians. Neutral estimates come closer to the Iranian estimate but are uncertain. The total number of people killed almost certainly exceeds 300,000. Wounded and captured soldiers push the casualty total over one million, and some estimates of total casualties exceed two million." See www.encarta.msn.com/encyclopedia_761580640_2/Iran-Iraq_War.html.

113. Henry Kissinger, quoted in Mehdi Hasan, "Farage v Bercow," *The New Statesman*, September 3, 2009, retrieved in October 2009 from: www.newstatesman.com/blogs/mehdi-hasan/2009/09/bercow-farage-lose-shame.

114. *Declaration of Howard Teicher to the United States District Court*, Southern District of Florida, January 31, 1995.

115. For a full discussion of U.S. calculations with regard to accessing the Strait of Hormuz during the Iran–Iraq War, see Sheldon L. Richman, "Where Angels Fear to Tread: The United States and the Persian Gulf Conflict," Cato Policy Analysis No. 90 (September 1978). See also Martin S. Navias and E. R. Hooton, *Tanker Wars: The Assault on Merchant Shipping During the Iran–Iraq Conflict, 1980–1988* (London: I. B. Tauris Publishers, 1996).

116. According to the *Final Report of the Independent Counsel for Iran/Contra Matters*, the price rise was attributable to the markups imposed by both North and Ghorbanifar, the Iranian expatriate businessman who negotiated the deal with the so-called Iranian moderates. See Lawrence E. Walsh, *Final Report of the Independent Counsel for Iran/Contra Matters* (Washington, DC: August 4, 1993), retrieved on October 20, 2009, from: www.fas.org/irp/offdocs/walsh/.

117. This figure was calculated on the basis of a 1987 article: "Iran-Contra Report; Arms, Hostages and Contras: How a Secret Foreign Policy Unraveled." *The New York Times*, November 19, 1987, retrieved on October 20, 2009, from: www.nytimes .com/1987/11/19/world/iran-contra-report-arms-hostages-contras-secret-foreign-policy-unraveled.html.

118. William Buckley was the head of the CIA station in the Beirut U.S. Embassy and was kidnapped in March 1984. He died around June 1985, and although Islamic Jihad claimed to have killed him, it seems that he probably died of pneumonia-related symptoms. Due to his intelligence value and his personal links with senior U.S. officials, Buckley was a one of the prime reasons for concerted U.S. operations to release U.S. hostages in Lebanon. See Gordon Thomas, "The Spy Who Never Came in from

the Cold," *Canada Free Press*, October 25, 2006, retrieved in October 2009 from: www.canadafreepress.com/2006/thomas102506.htm.

119. It was never established that Islamic Jihad was responsible for the Arrow Air 1285 crash. The Canadian Aviation Safety Board (CASB) investigated the accident and attributed it to the aircraft's high drag and reduced lift condition, but a minority report concluded that fire had broken out on board the aircraft possibly due to a detonation in a cargo compartment. See the CASB minority report, October 28, 1988; retrieved in October 2009 from www.sandford.org/gandercrash/investigations/minority_report/html/_1.shtml.

120. In November 2006 the FSLN leader, Daniel Ortega, once again won the Presidency.

121. www.wordiq.com/definition/Boland_Amendment

122. "The Oliver North File," *The National Security Archive*, February 26, 2004, Retrieved in October 2009, from: www.gwu.edu/~nsarchiv/NSAEBB/NSAEBB113/index.htm.

123. "The Iran-Contra Affair 20 Years On, Documents Spotlight Role of Reagan, Top Aides," Document One, *The National Security Archive*, November 24, 2006, retrieved from: www.gwu.edu/-nsarchiv/NSAEBB210/index.htm.

124. Document Two, Ibid.

125. Document Nine, Ibid.

126. See: "October 5, 1986: CIA Transport Plane Shot Down in Nicaragua; Story Reveals Illegal Contra-Arms Program," retrieved on October 20, 2009, from: www.historycommons.org/entity=Eugene_hasenfus_1&printerfreindly=true; "Hasenfus Says Agents Didn't Work on Flights," *The New York Times*, November 5, 1986, retrieved on October 20, 2009, from: www.nytimes.com/1986/11/05/hasenfus-says-agents-didn-t-work-on-flights.html; Stephen Kinzer, "Hasenfus Is Freed by Nicaraguans and Heads Home," *The New York Times*, December 18, 1986, retrieved on October 20, 2009, from: www.nytimes.com/198612/18/world/hasenfus-is-freed-by-nicaraguans-and-heads-home.html.

127. David Johnston, "Bush Pardons Six in Iran Affair, Aborting a Weinberger Trial; Prosecutor Assails 'Cover-Up,'" *The New York Times*, December 25, 1992, retrieved on October 24, 2009, from: www.nytimes.com/books/97/06/29/reviews/iran-pardon.html.

128. Walsh, 1993.

129. Eunkyung Park and Gerald M. Kosicki, "Presidential Support during the Iran-Contra Affair: People's Reasoning Process and Media Influence," *Communication Research* (1995): 22; 207, retrieved on October 18, 2009, from: http://crx.sagepub.com/cgi/content/abstract/22/2/207.

130. A number of academic articles have examined the media's handling of the Iran-Contra affair and the resulting public reaction to it. See, for example, Park and

Kosicki, 1995; see also Richard A. Brody and Catherine R. Shapiro, "Policy Failure and Public Support: The Iran-Contra Affair and Public Assessment of President Reagan," *Political Behavior* 11, 4 (1989).

131. A 1987 *New York Times* article by Stephen Engelberg reported that "to this day, present and former American officials say they are uncertain whether the request for aid came from real dissidents or was merely part of a complex deception." At any rate, in the subsequent House Iran-Contra investigation, it was established that the names of the Iranians involved in talks with the United States would not be revealed for security reasons. See Stephen Engelberg, "Iran 'Moderates': Genuine or Fraud?," Special to *The New York Times*, June 28, 1987, retrieved in October 2009 from: www.nytimes.com/1987/06/28/world/iran-moderates-genuine-or-fraud.html; Patrick Clawson, "Khatemi, the Search for Iranian 'Moderates,' and U.S. Policy," The Washington Institute (1997), retrieved in October 2009 from: www.iran.org/news/WI_970604.htm.

132. According to the same *New York Times* article, "after talks in Israel with Mr. Ledeen, Mr. Ghorbanifar struck a deal: Iran would stop supporting terrorism against Americans and work to free the hostages, and the United States would ship arms to Tehran. At the same time, Mr. Ghorbanifar was apparently working separately to advance the cause of his so-called moderate political allies inside Iran by arranging separate, private meetings with Israeli and American officials that may not have been officially authorized by the Iranian Government." See Engelberg, 1987.

133. Overall, however, both sides relied heavily on U.S. weaponry. As noted above, Iraq was a beneficiary during the war itself, while Iran maintained arms it had received from the United States while it was under the shah's rule.

134. A third anti-Sandinista group that emerged among native Nicaraguans also fought the FSLN for some time. See Christopher Dickey, *With the Contras: A Reporter in the Wilds of Nicaragua* (New York: Simon and Schuster, 1985); Sam Dillon, *Commandos: The CIA and Nicaragua's Contra Rebels* (New York: Henry Holt, 1991): 49–56.

135. Marty Jezer, "Nicaraguan Lesson," *CommonDreams.org*, November 30, 2001, retrieved in October 2009 from: www.commondreams.org/views01/1130-08.htm.

136. The Boland Amendment, passed in December 1983, applied initially to the Department of Defense and the CIA but was later extended to apply to all U.S. government departments.

137. See Document 11 of "The Iran-Contra Affair 20 Years On," 2006.

138. Lora Lumpe, *The US Arms Central America—Past and Present, Norwegian Initiative on Small Arms Transfers* (Oslo: Peace Research Institute, May 1999). Retrieved in October 2009 from: www.prio.no/NISAT/Publications/The-US-Arms-Central-AmericaPast-and-Present/.

139. Online Encyclopedic entry on Nicaragua. Retrieved in October 2009 from: www.tiscali.co.u.k/reference/encyplopaedia/hutchinson/m0019831.html.

140. Although, as noted, FSLN leader Daniel Ortega regained the presidency in November 2006.

Chapter 5: Historical Insights: Mercenary and Auxiliary Forces Integrated into National Militaries

1. Chapter 1 highlights three ways that PSCs are distinct from the classical notion of a "mercenary": (1) PSCs are backed by a corporate infrastructure designed to select, train, and deploy them; (2) the modern PSC industry is unique from historical mercenaries in its scale and transnational nature; and (3) many reputable PSCs today, at least in the United States and United Kingdom, espouse company ideologies in line with liberal Western ideals, showing that PSCs do not appear to be as apolitical as a classical "mercenary" is thought to be.

2. The word *condottieri* refers to those who had accepted a contract, or *condotte*, for a fixed term of employment. In this period the term referred specifically to those employed on a non-permanent basis by a government to fight. These *condotte* were precise agreements, but an almost infinite variety of terms was possible. For instance, they could be for short or long duration, and for either an aggressive or defensive campaign (with a purely defensive campaign bringing in significantly lower sums of money). Geoffrey Trease, *The Condotttieri: Soldiers of Fortune* (London: Thames and Hudson, 1970): 17.

3. Machiavelli, 1950: Chapter XII, 48. Machiavelli was not alone in making such criticisms. Flavio Biondo (1392–1463), the chancellor of papal captain Giovanni Vitelleschi in 1432, and Antonio Giacomini, a Florentine commissioner who had witnessed the failure of the republic's condottieri to retake the rebel city of Pisa in the early sixteenth century, equally criticized the condottieri for their alleged lack of military professionalism. See Denis Hay and John Law, *Italy in the Age of the Renaissance 1530–1830* (London and New York: Longman, 1989): 84–85.

4. Joseph Jay, *Captains of Fortune: Profiles of Six Italian Condottieri* (London: Deiss, 1996): 16–17.

5. Jay, 1996: 17.

6. Trease, 1970: 21. Trease dismisses the temporal power of both the Holy Roman Emperor and the popes of Avignon, claiming these figures had minimal impact on the lives of the Italian city-state populace. He furthermore claims with regard to the kingdom of Southern Italy, ruled from Naples, "for much of the time this region was so riven with strife that its weak rulers were as dependent on *condottieri* as were any of the little duchies and republics into which the rest of the peninsula was fragmented."

7. Daniel Waley, *The Italian City-Republics* (London: World University Library, 1969): 83.

8. Waley refers to men between the ages of fourteen and seventy, "though more humane limits (such as 18 to 60) were also known." See Waley, 1969: 84.

9. Jay, 1996: 17.

10. Waley, 1969: 132–133.

11. It should be noted that "foreign" does not necessarily mean non-Italian, but rather Italians who were not from the same city-state. Trease says in the early days condottieri were mostly foreigners in the conventional sense of the term—Germans, Swiss, Provencals, Bretons, Burgundians, Gascons—"soldiers rendered redundant by the outbreak of peace in other lands." However, by the close of the fourteenth century, Italians from every region were taking over as condottieri (Trease, 1970: 23).

12. Mockler, 1969: 30.

13. C. C. Bayley, *War and Society in Renaissance Florence: The "De Militia" of Leonardo Bruni* (Toronto: University of Toronto Press, 1961): 14.

14. Eugene B. Smith, "The New Condottieri and U.S. Policy: The Privatization of Conflict and its Implications," *Parameters* (Winter 2002–2003): 106.

15. Michael Mallett, *Mercenaries and Their Masters* (London: The Bodley Head, 1974): 225.

16. See Herfried Munkler, "The Wars of the 21st Century," *RICR Mars IRRC March*, Vol. 85, No. 849 (2003): 88.

17. Mockler, 1969: 64–65.

18. Mallett, 1974: 38.

19. William Caferro, "Italy and the Companies of Adventure in the Fourteenth Century," *The Historian* 58, 4 (June 1996): 799. See also Trease, 1970: 68–69.

20. Trease, 1970: 24.

21. Machiavelli, 1950: 49.

22. Mallett, 1974: 197–198, 200.

23. Mockler, 1969: 70.

24. Caferro, 1996: 795–810.

25. Hay and Law, 1989: 84.

26. Mallett, 1974: 44.

27. Mallett, 1974: 35–36.

28. Mockler, 1969: 63; Trease, 1970: 206, 283.

29. Mallett, 1974: 38.

30. Mockler, 1969: 70.

31. Mallett, 1974: 13.

32. Waley, 1969: 134–135.

33. Mallett, 1974, 21.

34. Quoted in Mallett, 1974: 130.

35. R. Davidsohn, *Storia di Firenze* (1957): 458–465, cited in Mallett, 1974: 22–23.

36. Trease, 1970: 68–69.

37. Trease, 1970: 68–69.

38. Mallett, 1974: 107–108.

39. Mockler, 1969: 50.

40. Mockler, 1969: 61.

41. Hay and Law, 1989: 85.

42. Anthony Mockler, *The New Mercenaries* (London: Sidgwick & Jackson, 1985), 3.

43. Mockler, 1985: 3.

44. Edward J. Lowell, *The Hessians* (New York: Harper and Brothers, 1884), Chapter 2, retrieved on October 18, 2007, from: www.americanrevolution.org/hessindex.html.

45. Lanning, 2005: 81.

46. Joseph George Rosengarten, *Defence of the Hessians* (Philadelphia: Reprinted From the *Pennsylvania Magazine of History and Biography*, July 1899): 11–12.

47. Rosengarten, 1899: 12.

48. Lowell, 1884: Chapter 4.

49. Johann Ernst Prechtel, *A Hessian Officer's Diary of the American Revolution*, trans. Bruce E. Burgoyne (Bowie, MD: Heritage Books, 1994), 95.

50. Prechtel, 1994: 46. Running the gauntlet is a form of physical punishment entailing a person being made to run through a double line of soldiers who attempt to strike him or her as he or she passes. See "Gauntlet," *Dictionary.com Unabridged (v.1.1)*, Random House, Inc., retrieved on May 22, 2008 from: http://dictionary.reference.com/browse/gauntlet.

51. Lanning, 2005: 85.

52. Due to the relatively poor morale of the Hessian troops, integration with the British forces did raise the possibility that British morale would be negatively influenced by Hessian views of the conflict. The data to support such a view, however, are rather minimal.

53. Rosengarten, 1899: 5.

54. Ingrao, 1987, 137.

55. Ingrao, 1987: 131–132, 137.

56. Frieherr von der Lith Friedrich, "Fedzug der Hessen nach Amerika," *Ephemeriden uber Aufklarung, Litteratur, und Kunst* (Marburg, 1785), II, p. 4. See also Samuel Pufendorf, *An Introduction to the History of the Principal Kingdoms and States of Europe* (London, 1697): 301-302; Rodney Atwood, *The Hessians* (New York: Cambridge University Press, 1980): 7.

57. Ingrao, 1987: 132.

58. Mark Mayo Boatner, *Encyclopedia of the American Revolution* (New York: David McKay, 1969), 425.

59. Boatner, 1969: 424–425.

60. Johann Georg Zinn, "Journal Entry," in Bruce E. Burgoyne, ed. and trans., *Enemy Views: The American Revolutionary War as Recorded by the Hessian Participants* (Bowie, MD: Heritage Books, Inc., 1996), 71.

61. Carl Friedrich Rueffer, "Journal Entry," in Bruce E. Burgoyne, ed. and trans., *Enemy Views: The American Revolutionary War as Recorded by the Hessian Participants* (Bowie, MD: Heritage Books, 1996), 79–80.

62. R. L. S., "Letter to the Editor: Cruelty of the Hessians: A Revolutionary War Episode of Present-Day Significance," *The New York Times* (letter dated May 27, 1819; published May 29, 1819), retrieved on March 13, 2008, from: http://query.nytimes.com/mem/archive-free/pdf?res=9B00E2DD1238EE32A2575AC2A9639C946996D6CF. All spelling original.

63. For more on the ineffectiveness of military cruelty against civilians in occupied territories and civilian reactions to it at home, see Isabel Hull on the British military's conduct toward the Boer civilians and the later results of British civilian oversight of the military. Isabel Hull, *Absolute Destruction: Military Culture and the Practices of War in Imperial Germany* (Ithaca, NY: Cornell University Press, 2005): 183–187.

64. Boatner, 1969: 425.

65. Varnum Lansing Collins, ed., *A Narrative of the British and Hessians at Princeton in 1776–77: A Contemporary Account of the Battles of Trenton and Princeton* (Princeton, NJ: The University Library, 1906): 12.

66. Collins, 1906: 9.

67. Lowell, 1884: Chapter 6, quoting the editor of the *Frankfurt Magazine*.

68. Lowell, 1884: Chapter 6.

69. Lanning, 2005: 83.

70. Lanning, 2005: 84.

71. Lowell, 1884: Chapter 3.

72. Lowell, 1884: Chapter 3.

73. Note that the directions of the arrows depicted in Figure 5.1 indicate an actor seeking out another actor for employment. Thus, the depiction of the Hessian case illustrates that one state approached another state about hiring a military force, and that state then recruited soldiers for that deployment. In both the condottieri and modern cases, the arrows point both ways: The state or city-state approaches certain PSCs or Free/Great Companies for particular tasks, and the companies also approach the state at times with proposals for work in a certain area. Furthermore, the individuals approach the companies when they hear of an employment opportunity, but the companies also approach particular individuals with whom they are familiar for certain jobs.

Chapter 6: Concluding Lessons and Recommendations

1. Interview with high-level PSC official, January 24, 2007.

2. U.S. Government Accountability Office, July 2005: 43–44; U.S. Government Accountability Office, June 13, 2006: 14–15.

3. James Schmitt (former U.S. Army officer; 2006–2007 President of the International Peace Operations Association; then-Senior Vice President for Strategy, Armor

Group North America Inc.), in interview with the author, July 18, 2007; Colonel Timothy Cornett (Commander of the Standing Joint Force Headquarters, U.S. Southern Command), in correspondence with the author, January 10, 2007.

4. Schwartz, 2009: 10. See also Moshe Schwartz, "Training the Military to Manage Contractors during Expeditionary Operations: Overview and Options for Congress," CRS Report R40057 (December 17, 2008); U.S. Army, *Contracting Basics for Leaders and the Deployed COR* (February 2008). Schwartz reported in August 2009 that the Army was also drafting a handbook on armed private security contracting at that time.

5. Joshua Partlow, "Taliban Targeting U.S. Contractors," *Washington Post*, April 17, 2010: 6.

6. U.S. Government Accountability Office, 2006: 15.

7. Interview with high-level PSC official, April 2, 2007.

8. Schwartz, 2009: 10, 15.

9. Schwartz, 2009: 16.

10. See for instance Article 47.2, Protocol Additional to the Geneva Conventions of 12 August 1949, and relating to the Protection of Victims of International Armed Conflicts (Protocol 1)" (Adopted on June 8, 1977, Entry into force December 7, 1979), retrieved on November 20, 2007, from: www.unhchr.ch/html/menu3/b/93.htm. See also Article 1 of the Draft Luanda Conventions, as explored in Katherine Fallah, "Corporate Actors: The Legal Status of Mercenaries in Armed Conflict," *ICRC Review* 88, 863 (September 2006): 607–608; OAU Convention for the Elimination of Mercenaries in Africa, O.A.U. Doc. CM/433/Rev.L, Annex 1 (1972), retrieved on November 20, 2007, from: www1.umn.edu/humanrts/instree/mercenaryconvention.html.

11. As noted in Chapter 1, Article 47.2 of Additional Protocol I defines a mercenary as any person who:

    (a) is specially recruited locally and abroad in order to fight in an armed conflict;

    (b) does, in fact, take a direct part in hostilities;

    (c) is motivated to take part in the hostilities essentially by the desire for private gain and, in fact, is promised by or on behalf of a Party to the conflict material compensation substantially in excess of that promised or paid to combatants of similar rank and functions in the armed forces of that Party;

    (d) is neither a national of a Party to the conflict nor a resident of territory controlled by a Party to the conflict;

    (e) is not a member of the armed forces of a Party to the conflict; and

    (f) has not been sent by a State which is not a Party to the conflict on official duty as a member of its armed forces.

12. "A New Legal Framework for Military Contractors?" Princeton Problem-Solving Workshop Series in Law and Security, Woodrow Wilson School of Public and International Affairs, Princeton University (June 8, 2007): 8, retrieved on October 15,

2007, from: http://lapa.princeton.edu/conferences/military07/MilCon_Workshop _Summary.pdf.

13. Avril McDonald, "The Legal Status of Military and Security Subcontractors," in Roberta Arnold and Pierre-Antoine Hildbrand, eds., *International Humanitarian Law and the 21st Century's Conflicts: Changes and Challenges* (Lausanne: Editions Interuniversitaires Suisses, 2005), 226–227; Michael N. Schmitt, "Humanitarian Law and Direct Participation in Hostilities by Private Contractors or Civilian Employees," *Chicago Journal of International Law* (Winter 2005): 522.

14. In the absence of a legally binding international convention to regulate PSC activities, the Swiss Federal Council instructed the Swiss Federal Department of Foreign Affairs (FDFA) in December 2005 to launch an initiative to "confirm existing legal obligations of the actors and develop non-binding good practices." The FDFA did this in cooperation with the International Committee of the Red Cross (ICRC) and in September 2008 produced the *Montreux Document* containing non-binding recommendations and best-practice guidance for PSCs. While it is promising that most major contracting states have approved the document—Israel being a notable exception— the *Montreux Document* cannot be considered a lasting solution to the problem of contractor accountability, as it lacks an enforcement mechanism. See the Swiss Initiative and International Committee of the Red Cross, *Montreux Document on Pertinent International Legal Obligations and Good Practices for States Related to Operations of Private Military and Security Companies During Armed Conflict* (Montreux: Swiss Initiative, September 17, 2008).

15. Robert Vainshtein, "UCMJ v. MEJA: Two Options for Regulating Contractors," *Journal of International Peace Operations* 2, 4 (January 2007): 11.

16. A New Legal Framework for Military Contractors?" 4. See also Vainshtein, 2007: 3.

17. A New Legal Framework for Military Contractors?," 4; retrieved on October 15, 2007, from: http://lapa.princeton.edu/conferences/military07/MilCon_Workshop _Summary.pdf.

18. A New Legal Framework for Military Contractors?" 11.

19. Ginger Thompson and James Risen, "Plea by Blackwater Guard Helps Indict Others," *The New York Times* (December 8, 2008), retrieved on November 2, 2009, from: www.nytimes.com/2008/12/09/washington/09blackwater.html; "The Underside of War: CIA Interrogations and the Blackwater Affair," *The Economist* (August 27, 2009), retrieved on November 2, 2009, from: www.economist.com/displaystory.cfm?story _id=14323104; Anthony Shadid, "Biden Says U.S. Will Appeal Blackwater Case Dismissal," *The New York Times* (January 23, 2010).

20. *Agreement between the United States of America and the Republic of Iraq on the Withdrawal of United States Forces from Iraq and the Organization of Their Activities during Their Temporary Presence in Iraq* ("Iraq Status of Forces Agreement"),

(November 17, 2008), retrieved on November 17, 2009, from: http://graphics8.nytimes .com/packages/pdf/world/20081119_SOFA_FINAL_AGREED_TEXT.pdf.

21. Michael Cottier, "Elements for Contracting and Regulating Private Security and Military Companies," *ICRC Review* 88, 863 (September 2006): 642.

22. U.S. Department of Defense, Office of the Secretary, 32 CFR Part 159, "Private Security Contractors (PSCs) Operating in Contingency Operations," *Federal Register* Vol. 74, No. 136 (July 17, 2009): 34690–34691.

23. Andrew Bearpark and Dr. Sabrina Schulz, "The Regulation of the Private Security Industry and the Future of the Market," in Simon Chesterman and Chia Lenhardt, eds., *From Mercenaries to Market: The Rise and Regulation of Private Military Companies* (Oxford, UK: Oxford University Press, 2009), 13–14.

24. Furthermore, at least a few ISOA member companies appear to have internalized the norms of ethical conduct outlined in the ISOA Code of Conduct beyond what is required by ISOA membership. Such firms reflect these norms in their own company practices, making an effort to transform the industry into a model for ethical wartime practices. For instance, EOD Technology, Inc. (EODT) held its own internal symposium on ethical security practices in the fall of 2007. The event was titled the "Ethics Stand Down," and was said to be part of EODT's "continuous improvement process." J. J. Messner of ISOA, who attended the event, reflected that the very sponsorship of such an event, as well as the content of the panels themselves, made the EODT symposium an ideal toward which ISOA hoped all of its member companies would strive. The fact that member companies demonstrate compatibility with ISOA norms of ethical conduct—whether for public-relations purposes or because they actually internalize these norms—is significant, for it means that the ISOA operates through both market-oriented mechanisms and learning processes.

25. August Cole, "Blackwater Quits Security Association," *The Wall St. Journal* (October 11, 2007). retrieved on January 15, 2008, from: http://online.wsj.com/article/ SB119207104012555696.html?mod=googlenews_wsj.

REFERENCES

Abbott, Andrew. *The System of Professions: An Essay on the Division of Expert Labor.* Chicago: University of Chicago Press, 1988.

Abbott, Andrew. "The Army and the Theory of Professions." In Don M. Snider and Gayle L. Watkins *The Future of the Army Profession*, 523–536. Boston: McGraw-Hill, 2002.

Abdelal, Rawi, et al. "Identity as a Variable." *Perspectives on Politics* 4 (2006): 695–711.

Abraham, Antoine J. *The Lebanon War.* Westport, CT: Praeger, 1996.

Abrams, Fran, and Alex Duval Smith. "Foreign Office 'Victimised' Penfold." *London Independent*, June 3, 2000.

Agreement between the United States of America and the Republic of Iraq on the Withdrawal of United States Forces from Iraq and the Organization of Their Activities during Their Temporary Presence in Iraq ("Iraq Status of Forces Agreement"). November 17, 2008. Retrieved on November 17, 2009, from: http://graphics8.nytimes.com/packages/pdf/world/20081119_SOFA_FINAL_AGREED_TEXT.pdf.

Alberts, Colin M., Gerard J. Christman, and Michael P. Dowdy. "Achieving Interoperability: Information Sharing via DoD's Extranet in Stability Operations," *Journal of International Peace Operations* 3, 2 (September–October, 2007): 10.

Allison, Olivia, and Martha Clark Dunigan. "Ensuring Effective Use of Private Forces: Domestic, International, and Transnational Regulatory Options in the Face of Changing Warfare." In Isaiah Wilson III and James J. F. Forest, eds., *Handbook of Defence Politics.* London: Routledge, 2008.

"Annex A: The Berwin Letter." In Sir Thomas Legg KCB QC and Sir Robin Ibbs KBE, *Report of the Sierra Leone Arms Investigation.* Return to an Address of the Honorable the House of Commons. London: The Stationary Office: July 27, 1998.

Arnold, Guy. *Mercenaries: The Scourge of the Third World.* London: MacMillan Press, 1999.

Aslund, Anders. *Post-Communist Economic Revolutions: How Big a Bang?* Washington, DC: The Center for Strategic and International Studies, 1992.

Associated Press. "Blackwater Blamed for Fallujah Bloodshed." *Newser*, September 28, 2007. Retrieved on January 9, 2008, from: www.newser.com/story/8370.html.

Associated Press. "Legal Avenues against Blackwater Murky." *The New York Times*, October 3, 2007. Retrieved on October 3, 2007, from: www.nytimes.com/aponline/us/AP-Blackwater-Legal.html?pagewanted=print.

Atwood, Rodney. *The Hessians*. New York: Cambridge University Press, 1980.

Avant, Deborah. "Losing Control of the Profession Through Outsourcing?" In Don M. Snider and Lloyd J. Matthews, eds., *The Future of the Army Profession*, 271–290. Boston: McGraw Hill, 2005a.

Avant, Deborah. *The Market for Force: The Consequences of Privatizing Security*. New York: Cambridge University Press, 2005b.

Avant, Deborah. "Private Security and the Prospects for Institution Building and Democracy in Transitional States." Paper presented at the annual meeting of the American Political Science Association, Washington, DC (September 1, 2005c). Retrieved on November 14, 2007, from: www.allacademic.com/meta/p41783_index.html.

Avant, Deborah. "The Implications of Marketized Security for IR Theory: The Democratic Peace, Late State Building, and the Nature and Frequency of Conflict." *Perspectives on Politics* 4 (2006): 507–528.

Avant, Deborah. "After Blackwater, Four Fundamental Questions about Our Democracy." *San Francisco Chronicle*, October 8, 2007. Retrieved on November 14, 2007, from: www.pacificcouncil.org/pdfs/Avant_10.08.pdf.

Aylwin-Foster, Brigadier Nigel. "Changing the Army for Counterinsurgency Operations." *Military Review* (November-December 2005). Retrieved on May 1, 2009, from: www.army.mil/professionalwriting/volumes/volume4/february_2006/2_06_1_pf.html.

Bard, Mitchell G. *Myths & Facts: A Guide to the Arab–Israeli Conflict*. Chevy Chase, MD: American-Israeli Cooperative Enterprise, 2002.

Barstow, David. "Security Companies: Shadow Soldiers in Iraq." *The New York Times*, April 19, 2004.

Bayley, C. C. *War and Society in Renaissance Florence: The "De Militia" of Leonardo Bruni*. Toronto: University of Toronto Press, 1961.

Bearpark, Andrew, and Sabrina Schulz. "The Regulation of the Private Security Industry and the Future of the Market." In Simon Chesterman and Chia Lenhardt, eds., *From Mercenaries to Market: The Rise and Regulation of Private Military Companies*. Oxford, UK: Oxford University Press, 2009.

Berndtsson, Joakim. "Private Military Companies and the Privatisation of Violence and Security: Rethinking the Monopoly of Violence and the Role of the State."

Paper presented at the Annual Meeting of the International Studies Association. San Diego: March 2006.

Beutel, M. Dee. "Buying Our Decline: Mercenaries and Modernity." Paper Presented at the Annual Meeting of the International Studies Association's 49th Annual Convention. San Francisco, March 26, 2008.

Biddle, Stephen. "Rebuilding the Foundations of Offense-Defense Theory." *The Journal of Politics* 63, 3 (August 2001): 741–774.

Biddle, Stephen. *Military Power: Explaining Victory and Defeat in Modern Battle.* Princeton, NJ: Princeton University Press, 2004.

Biddle, Stephen. "Explaining Military Outcomes." In Risa A. Brooks and Elizabeth A. Stanley, eds., *Creating Military Power.* Stanford, CA: Stanford University Press, 2007.

Biddle, Stephen, and Stephen Long. "Democracy and Military Effectiveness: A Deeper Look." *The Journal of Conflict Resolution* 48, 4 (August 2004): 525–546.

"Blackwater 5: Case Dismissed." *The Washington Post*, January 6, 2010: 14.

"Blackwater by Numbers: A Statistical Index." *Mother Jones Blog* (October 3, 2007). Retrieved on March 21, 2008 from: www.motherjones.com/cgi-bin/print_mojoblog .pl?url=http://www....archives/2007/10/5663_blackwater_by_numbers_a_statistical _index.html.

"Blackwater Christmas Eve Shooting and Immunity." September 12, 2007. Retrieved on October 14, 2007, from: www.blackwaterblogger.com/2007/09/accountability1 .html.

Blackwater Foundation. "Blackwater Worldwide Provides Relief within a Fire." Retrieved on March 18, 2008, from: www.blackwaterusa.com/foundation/Wildfire _Victim_Relief.html.

Blackwater Foundation. "Kenya Rescue 2008." Retrieved on March 18, 2008, from: www.blackwaterusa.com/foundation/Kenya_Rescue.html.

Blackwater Global Peace and Stability Operations Institute website. Retrieved on October 22, 2007, from: http://gpsoi.org/index.html.

Blanford, Nicholas. "U.S. Warship Stirs Lebanese Fear of War: The USS *Cole* Has Deployed off the Coast of Lebanon as That Nation's Political Crisis Deepens." *Christian Science Monitor* (March 4, 2008). Retrieved on July 3, 2009, from: www.csmonitor .com/2008/0304/p01s01-wome.html.

Boatner, Mark Mayo. *Encyclopedia of the American Revolution.* New York: David McKay, 1969.

Bonner, Raymond. "War Crimes Panel Finds Croat Troops Cleansed the Serbs." *New York Times*, March 21, 1999.

Boot, Max. "The Lessons of a Quagmire." *The New York Times*, November 16, 2003. Retrieved on February 8, 2008, from: http://query.nytimes.com/gst/fullpage.html ?res=9803E5DD1038F935A25752C.

Boot, Max. "An Iraq To-Do List: How We Can Help the Surge Succeed." *The Weekly Standard* 12, 34 (May 21, 2007). Retrieved on February 8, 2008, from www.weeklystandard .com/Utilities/printer_preview.asp?idArticle=13643&R=139501DB68.

Boozell, Lieutenant Colonel James. Presentation for Session on "Personal Security and Safety in the Field: Safety in a Hostile Environment." *International Peace Operations Association Annual Summit*, October 29, 2007.

Bowker, N. and Tuffin, K. "Using the Online Medium for Discursive Research about People with Disabilities." *Social Science Computer Review* 22, 2 (2004): 228–241.

Bradford, Gillian. "20 Year Anniversary of the Bombing of the Rainbow Warrior." *ABC News*. Retrieved on April 2, 2010, from: www.abc.net.au/am/content/2005/ s1410516.htm.

Broder, John M. and James Risen. "Contractor Deaths in Iraq Soar to Record." *The New York Times*, May 19, 2007. Retrieved on May 19, 2007, from: www.nytimes .com/2007/05/19/world/middleeast/19contractors.html?hp=&pagewanted=print.

Brody, Richard A. and Catherine R. Shapiro. "Policy Failure and Public Support: The Iran-Contra Affair and Public Assessment of President Reagan." *Political Behavior* 11, 4 (1989).

Brooks, Doug. "Hope for the 'Hopeless Continent': Mercenaries." *Traders: Journal for the Southern African Region* 3 (July–October 2000).

Brooks, Risa A. "Making Military Might: Why Do States Fail and Succeed? A Review Essay." *International Security* 28, 2 (Fall 2003): 149–191.

Brooks, Risa A. "The Impact of Culture, Society, Institutions, and International Forces on Military Effectiveness." In Risa Brooks and Elizabeth Stanley, eds., *Creating Military Power: The Sources of Military Effectiveness*, 1–26 (Stanford, CA: Stanford University Press, 2007).

Bueno de Mesquita, Bruce. *The War Trap*. New Haven, CT: Yale University Press, 1981.

Bueno de Mesquita, Bruce. "The War Trap Revisited: A Revised Expected Utility Model." *American Political Science Review* 79, 1 (1985).

Bueno de Mesquita, Bruce, and D. Lalman. *War and Reason, Domestic and International Imperatives*. New Haven, CT: Yale University Press, 1992.

Caferro, William. "Italy and the Companies of Adventure in the Fourteenth Century." *The Historian* 58, 4 (June 1996).

Carroll, James. "Outsourcing Intelligence." *The Boston Globe*, August 27, 2007. Retrieved on February 4, 2008 from: www.boston.com/news/globe/editorial_opinion/ oped/articles/2007/08/27/outsourcing_intelligence/

CASB Minority Report (October 28, 1988). Retrieved on October 20, 2009, from: www .sandford.org/gandercrash/investigations/minority_report/html/_1.shtml.

Center for International Development at Harvard University. "Washington Consensus." Retrieved on April 23, 2008, from: www.cid.harvard.edu/cidtrade/issues/ washington.html.

Checkel, Jeffrey. "Why Comply? Social Learning and European Identity Change." *International Organization* 55, 3 (September 2001): 553–588.

Chojnacki, Sven. "Democratic Wars and Military Interventions, 1946–2002: The Monadic Level Reconsidered." In Anna Geis, Lothar Brock, and Harald Muller, eds., *Democratic Wars: Looking at the Dark Side of Democratic Peace*. New York: Palgrave, 2006.

Chossudovsky, Michel. "NATO Has Installed a Reign of Terror in Kosovo." Paper Presented to the Independent Commission of Inquiry to Investigate U.S./NATO War Crimes against The People of Yugoslavia. International Action Center, New York, July 31, 1999. Retrieved on September 1, 2009, from: www.iacenter.org/warcrime/chossu.htm.

Clawson, Patrick. "Khatemi, the Search for Iranian 'Moderates,' and U.S. Policy." The Washington Institute (1997). Retrieved in October 2009 from: www.iran.org/news/WI_970604.htm.

Cockayne, James. "The Global Reorganization of Legitimate Violence: Military Entrepreneurs and the Private Face of International Humanitarian Law," *ICRC Review* 88, 863 (September 2006): 459–490.

Cohen, Roger. "U.S. Cooling Ties to Croatia after Winking at Its Buildup." *The New York Times*, October 28, 1995. Retrieved on January 18, 2008, from: http://query.nytimes.com/gst/fullpage.html?res=9503E5DB1F39F93BA15753C1A963958260&scp=1&sq=US+cooling+ties+with+croatia+after+winking+at+its+buildup.

Cole, August. "Blackwater Quits Security Association." *The Wall St. Journal*, October 11, 2007. Retrieved on January 15, 2008, from: http://online.wsj.com/article/SB119207104012555696.html?mod=googlenews_wsj

Cole, August. "Blackwater Dismissal Risks Hurting Iraq Relations." *The Wall Street Journal*, January 2, 2010: 7.

Collelo, Thomas, ed. "Phalange Party." *Lebanon: A Country Study*. Washington, DC: GPO for the Library of Congress, 1987. Retrieved on September 1, 2009, from: http://countrystudies.us/lebanon/85.htm.

Collins, Varnum Lansing, ed. *A Narrative of the British and Hessians at Princeton in 1776–77: A Contemporary Account of the Battles of Trenton and Princeton*. Princeton, NJ: The University Library, 1906.

Congressional Budget Office. *Contractors' Support of U.S. Operations in Iraq*. August 2008. Retrieved on December 23, 2008, from: www.cbo.gov/ftpdocs/96xx/doc9688/08-12-IraqContractors.pdf.

Cordesman, Anthony. "Iraq: Too Uncertain to Call." Center for Strategic and International Studies (November 2003). Retrieved on April 25, 2008, from: www.csis.org/media/csis/press/pro3_65[1].pdf.

Cottier, Michael. "Elements for Contracting and Regulating Private Security and Military Companies." *ICRC Review* 88, 863 (September 2006).

Cotton, Sarah, Ulrich Petersohn, Molly Dunigan, Q Burkhart, Ed O'Connell, and Michael Webber. *Hired Guns: Views about Armed Contractors in Operation Iraqi Freedom.* Santa Monica, CA: RAND Corporation, MG-987, 2010.

"Croatian Atrocities Being Forgotten." CBC Report, July 21, 2003. Retrieved on September 1, 2009, from: www.globalresearch.ca/articles/CHO307D.html.

"Criminal Trials of Blackwater Contractors: Chapter 8—The Queen's Croquet-Ground." *The White Rabbit.* September 12, 2007. Retrieved on October 14, 2007, from: www.blackwaterblogger.com.

Danner, Mark. "Operation Storm." *New York Review of Books,* Oct. 22, 1998.

Declaration of Howard Teicher to the United States District Court, Southern District of Florida, January 31, 1995.

Deeb, Marius. *The Lebanese Civil War.* Santa Barbara, CA: Praeger Publishers, 1980.

Defense Science Board. *Report of the Defense Science Board Task Force on Outsourcing and Privatization.* August 1996. Retrieved on May 15, 2007, from: www.acq.osd.mil/dsb/reports/outsourcing.pdf.

Desch, Michael C. "Democracy & Victory: Why Regime Type Hardly Matters." *International Security* 27, 2 (Fall 2002): 5–47.

De Vaux, Roland. *Ancient Israel: Its Life and Institutions.* Grand Rapids, MI: Wm. B. Eerdmans Publishing Co., 1997.

Dickey, Christopher. *With the Contras: A Reporter in the Wilds of Nicaragua.* New York: Simon and Schuster, 1985.

Dillon, Sam. *Commandos: The CIA and Nicaragua's Contra Rebels.* New York: Henry Holt, 1991.

Downes, Alexander. "Desperate Times, Desperate Measures: The Causes of Civilian Victimization in War." *International Security* 30, 4 (Spring 2006): 152–195.

Elsea, Jennifer K., and Nina M. Serafino. "Private Security Contractors in Iraq: Background, Legal Status, and Other Issues." *CRS Report for Congress.* Washington, DC: Congressional Research Service, July 11, 2007.

Engelberg, Stephen. "Iran 'Moderates': Genuine or Fraud?" Special to *The New York Times,* June 28, 1987. Retrieved in October 2009 from: www.nytimes.com/1987/06/28/world/iran-moderates-genuine-or-fraud.html.

Evoe, Patrick J. "Operation Palliser: The British Military Intervention into Sierra Leone, A Case of a Successful Use of Western Military Interdiction in a Sub-Sahara African Civil War." Thesis Presented to the Graduate Council of Texas State University-San Marcos in Partial Fulfillment of the Requirements for the Degree of Master of Arts. San Marco, Texas: December 2008.

"Executive Outcomes." *SourceWatch.* Accessed June 10, 2008, from: www.sourcewatch.org/index.php?title=Executive_Outcomes.

Fainaru, Steve. "Iraq Contractors Face Growing Parallel War." *The Washington Post,* June 16, 2007. Retrieved on January 11, 2008, from: www.washingtonpost.com/wpdyn/content/article/2007/06/15/AR2007061502602.html

Fainaru, Steve, and Alec Klein. "In Iraq, a Private Realm of Intelligence-Gathering." *The Washington Post*, July 1, 2007. Retrieved on December 18, 2007, from: www.washingtonpost.com/wp-dyn/content/article/2007/06/30/AR2007063001075_pf.html.

Fallah, Katherine. "Corporate Actors: The Legal Status of Mercenaries in Armed Conflict." *ICRC Review* 88, 863 (September 2006).

Felter, Joseph H. "Taking Guns to a Knife Fight: Effective Military Support to Counterinsurgency." Draft Paper, U.S. Military Academy (February 16, 2007).

Forsythe, David P. "Democracy, War, and Covert Action," *Journal of Peace Research* 29, 4 (1992): 385–395.

Fowler, Kenneth. "Sir John Hawkwood and the English Condottieri in Trecento Italy." *Renaissance Studies* 12, 1 (1998).

Frank, Benis M. *U.S. Marines in Lebanon: 1982–84* (Washington, DC: History and Museums Division, Headquarters, U.S. Marine Corps, 1987). Retrieved from: www.ibiblio.org/hyperwar/AMH/XX/MidEast/Lebanon-1982-1984/USMC-Lebanon82/USMC-Lebanon82-4.html#cn21.

Friedrich, Frieherr von der Lith. "Fedzug der Hessen nach Amerika." *Ephemeriden uber Aufklarung, Litteratur, und Kunst* (Marburg, 1785), II.

Frye, David G. "Rome's Barbarian Mercenaries." American History (Spring 2007). Retrieved on March 21, 2008, from: www.thehistorynet.com/historical_conflicts/7311986.html?showAll=y&c=y.

Gartzke, Erik. "Democracy and the Preparation for War: Does Regime Type Affect States' Anticipation of Casualties?" *International Studies Quarterly* 45, 3 (September 2001).

Gawrych, George W. "Siege of Beirut." *GlobalSecurity.org*. Retrieved on Sept. 1, 2009 from: www.globalsecurity.org/military/library/report/2002/MOUTGawrych.htm.

Glanz, James, and Alissa J. Rubin. "From Errand to Fatal Shot to Hail of Fire to 17 Deaths." *The New York Times*, October 2, 2007. Retrieved on January 9, 2008, from: www.nytimes.com/2007/10/03/world/middleeast/03firefight.html?scp=4&sq=nisour+square+blackwater.

Glanz, James, and Alissa J.Rubin. "Blackwater Shootings 'Murder,' Iraq Says." *The New York Times*, October 8, 2007. Retrieved on January 9, 2007, from: www.nytimes.com/2007/10/08/world/middleeast/08blackwater.html?scp=1&sq=nisour+square+blackwater.

Glaser, Charles L., and Chaim Kaufmann. "What Is the Offense-Defense Balance and Can We Measure It?" *International Security* 22, 4 (Spring 1998): 44–82.

Glass, Jon W. "Blackwater Aims High with Unmanned Aircraft." *The Virginian-Pilot*, November 23, 2007. Retrieved on August 28, 2009, from: http://hamptonroads.com/node/433181.

Goulet, Yves. "MPRI: Washington's Freelance Advisors." *Jane's Intelligence Review* 10, 7 (July 1998).

Gourevitch, Peter. "The Second Image Reversed: The International Sources of Domestic Politics." *International Organization* 32, 4 (Autumn 1978): 881–912.

Greider, William. "The Education of David Stockman." *The Atlantic Monthly* (December 1981). Retrieved on March 21, 2008, from: www.theatlantic.com/politics/budget/stockman.htm.

Grigg, William Norman. "Why Kosovo?" *New American* (May 10, 1999).

The Hague Convention IV. "Convention Respecting the Laws and Customs of War on Land." October 18, 1907. Retrieved on November 20, 2007, from: http://net.lib.byu.edu/rdh7/wwi/hague/hague5.html.

Hallenbeck, Ralph A. *Military Force as an Instrument of U.S. Foreign Policy (Intervention in Lebanon, August 1982–February 1984)*. New York: Praeger, 1991.

Hammes, Thomas. "Foreword." In Eric Hammel, *The Root: The Marines in Beirut, August 1982–February 1984*. Osceola, WI: Zenith Press, 2005.

Hasan, Mehdi. "Farage v Bercow." *The New Statesman* (September 3, 2009). Retrieved in October 2009 from: www.newstatesman.com/blogs/mehdi-hasan/2009/09/bercow-farage-lose-shame.

"Hasenfus Says Agents Didn't Work on Flights." *The New York Times*, November 5, 1986. Retrieved on October 20, 2009, from www.nytimes.com/1986/11/05/hasenfus-says-agents-didn-t-work-on-flights.html.

Hay, Denis, and John Law. *Italy in the Age of the Renaissance 1530–1830*. London and New York: Longman, 1989.

Held, David. "Central Perspectives on the Modern State." In David Held et al., eds., *States and Societies*, 1–55. New York: New York University Press, 1983.

Hemingway, Mark. "Blackwater's Legal Netherworld: Private Contractors Are Subject to Military Justice—Or Are They?" *National Review Online* (September 26, 2007). Retrieved on January 15, 2008, from: http://article.nationalreview.com/?q=MmYzMTkwMzQ2OTVhNGY2MGQzMDY0MTJiM2ExYmY3YmY

Hoffman, Bruce. *Insurgency and Counterinsurgency in Iraq*. RAND Occasional Paper OP-127-IPC/CMEPP (June 2004). Retrieved on April 25, 2008, from: http://rand.org/pubs/occasional_papers/2005/RAND_OP127.pdf.

Horsley, Richard A. *Galilee: History, Politics, People*. New York: Trinity Press International, 1995.

Hull, Isabel. *Absolute Destruction: Military Culture and the Practices of War in Imperial Germany*. Ithaca, NY: Cornell University Press, 2005.

Human Rights First. *Private Security Contractors at War: Ending the Culture of Impunity*. Washington, DC: Human Rights First, 2008.

Hunt, Richard A. *Pacification: The American Struggle for Vietnam's Hearts and Minds*. Boulder, CO: Westview Press, 1995.

Huntington, Samuel P. *The Soldier and the State*. Cambridge, MA: Belknap Press, 1959.

Ingrao, Charles W. *The Hessian Mercenary State.* New York: Cambridge University Press, 1987.

International Convention against the Recruitment, Use, Financing, and Training of Mercenaries ("UN Convention"). December 4, 1989. Retrieved on November 20, 2007, from: www.icrc.org/ihl.nsf/FULL/530?OpenDocument.

International Peace Operations Association. "IPOA Endorsement of H.R. 2740 'MEJA Expansion and Enforcement Act of 2007." Press Release. October 3, 2007.

"The Iran-Contra Affair 20 Years On: Documents Spotlight Role of Reagan, Top Aides." Documents One, Two, Nine. *The National Security Archive*, November 24, 2006. Retrieved on October 20, 2009, from: www.gwu.edu/-nsarchiv/NSAEBB210/index.htm.

"Iran-Contra Report; Arms, Hostages and Contras: How a Secret Foreign Policy Unraveled." *The New York Times*, November 19, 1987. Retrieved on October 20, 2009, from: www.nytimes.com/1987/11/19/world/iran-contra-report-arms-hostages-contras-secret-foreign-policy-unraveled.html.

Ivanovich, David. "Contractor Deaths Up 17 Percent across Iraq in 2007." *Houston Chronicle*, February 9, 2008. Retrieved on April 14, 2008, from: www.chron.com/disp/story.mpl/front/5528613.html.

Jay, Joseph. *Captains of Fortune: Profiles of Six Italian Condottieri.* London: Deiss, 1996.

Jennings, Christian. "Private U.S. Firm Training Both Sides in Balkans." *Scotsman* (March 2, 2001).

Jervis, Robert. *Perception and Misperception in International Politics.* Princeton, NJ: Princeton University Press, 1976.

Jervis, Robert. "Cooperation under the Security Dilemma." *World Politics* 30, 2 (January 1978).

Jezer, Marty. "Nicaraguan Lesson." *CommonDreams.org*, November 30, 2001. Retrieved in October 2009 from: www.commondreams.org/views01/1130-08.htm.

Johnston, David. "Bush Pardons Six in Iran Affair, Aborting a Weinberger Trial; Prosecutor Assails 'Cover-Up.'" *The New York Times*, December 25, 1992. Retrieved on October 24, 2009, from: www.nytimes.com/books/97/06/29/reviews/iran-pardon.html.

Johnston, David, and John M. Broder. "FBI Says Guards Killed 14 Iraqis without Cause," *The New York Times*, November 14, 2007. Retrieved on January 9, 2008, from: www.nytimes.com/2007/11/14/world/middleeast/14blackwater.html?scp=10&sq=nisour+square+blackwater.

Kaldor, Mary. *New & Old Wars: Organized Violence in a Global Era.* Cambridge, UK: Polity Press, 1999.

Kampfner, John. *Blair's War.* London: The Free Press, 2003.

Karsh, Efraim. *The Iran–Iraq War: 1980–1988.* Oxford, UK: Osprey, 2002.

Katzenstein, Peter J. "Introduction." In Peter J. Kazenstein, ed., *The Culture of National Security*, 1–32. New York: Columbia University Press, 1996.

Kelley, John H. "Lebanon: 1982–1984." In Jeremy R. Azrael and Emil A. Payin, eds., *U.S. and Russian Policymaking with Respect to the Use of Force*, Chapter 6. Santa Monica, CA: RAND Corporation, 1996.

Kelty, Ryan, Darcy Schnack, and Keke Langkamp. "Attitudes on the Ground: What Soldiers Think about Civilian Contractors." *Paper Presented at the Annual Meeting of the International Studies Association* (San Francisco, March 2008).

King, Gary, Robert O. Keohane, and Sidney Verba. *Designing Social Inquiry*. Princeton, NJ: Princeton University Press, 1994.

Kinsey, Christopher. *Corporate Soldiers and International Security: The Rise of Private Military Companies*. London: Routledge, 2006.

Kinzer, Stephen. "Hasenfus Is Freed by Nicaraguans and Heads Home." *The New York Times*, December 18, 1986. Retrieved on October 20, 2009, from: www .nytimes.com/198612/18/world/hasenfus-is-freed-by-nicaraguans-and-heads-home .html.

Korbani, Agnes G. *U.S. Intervention in Lebanon, 1958 and 1982*. New York: Praeger: 1991.

Krasner, Stephen D. "Westphalia and All That." In Judith Goldstein and Robert O. Keohane, eds., *Ideas and Foreign Policy*, 235–264. Ithaca, NY: Cornell University Press, 1993.

Lacquement, Richard. "Mapping Army Professional Expertise and Clarifying Jurisdictions of Practice." In Don M. Snider and Lloyd J. Matthews, eds, *The Future of the Army Profession*, 251–270. Boston: McGraw Hill, 2005.

Laffin, John. *The War of Desperation—1982–85*. Oxford, UK: Osprey Publishing Ltd, 1985.

Lake, David A. "Powerful Pacifists: Democratic States and War." *The American Political Science Review* 86, 1 (March 1992): 24–37.

Lanning, Michael Lee. *Mercenaries: Soldiers of Fortune, from Ancient Greece to Today's Private Military Companies*. New York: Ballantine Books, 2005.

"Lebanon Civil War: 1975–1991." *GlobalSecurity.org*. Retrieved on September 1, 2009, from: www.globalsecurity.org/military/world/war/lebanon.htm.

"Lebanon: The Lebanese Armed Forces in the 1980s." Library of Congress Country Studies, *CIA World Factbook*. Washington, DC: Central Intelligence Agency, n.d. Retrieved on July 3, 2009, from: www.photius.com/countries/lebanon/national _security/lebanon_national_security_the_lebanese_armed_f107.html.

"Lebanon: World War I and the French Mandate, 1914–1941." Retreived on September 1, 2009, from: www.country-data.com/cgi-bin/query/r-7940.html.

Lee, Matthew. "U.S. Contractors Lose Immunity in Iraq Security Deal." *The Seattle Post-Intelligencer*, November 20, 2008. Retrieved on November 24, 2008, from: http://seattlepi.nwsource.com/national/1152ap_iraq_security_contractors.html.

Legg, Sir Thomas KCB QC, and Sir Robin Ibbs, KBE. *Report of the Sierra Leone Arms Investigation*. Return to an Address of the Honorable the House of Commons. London: The Stationary Office: July 27, 1998.

Lewis, Paul G. "Introduction." In David Held et al., eds., *States and Societies*, 413–417. New York: New York University Press, 1983.

Logan, Lara. "Interview with Erik Prince." *60 Minutes*, October 13, 2007a.

Lowell, Edward J. *The Hessians*. New York: Harper and Brothers, 1884. Retrieved on October 18, 2007, from: www.americanrevolution.org/hessindex.html.

Luban, Daniel. "Blackwater Pays Price for Iraqi Firefight," *Asia Times* (September 19, 2007). Retrieved on December 30, 2008, from: www.atimes.com/atimes/Middle _East/II19Ako4.html.

Lumpe, Lora. *The US Arms Central America—Past and Present, Norwegian Initiative on Small Arms Transfers*. Oslo: Peace Research Institute, May 1999. Retrieved in October 2009 from: www.prio.no/NISAT/Publications/The-US-Arms-Central-AmericaPast-and-Present/.

Lynn-Jones, Sean M. "Offense-Defense Theory and Its Critics." *Security Studies* 4, 4 (1995): 660–691.

Machiavelli, Niccolo. *The Prince*. New York: Random House, 1950.

"Making a Living With a Gun." *Fiji Times*. February 26, 2008. Retrieved on June 3, 2008, from: www.fijitimes.com/print.aspx?id=82373.

Mallett, Michael. *Mercenaries and Their Masters*. London: The Bodley Head, 1974.

McCarthy, Roy. "Uneasy Truce in the City of Ghosts." *The Guardian*, April 24, 2004. Retrieved on February 11, 2008, from: www.guardian.co.uk/Iraq/Story/0,2763, 1202163,00.html.

McDonald, Avril. "The Legal Status of Military and Security Subcontractors." In Roberta Arnold and Pierre-Antoine Hildbrand, eds., *International Humanitarian Law and the 21st Century's Conflicts: Changes and Challenges*. Lausanne: Editions Interuniversitaires Suisses, 2005.

Mearsheimer, John. *The Tragedy of Great Power Politics*. New York: W. W. Norton & Company, 2001.

Meho, Lokman I. "E-Mail Interviewing in Qualitative Research: A Methodological Discussion." *Wiley Interscience* (May 25, 2006). Retrieved on October 20, 2007, from: www.interscience.wiley.com.

Merom, Gil. *How Democracies Lose Small Wars*. New York: Cambridge University Press, 2003.

Messner, J. J., and Ylana Gracielli. *State of the Peace and Stability Operations Industry: Second Annual Survey*. Peace Operations Institute, International Peace Operations Association, 2007. Retrieved from: www.ipoaonline.org.

Miller, T. Christian. "Private Contractors Outnumber U.S. Troops in Iraq." *The Los Angeles Times*, July 4, 2007. Retrieved on January 11, 2008, from: www.common-dreams.org/archive/2007/07/04/2284/.

Millet, Allan, Williamson Murray, and Kenneth Watman. "The Effectiveness of Military Organizations." *International Security* 11, 1 (Summer 1986).

Mockler, Anthony. *The Mercenaries*. New York: Macmillan, 1969.

Mockler, Anthony. *The New Mercenaries*. London: Sidgwick & Jackson, 1985.

Morgenthau, Hans J. "Alliances in Theory and Practice." In Arnold Wolfers, ed., *Alliance Policy in the Cold War*. Baltimore: Johns Hopkins Press, 1959.

Muller, Harald. "The Antinomy of Democratic Peace." *International Politics* 41, 4 (2004: Special Issue: The Dynamics of Democratic Peace).

Munkler, Herfried. "The Wars of the 21st Century." *RICR Mars IRRC March* 85, 849 (2003).

Murphy, Jarrett. "Beirut Barracks Attack Remembered." *CBS News*, October 23, 2003. Retrieved on September 1, 2009, from: www.cbsnews.com/stories/2003/10/23/world/main579638.shtml.

Nagl, John A. *Learning to Eat Soup with a Knife: Counterinsurgency Lessons from Malaya and Vietnam*. Chicago: University of Chicago Press, 2002.

"A Nation Resolved to Overcome Its Tough Heritage." International Special Reports. *The Washington Times*. Retrieved on January 16, 2008, from: www.international specialreports.com/europe/01/croatia/anationresolved.html.

Navias, Martin S., and E. R. Hooton. *Tanker Wars: The Assault on Merchant Shipping During the Iran–Iraq Conflict, 1980–1988*. London: I. B. Tauris Publishers, 1996.

"A New Legal Framework for Military Contractors?" Princeton Problem-Solving Workshop Series in Law and Security. Woodrow Wilson School of Public and International Affairs, Princeton University. June 8, 2007. Retrieved on October 15, 2007, from: http://lapa.princeton.edu/conferences/military07/MilCon_Workshop_Summary.pdf

OAU Convention for the Elimination of Mercenaries in Africa. O.A.U. Doc. CM/433/Rev.L, Annex 1. 1972. Retrieved on November 20, 2007, from: www1.umn.edu/humanrts/instree/mercenaryconvention.html.

O'Ballance, Edgar. *Civil War in Lebanon, 1975–1992*. New York: Palgrave, 2002.

O'Brien, Kevin. "PMCs, Myths, and Mercenaries: The Debate on Private Military Companies." *Royal United Services Institute Journal* (February 2002). Retrieved on June 10, 2008, from: www.globalpolicy.org/nations/sovereign/military/02debate.htm.

"October 5, 1986: CIA Transport Plane Shot Down in Nicaragua; Story Reveals Illegal Contra-Arms Program." Retrieved on October 20, 2009, from: www.history commons.org/entity=Eugene_hasenfus_1&printerfreindly=true.

Office of the Special Inspector General for Iraq Reconstruction. *Field Commanders See Improvements in Controlling and Coordinating Private Security Contractor Missions in Iraq*. SIGIR 09-022, July 28, 2009. Retrieved on October 19, 2009, from: www.sigir.mil/reports/pdf/audits/09-022.pdf.

"The Oliver North File." *The National Security Archive*, February 26, 2004. Retrieved in October 2009 from: www.gwu.edu/nsarchiv/NSAEBB/NSAEBB113/index.htm.

Oppel, Richard A. Jr., and Michael R. Gordon. "U.S. Military and Iraqis Say They Are Shut Out of Inquiry." *The New York Times*, October 11, 2007. Retrieved on January 9, 2008, from: www.nytimes.com/2007/10/11/world/middleeast/11blackwater .html?scp=3&sq=nisour+square+blackwater.

Park, Eunkyung, and Gerald M. Kosicki. "Presidential Support during the Iran-Contra Affair: People's Reasoning Process and Media Influence." *Communication Research* (1995). Retrieved on October 18, 2009, from: http://crx.sagepub.com/cgi/ content/abstract/22/2/207.

Partlow, Joshua. "Taliban Targeting U.S. Contractors." *The Washington Post*, April 17, 2010: 6.

Pelton, Robert Young. *Licensed to Kill: Hired Guns in the War on Terror*. New York: Crown, 2006.

Percy, Sarah. *Mercenaries: The History of a Norm in International Relations*. Oxford, UK: Oxford University Press, 2007.

Percy, Sarah V. "Mercenaries: Strong Norm, Weak Law." *International Organization* 61 (Spring 2007).

Phinney, David. "Marines Jail Contractors in Iraq: Tension and Confusion Grow amid the 'Fog of War.'" *CorpWatch*. June 7, 2005. Retrieved on December 13, 2005, from: www.corpwatch.org/article?php.id=12349.

Prechtel, Johann Ernst. *A Hessian Officer's Diary of the American Revolution*. Translated by Bruce E. Burgoyne. Bowie, MD: Heritage Books, 1994.

"Press Statement of Minister of Defense Mediu." Retrieved on August 12, 2009, from: www.mod.gov.al/botime/html/revista/2007/5/faqe13.htm.

Prince, Rosa and Massie-Blomfield, Adrian. "David Miliband Attacks 'Intolerable' Israeli Cloning of British Passports." *London Daily Telegraph*. Retrieved on April 2, 2010, from: www.telegraph.co.uk/news/newstopics/politics/7506701/David-Miliband-attacks-intolerable-Israeli-cloning-of-British-passports.html.

"Protocol Additional to the Geneva Conventions of 12 August 1949, and relating to the Protection of Victims of International Armed Conflicts (Protocol 1)." Adopted on June 8, 1977, Entry into force December 7, 1979. Retrieved on November 20, 2007, from: www.unhchr.ch/html/menu3/b/93.htm.

Pufendorf, Samuel. *An Introduction to the History of the Principal Kingdoms and States of Europe*. London, 1697.

Pullan, Wendy. "Structuring Structure." In Wendy Pullan and Harshad Bhadeshia, eds., *Structure in Science and Art* New York: Cambridge University Press, 2000.

Rabinovich, Itamar. *The War for Lebanon, 1970–1985*. Ithaca, NY: Cornell University Press, 1985.

"The Reagan Years: Reaganomics." CNN.com In-Depth Specials. Retrieved on February 4, 2008, from: www.cnn.com/SPECIALS/2001/reagan.years/whitehouse/reaganomics .html

Reitan, Earl A. *The Thatcher Revolution: Margaret Thatcher, John Major, Tony Blair, and the Transformation of Modern Britain, 1979–2001*. Lanham, MD: Rowman & Littlefield, 2003.

Reiter, Dan, and Allan C. Stam III. "Democracy and Battlefield Military Effectiveness." *The Journal of Conflict Resolution* 42, 3 (June 1998): 271–272.

Reiter, Dan, and Allan C. Stam. *Democracies at War*. Princeton, NJ: Princeton University Press, 2002.

Reno, William. "Privatizing War in Sierra Leone." *Current History* 96, 610 (May 1997).

Reno, William. "The Clinton Administration and Africa: Private Corporate Dimension." *Issue: A Journal of Opinion* 26, 2 (1998).

Richman, Sheldon L. "Where Angels Fear to Tread: The United States and the Persian Gulf Conflict." Cato Policy Analysis No. 90 (September 1978).

Ripley, Tim. *Operation Deliberate Force*. Lancaster, UK: Centre for Defence and International Security Studies, 1999.

Risse-Kappen, Thomas. "Democratic Peace–Warlike Democracies? A Social Constructivist Interpretation of the Liberal Argument." *European Journal of International Relations* 1, 4 (1995).

R. L. S. "Letter to the Editor: Cruelty of the Hessians: A Revolutionary War Episode of Present-Day Significance." *The New York Times*, May 29, 1918. Retrieved on March 13, 2008, from: http://query.nytimes.com/mem/archive-free/pdf?res=9B00 E2DD1238EE32A2575AC2A9639C946996D6CF

Rosen, Nir. "The Myth of the Surge." *Rolling Stone* Issue 1047 (March 6, 2008): 46–53.

Rosen, Stephen Peter. "Military Effectiveness: Why Society Matters." *International Security* 19, 4 (Spring 1995), 5–31.

Rosen, Stephen Peter. *Societies and Military Power: India and Its Armies*. Ithaca, NY: Cornell University Press, 1996.

Rosengarten, Joseph George. *Defence of the Hessians*. Philadelphia: Reprinted From the *Pennsylvania Magazine of History and Biography* (July 1899).

Rubin, Alissa J., and Paul von Zielbauer. "Blackwater Case Highlights Legal Uncertainties." *The New York Times*, October 11, 2007. Retrieved on October 11, 2007 from: www.nytimes.com/2007/10/11/world/middleeast/11legal.html?_r=1&hp=& oref=slogin&pagewanted=print.

Rueffer, Carl Friedrich. "Journal Entry." In Bruce E. Burgoyne, ed. and trans., *Enemy Views: The American Revolutionary War as Recorded by the Hessian Participants*. Bowie, MD: Heritage Books, 1996.

Rumsfeld, Donald H. "Transforming the Military." *Foreign Affairs*, May/June 2002.

Salem, Paul E. "Superpowers and Small States: An Overview of American–Lebanese Relations." Retrieved on August 31, 2009, from: www.lcps-lebanon.org/pub/breview/ br5/psalembr5pt3.html. [Originally published 1992.]

Scahill, Jeremy. *Blackwater: The Rise of the World's Most Powerful Mercenary Army*. New York: Nation Books, 2007.

Schakowsky, Jan. "Schakowsky Uncovers 1,001 Contractor Deaths in Iraq." Press Release, August 6, 2007. Retrieved on September 4, 2007, from: www/house.gov/list/press/il09_schakowsky/pr_contractordeaths_080607.s.

Schmitt, Eric. "Accord Tightens Control of Security Contractors in Iraq." *The New York Times*, December 5, 2007.

Schmitt, Eric, and Thom Shanker. "Pentagon Sees One Authority over Contractors." *The New York Times*, October 17, 2007. Retrieved on November 14, 2007, from: www.nytimes.com/2007/10/17/washington/17blackwater.html?ei=5070&en=c257b0742b5a6103&ex=1193284800&adxnnl=1&emc=eta1&adxnnlx=1195045958-w7UnPIjzvdNLbjO6ySux3Q.

Schmitt, Eric, and Paul von Zielbauer. "Accord Tightens Control of Security Contractors in Iraq." *The New York Times*, December 5, 2007. Retrieved on December 18, 2007, from: www.nytimes.com/2007/12/05/washington/05blackwater.html?pagewanted=print.

Schmitt, Michael N. "Humanitarian Law and Direct Participation in Hostilities by Private Contractors or Civilian Employees." *Chicago Journal of International Law* (Winter 2005).

Schrader, Esther. "US Companies Hired to Train Foreign Armies." *The Los Angeles Times*, April 14, 2002. Retrieved on January 16, 2008, from: www.globalpolicy.org/security/peacekpg/training/pmc.htm.

Schultz, Kenneth A., and Barry R. Weingast. "The Democratic Advantage: The Institutional Sources of State Power in International Competition." *International Organization* 57, 1 (Winter 2003).

Schwartz, Moshe. "Training the Military to Manage Contractors during Expeditionary Operations: Overview and Options for Congress." *CRS Report for Congress* No. R40057 (December 17, 2008).

Schwartz, Moshe. "Department of Defense Contractors in Iraq and Afghanistan: Background and Analysis." *CRS Report for Congress* (August 13, 2009). Retrieved on September 2, 2009, from: www.crs.gov.

Sepp, Kalev I. "Best Practices in Counterinsurgency." *Military Review* (May–June 2005). Retrieved on April 25, 2008, from: www.maxwell.af.mil/au/awc/awcgate/milreview/sepp.pdf.

Serbian National Federation. "Kosovo: An Unjust and Unnecessary War." Serbian National Federation, 1999. Retrieved on September 1, 2009, from: www.balkanstudies.org/wordfiles/Kosovo/Aussie_Kosovo_Paper0899.htm.

Shadid, Anthony. "Biden Says U.S. Will Appeal Blackwater Case Dismissal." *The New York Times*, January 23, 2010.

Shearer, David. "Dial an Army." *The World Today* (August/September 1997).

Silber, Laura and Allan Little. *Yugoslavia: Death of a Nation*. New York: Penguin Books, 1997.

Silverstein, Ken. "Privatizing War: How Affairs of State Are Outsourced to Corporations beyond Public Control." *The Nation*, August 4, 1997.

Silverstein, Ken. *Private Warriors*. New York: Verso, 2000.

Silverstein, Ken. "Revolving Door to Blackwater Causes Alarm at CIA." *Harper's Magazine* (September 12, 2006). Retrieved on March 21, 2008, from: www.harpers.org/archive/2006/09/sb-revolving-door-blackwater-1158094722.

Singer, P. W. "Can't Win with 'Em, Can't Go to War without 'Em: Private Military Contractors and Counterinsurgency." *Policy Paper No. 4*. Washington, DC: Brookings Institution, September 2007.

Singer, Peter W. *Corporate Warriors: The Rise of the Privatized Military Industry*. Ithaca, NY: Cornell University Press, 2003.

Singer, Peter W. "Should Humanitarians Use Private Military Services?" *Small Wars Journal*. Retrieved on February 11, 2008, from: http://smallwarsjournal.com/documents/petersinger.pdf.

Siverson, R. M. "Thinking about Puzzles in the Study of International War." *Conflict Management and Peace Science* 15, 2 (1996).

Sizemore, Bill, and Joanne Kimberlin. "Blackwater: When Things Go Wrong." *The Virginian-Pilot*, July 26, 2006.

Skocpol, Theda. "Bringing the State Back In: Strategies of Analysis in Current Research." In Peter B. Evans, Dietrich Rueschemeyer, and Theda Skocpol, eds., *Bringing the State Back In*, 3–37. New York: Cambridge University Press, 1985.

Smith, Charles D. *Palestine and the Arab–Israeli Conflict*. Boston and New York: Bedford/St. Martin's, 2004.

Smith, Eugene B. "The New Condottieri and U.S. Policy: The Privatization of Conflict and Its Implications." *Parameters* (Winter 2002–2003).

Smith, General Rupert. *The Utility of Force: The Art of War in the Modern World*. New York: Alfred A. Knopf, 2007.

Snow, Keith Harmon. "Chloe's Blood Diamond: Angola Rock Sold for $16 Million to June 3, 2008, from: www.globalresearch.ca/PrintArticle.php?articleid=7423.

Sobel, Richard. "U.S. and European Attitudes toward Intervention in the Former Yugoslavia: *Mourir Pour la Bosnie*?" In Richard Henry Ullman, ed., *The World and Yugoslavia's Wars*. New York: Council on Foreign Relations, 1996.

Spearin, Christopher. "Special Operations Forces a Strategic Resource: Public and Private Divides." *Parameters* (Winter 2006-07): 59–65.

Spicer, Lieutenant Colonel Tim. *An Unorthodox Soldier: Peace and War and the Sandline Affair*. London: Mainstream Publishing, 2000.

Steinberg, Jeffrey. "Rohatyn, Shultz, Cheney 'Privatization' Scheme to Wreck U.S. National Security." *Executive Intelligence Review* (March 31, 2006). Retrieved on October 26, 2009, from: www.larouchepub.com/other/2006/3313rohatyn_privatiz.html.

Stout, David. "House Bill Would Allow Prosecution of Contractors." *The New York Times.* October 4, 2007. Retrieved on October 4, 2007, from: www.nytimes .com/2007/10/04/washington/05cong.html?_r=1&hp=&oref=slogin&pagewanted= print.

Stout, David, and John M. Broder. "Report Depicts Recklessness at Blackwater." *The New York Times,* October 1, 2007. Retrieved on October 1, 2007, from: www .nytimes.com/2007/10/01/washington/01cnd-blackwater.html?_r=1&hp=&oref= slogin&pagewanted=print.

"Swiss Initiative on Private Military and Security Companies." Swiss Federal Department of Foreign Affairs. Retrieved on September 26, 2008, from: www.eda.admin .ch/eda/en/home/topics/intla/humlaw/pse.html.

Swiss Initiative on Private Military and Security Companies and the International Committee of the Red Cross. *Montreux Document on Pertinent International Legal Obligations and Good Practices for States Related to Operations of Private Military and Security Companies During Armed Conflict.* Montreux: Swiss Initiative, September 17, 2008.

Tabarrok, Alexander. "The Rise, Fall, and Rise Again of Privateers." *The Independent Review* XI, 4 (Spring 2007): 565–577.

Tajfel, Henri. "Aspects of National and Ethnic Loyalty." *Social Science Information* 9 (1970): 119–144.

Tajfel, Henri. *Human Groups and Social Categories.* Cambridge, UK: Cambridge University Press, 1981.

Testimony of Ambassador Richard J. Griffin, Assistant Secretary of State, Bureau of Diplomatic Security, Department of State. "Private Security Contracting in Iraq and Afghanistan." House Committee on Oversight and Government Reform, October 2, 2007. Retrieved on October 5, 2008 from: http://oversight.house.gov/documents/ 20071002145249.pdf.

Testimony of Ginger Cruz, Deputy Special Inspector General for Iraq Reconstruction. "The Role of the Department of Defense in Provincial Reconstruction Teams." House Committee on Armed Services, Subcommittee on Oversight and Investigations, September 5, 2007. Retrieved on December 23, 2008, from: http://armedservices .house.gov/pdfs/OI090507/Cruz%20_Testimony090507.pdf.

Thomas, Gordon. "The Spy Who Never Came in from the Cold." *Canada Free Press,* October 25, 2006. Retrieved in October 2009 from: www.canadafreepress.com/ 2006/thomas102506.htm.

Thompson, Ginger and Risen, James. "Plea by Blackwater Guard Helps Indict Others." *The New York Times,* December 8, 2008. Retrieved on November 2, 2009, from: www.nytimes.com/2008/12/09/washington/09blackwater.html.

Thomson, Janice E. *Mercenaries, Pirates, and Sovereigns: State-Building and Extraterritorial Violence in Early Modern Europe.* Princeton, NJ: Princeton University Press, 1994.

Tilly, Charles. "War Making and State Making as Organized Crime." In Peter B. Evans, Dietrich Rueschemeyer, and Theda Skocpol, eds., *Bringing the State Back In*, 169–193. New York: Cambridge University Press, 1985.

Townsend, Mark. "Why Won't the US Tell Us How Matty Died?" *The Guardian*, February 4, 2007. Retrieved on June 10, 2008, from: www.guardian.co.uk/2007/feb/04/iraq.military/print.

Trease, Geoffrey. *The Condotttieri: Soldiers of Fortune*. London: Thames and Hudson, 1970.

Turner, John C. "Social Categorization and the Self-Concept: A Social Cognitive Theory of Group Behavior." In E. J. Lawler, ed., *Advances in Group Processes, Vol. 2*, 77–121. Greenwich, CT: JAI Press, 1985.

Turner, John C., et al. *Rediscovering the Social Group: A Self-Categorization Theory*. New York: Blackwell, 1987.

"The Underside of War: CIA Interrogations and the Blackwater Affair." *The Economist* (August 27, 2009). Retrieved on November 2, 2009, from: www.economist.com/displaystory.cfm?story_id=14323104.

U.N. Security Council Resolution 1132, Paragraph 6, October 8, 1997. Retrieved on September 28, 2009, from: www.customs.gov.sg/NR/rdonlyres/876D72D9-7B10-4881-9189-CC5E76B07CAC/24002/UNSCResolution11321997.pdf.

U.S. Army, *Contracting Basics for Leaders and the Deployed COR*. February 2008.

U.S. Department of the Army. *Civil Affairs Operations*. Field Manual 41-10, January 1993.

U.S. Department of Defense Directive 3000.05. "Military Support for Stability Security, Transition, and Reconstruction (SSTR) Operations." November 28, 2005. Retrieved on October 31, 2007, from: www.dtic.mil/whs/directives/corres/pdf/300005p.pdf.

U.S. Department of Defense, Office of the Secretary. 32 CFR Part 159, "Private Security Contractors (PSCs) Operating in Contingency Operations." *Federal Register* Vol. 74, No. 136. July 17, 2009.

U.S. Department of State, Bureau of African Affairs. "Background Note: Sierra Leone." August 2009. Retrieved on September 29, 2009, from: www.state.gov/r/pa/ei/bgn/5475.htm.

U.S. General Accounting Office. "Outsourcing DOD Logistics: Savings Achievable but Defense Science Board's Projections Are Overstated." Publication No. GAO/NSIAD-98-48. Washington, DC: December 1997.

U.S. Government Accountability Office. "Rebuilding Iraq: Actions Needed to Improve Use of Private Security Providers." Publication No. GAO-05-737. Washington, DC: July 2005.

U.S. Government Accountability Office. "Rebuilding Iraq: Actions Still Needed to Improve Use of Private Security Providers." Publication No. GAO-06-865T. Washington, DC: June 13, 2006.

U.S. Government Accountability Office. "Rebuilding Iraq: DOD and State Department Have Improved Oversight and Coordination of Private Security Contractors in Iraq, but Further Actions Are Needed to Sustain Improvements." Publication No. GAO-08-966. Washington, DC: July 2008.

U.S. House of Representatives, Committee on Oversight and Government Reform, Majority Staff. *Private Military Contractors in Iraq: An Examination of Blackwater's Actions in Fallujah*. September 2007.

U.S. Special Operations Command. "The History of the 10th Special Forces Group (Airborne)." Retrieved on April 2, 2010, from: www.soc.mil/SF/history.pdf.

"USMC Barracks Bombing." *The Patriotic Gentleman*. Retrieved on September 1, 2009, from: www.thepatrioticgentleman.com/USMC-barracks-bombing/USMC-barracks-bombing.html.

"U.S.-Trained Afghan Police Force Is Failing." *APS Diplomat News*, December 11, 2006. Retrieved on September 28, 2009, from: www.thefreelibrary.com/US-Trained +Afghan+Police+Force+Is+Failing-a0155719639.

Vainshtein, Robert. "UCMJ v. MEJA: Two Options for Regulating Contractors." *Journal of International Peace Operations* 2, 4 (January 2007).

Vaknin, Sam. "Analysis: Private Armies—II." *United Press International*, July 18, 2002.

Valentino, Benjamin, Paul Huth, and Dylan Balch-Lindsay. "'Draining the Sea': Mass Killing and Guerilla Warfare." *International Organization* 58 (Spring 2004): 375–407.

Van Creveld, Martin. *The Rise and Decline of the State*. New York: Cambridge University Press, 1999.

Van Evera, Stephen. *Causes of War: Power and the Roots of Conflict*. Ithaca, NY: Cornell University Press, 2001.

Waley, Daniel. *The Italian City-Republics*. London: World University Library, 1969.

Walsh, Lawrence E. *Final Report of the Independent Counsel for Iran/Contra Matters*. Washington, DC, August 4, 1993. Retrieved on October 20, 2009, from: www.fas .org/irp/offdocs/walsh/.

Walt, Stephen M. *The Origins of Alliances*. Ithaca, NY: Cornell University Press, 1987.

Waltz, Kenneth. *Theory of International Politics*. Reading, MA: Addison-Wesley, 1979.

Walzer, Michael. *Just and Unjust Wars: A Moral Argument with Historical Illustrations*. New York: Basic Books, 1977.

Watt, Nicholas, Philip Webster, and Michael Evans. "Arms Scandal Engulfs Cook." *The Times of London*, May 9, 1998. Retrieved on January 16, 2008, from: www .times-archive.co.uk/news/pages/tim/98/05/09/timnwsnws01020.html?1621558

Wayne, Leslie. "America's For-Profit Secret Army." *The New York Times*, October 13, 2002. Retrieved on January 16, 2008, from: www.globalpolicy.org/security/peacekpg/ training/mercenaries.htm.

Weber, Max. "Politics as a Vocation." In H. H. Gerth and C. W. Mills, eds., *From Max Weber*. Oxford, UK: Oxford University Press, 1972.

Weeks, Jessica L. "Autocratic Audience Costs: Regime Type and Signaling Resolve." *International Organization* 62 (Winter 2008): 35–64.

Weiner, Rebecca Ulam. "Peace Corp." *Boston Globe*, April 23, 2006. Retrieved on July 2, 2007, from www.boston.com.

Wendt, Alexander. "Anarchy Is What States Make of It: The Social Construction of Power Politics." In Charles Lipson and Benjamin J. Cohen, eds., *Theory and Structure in Political Economy: An International Organization Reader*. Cambridge, MA: The MIT Press, 1999.

West, Bing. *No True Glory*. New York: Bantam, 2005.

Westervelt, Eric. "Profile: Confusion in Iraq over Alleged Incident between Marines and Private Contractors." *National Public Radio: Morning Edition*. June 13, 2005. Retrieved on March 8, 2007, from: www.npr.org.

Wilson, LTC Isaiah III, and Jason Lyall. "Rage against the Machines: Explaining Outcomes in Counterinsurgency Warfare." *International Organization* 63 (2009): 67–106.

Woodward, Susan L. *Balkan Tragedy: Chaos and Dissolution after the Cold War*. Washington, DC: The Brookings Institution, 1995.

Wright, Derek. "Point of View: PSCs Like Saito Key to Peace." *The Asahi Shimbun*, July 15, 2005. Retrieved on November 14, 2007, from: http://ipoaonline.org/php/index.php?option=com_content&task=view&id=64&Itemid=82&date=2007-08-01

Yalichev, Serge. *Mercenaries of the Ancient World*. London: Constable, 1997.

Yermiya, Dov. *My War Diary: Lebanon June 5–July 1, 1982*. London: Pluto Press, 1984.

Zinn, Johann Georg. "Journal Entry." In Bruce E. Burgoyne, ed. and trans., *Enemy Views: The American Revolutionary War as Recorded by the Hessian Participants*. Bowie, MD: Heritage Books, 1996.

Zisser, Eyal, *Lebanon: The Challenges of Independence*. London and New York: I. B. Tauris, 2000.

Zunec, Ozren. "Civil–Military Relations in Croatia." In Constantine P. Danopoulos and Daniel Zirker, eds., *Civil–Military Relations in the Soviet and Yugoslav Successor States*. Boulder, CO: Westview, 1996.

INDEX